Successful Printing Management

SUCCESSFUL PRINTING MANAGEMENT

Edited by James F. Burns, Jr.
Printing Impressions

North American Publishing Company · Philadelphia

iv

Library of Congress catalog card number: 74-22957
ISBN: 0-912920-36-X
Order number: 112

Printed in the United States of America

Contents

Introduction vii

R. R. Donnelley & Sons Co., Inc. 1

Arcata National Corporation 46

Wallace Business Forms, Inc. 60

J. L. Clark Manufacturing Co. 72

W. A. Krueger Co. 82

Courier Corporation 120

Starline Corporation 130

George Banta Company, Inc. 140

Lee Enterprises, Inc. 158

Progressive Printing 170

Anyplant Printing Company 186

Introduction

What makes some printers soar while others slog? How did the Donnelleys, the Bantas, the Kruegers and their ilk shake the dust of the lowlands and reach the sunny plateaus of the high-volume Valhallas? Was it luck, or brainpower, or persistence, or was it some combination of those—the right man at the right time with the right formula?

Perhaps even more important, what are they doing now to keep going and keep growing?

The primary purpose of this volume is to answer those questions as much as possible through analysis and vivisection of the "stars" of the printing industry's galaxies as they gallop through their orbits in the Seventies, a time which is taxing their talents severely as any that has passed before.

How Donnelley has been blithely weathering storms that would sink the average enterprise—one suffering proportionate reversals—emerges through painstaking examination of how it disposes its men, machines and materiel. How Krueger rose from the depths of the Great Depression, through a long twilight of slow growth and into a steep upward sweep, is clocked and recorded—the more tellingly, perhaps, because this is a story in which the power of personalities to influence direction and growth is epitomized with an immediacy that offers guidelines as current and valid today as they were a year ago. And then there's the story of Arcata, the huge combine of diverse facilities which now amounts to the second largest commercial printing organization in America. How it was put together, when, by whom, and the whys and wherefores of its stormy history make for entirely different reading.

As a secondary theme, and largely by inference, this volume "sets the stage and draws the scenario" of what must be one of the most challenging eras the printing industry has ever faced. In the past half decade the technological revolution/evolution has affected profoundly every norm and ratio by which this industry had become accustomed to conducting business. Yet the looked-for wholesale dislocations, mergers, closings have not occurred. All the industry's prophets seem to share the faulty talents for prophecy that. clothe Marshall McLuhan so barely. The printing industry does not react according to geometric or slide-rule projections.

The publicly-owned segment of the commercial printing industry, which includes the majority of its giants, is composed of approximately 50 firms. They range in size from those earning $3 million a year to the aforementioned nine-figure sales heights. The list includes a dozen companies such as Jostens, Western Publishing and Meredith Corp. because they do more commercial printing than 90 percent of the industry's other units, even though such manufacturing might account for as little as 30 percent of their own total sales. Altogether, these publicly-held companies racked up 1974 sales in excess of $3.2 billion. Allowing for the income from other sources earned by companies such as the three just mentioned by name, *the commercial printing industry's public sector—while only 0.2 percent of the whole, numerically—contributed about one quarter of the industry's total 1974 sales volume.*

The truism that the best basic data sources of any industry are the public records of its publicly-held units is one that reaches its highest perfection when applied to the printing industry. That is so because it is the last of the major manufacturing industries to be composed of so many thousands of small units which are so overwhelmingly privately owned. And the truism applies most pervasively to the commercial printing sector because it is the most widely dispersed of all the printing industry's component parts. In no sector have we found an individual entrepreneur willing to "tell all" in anything like the depth the SEC demands of its wards, large and small.

Mainly for the above reasons, this volume concentrates on publicly-held companies. And mainly because those who wrote the individual success stories write also for Printing Impressions—*the North American Publishing Company periodical which is the largest graphic arts trade paper in the world—the profiles of commercial printers predominate. For the most part, the printers chosen include those whose track records are held in highest esteem, whose accomplishments serve as the industry's yard-sticks, and whose ups and downs are viewed as prime bellwethers of the health of the market and signposts of its trendings. While similarities will be found in some of the analyses, they trace mainly to style of authorship and the writers' natural bent for analysis and reportage, since no attempt was made to set a mold and follow it. Companies are as different inside and outside, in style, operation and motivation as are the people who shape them and run them. Our aim in this volume is to reflect such differences as accurately as possible.*

While commercial printers, publicly and privately owned, have been given center stage herein, we have reserved three prime spots for use as windows on three other aspects of the graphic arts scene. One of those windows surveys a business forms manufacturing scene, another a newspaper operation. Both profile a company widely recognized as a leader in its respective field. Because the first half of the Seventies was more a time of trial than of triumph, the third window reveals a darkling scene which was all too representative of the period in the experience of far too many printers. The "Anyplant" profile which synthesizes their story is fact-in-fiction form. Actually a composite model based on the chillingly similar tragedies of several noted printing establishments which went under in the early Seventies, "Anyplant" is a quasi-documentary which manages to reveal more of the treacherous aspects of the business clime of the era than a series of victim profiles would have done.

This volume begins with its most current success story, that of R. R. Donnelley. The choice for precedence rests solely on the subject's pre-eminence as the nation's leading printer in sales volume.

The "success story" is an action cameo, a candid "still" of the subject's corporate style coping with a specific environment at a specific time. As such it is as distinctive as a fingerprint, as informative as a strobe sequence of a runner's stride. Equally important, it is also a "slice of life and time" showing the ebb and flow of the beginning years of the Seventies.

We offer these ten in-depth analyses of what makes the successful printing companies tick in the form of cameos showing our subjects "as they were when visited." In some cases statistical data is updated, in others it is left to cover just that segment of time covered by the "success story."

A final comment: it may be a point of criticism of this foreword and perhaps this volume—which we hope to make a sustaining project—that the emphasis is on the narrower term "printing" rather than "graphic arts" or "the graphic communications industry." While we are fully in sympathy with the intent behind the use of those expressions, and meet it partially through variety, our main concern here is with those who manufacture the nation's printing, not those who perform services such as designing or publishing. While equally vital to the more inclusive terms, their contributions elude most of the tangible dimensions of the more limited target areas we use here.

We trust you will find these success stories rewarding, and wish you good reading.

—James F. Burns, Jr.

1

R. R. Donnelley & Sons Co., Inc.

R. R. Donnelley & Sons
Corporate Offices, Chicago, Illinois.

Two Decades of Donnelley's Vital Statistics

	Net Sales (000s)	Net Inc. (000s)	Share Earns	Div./ Share	Work'g Capital (000s)	L.T. Debt (000s)	Current Assets (000s)	Current Liabil's (000s)	Current Ratio
1954	$ 87,056	$ 5,730	$0.33	$0.04	$ 24,714	$ 5,176	n.a.	n.a.	n.a.
1955	94,404	6,600	.39	.05	22,342	3,877	31,180	8,530	3.7
1956	109,661	7,581	.41	.07	23,767	2,759	33,260	9,180	3.6
1957	120,042	8,092	.41	.11	30,909	1,477	41,020	9,290	4.2
1958	118,219	8,057	.41	.11	40,964	14,864	50,710	9,450	5.4
1959	130,165	9,180	.49	.12	43,723	14,500	54,600	10,570	5.2
1960	148,764	10,114	.53	.14	39,478	14,300	50,590	10,810	4.7
1961	149,831	10,167	.53	.16	39,984	13,600	53,160	12,880	4.1
1962	172,158	12,484	.65	.17	48,585	12,900	62,900	13,500	4.6
1963	184,137	14,272	.75	.21	53,515	9,203	69,466	15,951	4.4
1964	211,124	17,297	.90	.22	55,718	9,199	76,098	20,380	3.7
1965	228,725	20,486	1.06	.30	59,919	7,199	82,552	22,633	3.7
1966	247,921	20,695	1.07	.40	65,157	7,015	97,869	32,712	3.0
1967	261,533	22,093	1.14	.40	66,384	6,641	98,101	31,717	3.1
1968	272,905	20,776	1.07	.40	70,154	5,496	107,495	37,341	2.9
1969	307,879	21,235	1.10	.40	59,356	4,584	102,186	42,830	2.4
1970	331,163	22,938	1.19	.44	81,340	4,534	124,041	42,357	2.9
1971	339,992	24,382	1.27	.44	89,749	4,464	136,106	46,357	2.9
1972	353,565	26,125	1.37	.45	93,650	3,039	144,626	50,976	2.8
1973	378,817	31,109	1.64	.48	102,305	2,242	158,282	55,977	2.8
1974	453,868	28,778	1.52	.54	104,563	2,052	163,875	59,312	2.8

A Capsule Account of a Decade's Progress

Barring some outrageously unpredictable phenomenon—such as an instant Ice Age or a one-drop Great Flood—R. R. Donnelley & Sons Co. Inc. will be celebrating the end of the third quarter of the 20th Century by posting sales of well over $500 million. It'll be a great way for America's greatest commercial printer, now 111 years old, to prime itself for the Bicentennial.

As this report was being written, results of the Chicago-based giant's 1974 year were published. The data on sales were fine—a 19.8 percent gain over 1973 ($453,868,000 vs. $378,817,000). The data on earnings would have been almost as good had the company not switched to a LIFO (last in, first out) method of accounting for inventories—at a cost to net income of $7.3 million, or 39 cents a share. Had that changeover not been implemented, earnings would have been up 16.5 percent, with net income $36.1 million vs. 1973's $31.1 million, and net per share of $1.91 vs. $1.64. As 1974's books show them, however, net earnings were actually $28.8 million and net per share $1.52.

Although 1974 sales reflect impressive gains, well over any year in the preceding decade, they also reflect the effects of a similarly impressive inflationary period. The year's 10 to 12 percent erosion of the dollar brings the Donnelley sales-impetus picture much closer into focus with the company's track record for the 1964-73 decade, when the compound sales growth rate averaged 7.54 percent per annum. *(See Fig. A)*

In achieving that continuing growth rate, Donnelley's annual sales increases for the 1964-73 decade ranged from the series' high of 14.66 percent (increase of 1964 sales over 1963) to a low of 2.67 percent (1971's increase over 1970). In 1971, poor as business was anyway, Donnelley was further wounded by the loss of the Look Magazine account. The very next year, when sales at year-end toted up to a 3.99 percent increase, they did so despite the fact that Donnelley had suffered an even more grievous loss—the Life Magazine account, which expired at the close of 1972. Sales for 1973 were 7.14 percent ahead of 1972, re-establishing a far more characteristic curve, and Donnelley no longer has any comparable single-account factors the loss of which—in themselves—could be so calamitous.

While its 1974 sales represent only about 4 percent of that year's estimated total earnings of America's commercial printers ($10,928 million according to the Bureau of Domestic Commerce), R. R. Donnelley & Sons Co. Inc. is far and away the industry's leader in size and in "image." In an industry which calls "Profit Leaders" those members whose net before taxes is 8 percent or more, Donnelley posted twice that in 1973. Its average per annum, pre-tax net income yield for the 1964-73 decade has been 15.39 percent of net sales. Its *after*-tax net average 7.82 percent (*See Fig. B.*) By almost any of the vital norms—with the notable exception of those which equate the value of physical assets to yields such as sales or net income—the Chicago giant constantly coruscates.

	Fig. A — Annual Sales Growth Rate R. R. Donnelley			Fig. B — Donnelley's Earnings As a Percent of Sales	
	Sales (000s)	% Over Prior Yr.		Pre-Tax	Post-Tax
1964	$211,124	14.66	1964	16.38%	8.19%
1965	228,725	8.34	1965	17.22	8.96
1966	247,921	8.39	1966	16.06	8.35
1967	261,533	5.49	1967	16.25	8.45
1968	272,905	4.35	1968	16.01	7.61
1969	307,879	12.82	1969	14.04	6.90
1970	331,163	7.52	1970	13.79	6.93
1971	339,992	2.67	1971	13.88	7.17
1972	353,565	3.99	1972	14.29	7.39
1973	378,817	7.14	1973	16.00	8.21
Av. annual increase:		7.54	Av.	15.39	7.82
1974	453.868	19.81	1974	12.11	6.34

The effect of the changeover to the LIFO (last in, first out) method of accounting for inventory shows up sharply in the contrasts between 1974 pre-tax and post-tax net income percentages—as related to sales—and those for the prior decade (*Fig. B*). At 1974's 12.11 percent, the pre-tax earnings were. about 3.25 percentage points under the previous decade's average and, at 6.34 percent of sales, the 1974 after-tax net was almost 1.5 percentage points under the ten-year average. In no single year of the previous decade had either percentage been as low.

In the period 1963-73, R. R. Donnelley & Sons Co. accomplished the following: (*see Fig. C*):

It more than doubled its net sales—raising them from $184 million to close to $379 million, an increase of 10.57 percent;

It raised the value—net—of its land, buildings and equipment (l/b/e), by close to 113 percent (from $86 million in 1964 to $183 million in 1973);

It more than doubled the value of its stockholders' equity, raising the total by 113 percent (from $123.6 million to $263.8 million) and it boosted per share equity from the $6.44 it was at the end of 1963 to the $13.93 it was at the end of 1973—a gain of 116.3 percent.

The biggest increases for the decade, predictably perhaps, came in a favorite area of Donnelley's—net income, after taxes:

The company's 1963-73 period started at a net income level of $14.4 million and it ended at $31.1 million (up 118 percent);

Per share income went from 75¢ to $1.64 (up 119 percent).

Two things are especially noteworthy about the data in Fig. C: (1) the fact that twice as much growth in plant and capital equipment occurred in the first half of the decade as in the second, when the Life and Look accounts vanished, and (2) the fact that sales grew about 10 percent slower in the second half of the decade. While the sharp drops in the growth of stock equity reflect logically the cutback in capital investments in the 1968-73 period, the effect of the falloff in the sales growth rate during that period is somewhat curious. On less sales growth, the net income growth rate between 1968 and 1973 actually increased, while growth in the per share income was over 10 percent more in that second half of the decade than in the first.

Fig. C
Donnelley's Growth in Sales,
Facilities, Net Income, Equity

	1963 (millions)	1968 (millions)	1973 (millions)	Percent Growth 63-68	68-73	63-73
Net Sales	$184.14	$272.91	$378.82	48.21	38.81	105.70
Net Land/Bldg/Equip	86.03	142.58	183.11	65.72	28.43	112.80
Net Inc. (after Tax)	14.27	20.78	31.11	48.51	49.73	117.97
Working Capital	53.52	70.15	102.31	31.01	45.83	91.17
Stock Equity	123.57	190.83	263.78	54.43	38.23	113.47
	(dollars)	(dollars)	(dollars)			
Per Share Equity	6.44	9.85	13.93	53.00	41.40	116.30
Per Share Income	.75	1.07	1.64	42.67	53.27	118.67

It seems particularly worth repeating that on a 48 percent increase in its sales base between the end of 1963 and the end of 1968, management increased net income and per share income by 48.5 and 42.7 percent, respectively. In the second half of the decade, on a sales increase of only 38.8 percent, it boosted net income 49.7 percent and per share income 53.3 percent. It would seem that in the second half of the decade events conspired to make management considerably less growth-oriented in the physical sense than in terms of income. That is what the figures imply, anyway. Of course it's just as possible that the major inhibitors of capital growth were the loss of those major accounts* together with the recession of 1969-71 and the effect of inflation on the costs of construction and equipment.

Fig. C-a
1973-1974 Data Changes

| | $ Millions | | % Change |
	1973	1974	73-74
Net Sales	$378.82	$453.87	+19.81
Net L/B/E	183.11	204.35	+11.60
Net Inc.	31.11	28.78	- 7.49
Work. Cap.	102.31*	104.56	+ 2.20
Stock Eq.	263.78	281.90	+ 6.87
		(dollars)	
Eq./Share	13.93	14.91	+ 7.04
Inc./Sh.	1.64	1.52	- 7.32

*This is the figure quoted in the 1973 Annual Report. The 1974 AR restates it as $105.32, which would change the 2.20 percent gain to a decrease of 0.72 percent.

Land, Buildings, Equipment

Donnelley's ten manufacturing operations cover about 5,400,000 square feet of real estate in Illinois, Indiana, Ohio, Pennsylvania, Kentucky, Tennessee, Michigan and Connecticut. To the best of our knowledge, the Chicago headquarters installation—covering more than 1,300,000 square feet—is still the largest of the lot, although at 1,200,000 square feet the Crawsfordsville, Ind., plant is a close second. Those two plants are by far the largest; the next being the Willard, Ohio, and Warsaw, Inc., installations, which weigh in at 630,000 and 620,000 square feet respectively. Chicago's main produce is catalogs and magazines; Crawfordsville's and Willard's are books and directories; Warsaw's is catalogs. The Chicago installation dates from 1912 and grew to its present size mainly between that time and 1964. Crawfordsville started up in 1923; had grown to 500,000 square feet by 1957 and by 1967-68 reached its present size. Willard and Warsaw date back to 1956 and 1959 respectively and achieved their current muscularity in the past two years.

In order of size, the other plants are these: Mattoon, Ill., 300,000 square feet; Dwight, Ill., 274,000; Gallatin, Tenn., 250,000; Lancaster (West), Pa., 246,000; Glasgow, Ky., 204,000; Lancaster (East), Pa., 162,000 and Old Saybrook, Conn., 160,000. In addition, Donnelley has a new composition facility in Elgin, Ill., about 17,500 square feet, which it leases.

*Life's closing alone is reported to have cost Donnelley $3 million. The rotary letter-presses on which it was printed had to be junked, since no market for them could be found.—ED. NOTE

Besides Chicago, the Donnelley plants that specialize in catalogs and magazines are Old Saybrook, Lancaster East and Mattoon. Lancaster West and Dwight are directory plants and Glasgow specializes in magazines. The Elgin facility sets telephone directory yellow pages. Gallatin, which Donnelley calls its "new catalog module," was due on stream in 1975.

Old Saybrook was especially equipped to produce weekly magazines via web letterpress until Life Magazine went under and now web offset presses are being added to produce the shorter-run, special-interest magazines which are filling in nicely (People, Time Inc.'s new record-setting weekly is being produced there). Glasgow is primarily a web offset plant while Warsaw and Gallatin are primarily gravure plants. The huge Chicago and Crawfordsville plants are distinctly heteropressual.

Donnelley Printing Co., the Chicago behemoth's only wholly-owned subsidiary, operates the Lancaster, Pa. plants and the new one in Gallatin. Formerly Rudisill & Co., it was acquired by Donnelley in 1959. It is into Lancaster that Donnelley has been channeling most of the work coming from its recently established Wall Street financial printing sales office.

It was in 1959 that Lancaster East entered the Donnelley fold and the Old Saybrook and Warsaw plants went into operation. Both the Mattoon and Dwight facilities went onstream in 1968. Glasgow followed in 1970, Lancaster West in 1972, and Gallatin in 1975. Thus, since Willard's advent in 1956 Donnelley has added some 2,800,000 square feet of plant capacity, of which about 1,300,000 square feet are only about six or seven years old. It had taken Donnelley six decades to grow into the 2,600,000 square feet it occupied before 1956.

A Time to Tote Progress

1967 was something of a watershed-year for Donnelley in its own historians' eyes. In their annual report they noted that since 1957 the company "had expanded from three manufacturing divisions to six, with three more currently under development" (the Dwight and Mattoon plants and an addition in Crawfordsville). In that decade, Donnelley had spent $167 million to install new equipment and to add more than two million square feet of new facilities.

It was noted with considerable pride in that 1967 review that *"over 90 percent of capital requirements were* (sic) *generated from internal sources."* Another point of pride: "The operating investment (total assets) per employee was $10,600 at the end of 1957. This increased 70 percent to $19,000 per employee by the end of 1967." (What those historians could not foresee was that Donnelley's figures on net assets per employee would zoom another 62 percent in the next six years—to $30,740 per in 1973).

The introduction of the 1967 progress report was something of a background piece for the news that the Electronic Graphics Division had just been formed. The announcement declared that the division's purpose was to "serve the growing demand for film composition using a combination of electronic data processing, cathode ray tube and photographic devices." It added: "We expect the new equipment now on order, along with continuing development of skills, to advance our production capability in modern film composition techniques." In 1970, Donnelley declared that its Electronic Graphics operation "can produce a directory page on film in seconds—a job which formerly required hours."

The Crawfordsville operation, incidentally, was one of the first American printing establishments to install a Cameron book manufacturing system, and the Electronic Graphics Division was one of the first to install a cathode ray tube phototypesetting device, theirs being a VideoComp.

Equipment

In 1972, Donnelley made some uncharacteristic overtures to its stockholders in an annual report which discussed operations conducted during a disappointing year. The report was largely a "meet your company" type of morale piece, one quite out of the ordinary for a corporation whose annual reports tend to be somewhat patronizing (often whole paragraphs are picked up and repeated without a comma's change from one year to the next). Said the 1972 review:

"Our Computer Services Department serves all areas of the company. Teleprocessing equipment provides fast communication with our operations outside of Chicago. Our systems analysts have devised programs which enable us to most economically plan press forms and press imposition requirements. We have also developed computer programs to generate price estimates and determine paper and other material needs. We are extending these systems to shorten lead times and improve efficiency." The review added:

"Many Donnelley manufacturing operations use computer applications extensively. Our Electronic Graphics Division is a self-contained facility with its own systems and programming staff, in-house computers and high-speed character generators. Directory, catalog and magazine film composition is generated here for a number of the nation's leading publishers and manufacturers. On-line computers are used in other manufacturing operations, including color separation and platemaking, press instrumentation and binding operations."

Paying for Expansion

Between 1964 and 1973, Donnelley spent $242,084,000 on its land, building and equipment (l/b/e) requirements. In six out of ten of those years, what the company had budgeted for such expenditures was considerably exceeded by actual expenditures. For instance, in 1967 the budget for expansionary purposes was $20 million, but $26,205,000 was actually spent; in 1969, $22 million was budgeted for such expenses and $28.4 million was spent; in 1973, the expansion budget was $27 million and $32.8 million was spent—the 1974 expansion budget was $32 million but spending was in excess of $41 million. (*See Fig. D*) On the other hand, of the $24 million set aside for expansion in 1970, only $17.8 million was spent. Over the 1964-73 decade, however, the total of the budgeted estimates (sums planned for capital expansion) was $21 million short of what was actually spent, estimates averaging 10 percent below actuality. Over the decade, in only one year—1970—did Donnelley fail to spend at least 95 percent of budget goals for growth funding.

For the years 1964-73, the amounts Donnelley invested in physical facilities averaged out to 8.4 percent of its net sales per year, ranging from a low of 5.39 percent in 1970 to a high of 10.74 percent in 1964. (*See Fig. E*) In seven years of the decade more was spent on capital facilities than was earned after taxes; in two instances—the years 1964 and 1969— over 30 percent more. In no year during the decade did sums expended for 1/b/e additions or improvements fail to exceed 11 percent of the total value of such capital property as it stood, fully depreciated, at the end of the year. On the average, the monies spent during those years equated to over 17 percent of the net value of 1/b/e at the end of the years. The compounded annual growth rate in net value of 1/b/e for the decade 1964-73 averaged 7.93 percent.

Fig. D
Expansion Funds: R. R. Donnelley
Budget vs. Expenditures—1964-73

	Amount Budgeted (000s)	Amount Spent (000s)	Expenditures As % Budget For Expansion
1964	$ 20,000	$ 22,679	113.40%
1965	20,000	20,483	102.42
1966	22,000	19,794	89.97
1967	20,000	26,205	131.03
1968	20,000	23,158	115.79
1969	22,000	28,417	129.17
1970	24,000	17,834	74.31
1971	23,000	24,339	105.82
1972	23,000	26,414	114.84
1973	27,000	32,761	121.34
Total	$221,000	$242,084	Av. 109.70%
1974	32,000	41,018	128.18

Fig. E
Comparison of Donnelley's Annual
Expansion Expenditures with Annual Data for:

	Net Sales	Net Inc.[1]	Net L/B/E[2]
1964	10.74%	131.12%	22.82%
1965	8.96	102.40	18.73
1966	7.98	95.65	16.77
1967	10.02	118.61	19.78
1968	8.49	111.47	16.24
1969	9.23	133.82	18.14
1970	5.39	77.75	11.26
1971	7.16	99.82	14.96
1972	7.47	101.11	15.75
1973	8.65	105.31	17.89
Av. %	8.41	107.71	17.23
1974	9.04	142.53	20.07

[1] Net income *after* taxes.
[2] Relationship of year's expansion expenditures to net value of land, buildings, equipment at close of same year.

As noted before, a Donnelley tenet is that growth should be paid for out of internally-generated earnings. One of the recurrent verbatim-isms in annual reports the company publishes is this: "We are continuing our practice of returning the major part of earnings to finance growth." In *Fig. F* we have a clear picture of what that policy means to the money market. R. R. Donnelley's long-term debt as a percentage of its total liabilities and equity has been falling steadily since 1964, when it was 5.21 percent. The 0.65 percent figure for 1973, for instance, represents a long-term debt of $2,242,000 as contrasted with total liabilities and equity of $347,309,482. The notably consistent trend in *Fig. F* is the decade's steady decline in the size of long-term debt compared with the proportionate stability of the other debt and equity ratios.

Fig. F
Ratios of Major Elements of Donnelley Debt
to Total Liabilities for Years 1964-73

(NOTE: All columns total 100%)

	Current Liabil's	L. Term Debt	Defer'd Fed. Tax	Defer'd Inv. Cr.	Stock Equity
1964	11.55%	5.21%	4.57%	1.16%	77.51%
1965	11.66	3.71	4.90	1.48	78.25
1966	14.99	3.21	5.08	1.57	75.15
1967	13.64	2.85	5.38	1.65	76.48
1968	14.79	2.18	5.41	2.06	75.57
1969	15.77	1.69	5.77	2.08	74.70
1970	14.87	1.58	5.96	2.07	75.52
1971	15.29	1.47	5.51	1.75	75.98
1972	15.95	.95	5.48	1.79	75.84
1973	16.12	.65	5.45	1.84	75.95
Av.	14.46%	2.35%	5.35%	1.75%	76.10%
1974	15.97	.55	5.61	1.99	75.88

Figs. G, H, I and *J* outline the sources of Donnelley's l/b/e expansion-improvement capital. In *G* it can be seen that approximately a third of net income after taxes is paid out in dividends and for the most part the other two-thirds of the net goes into the retained earnings kitty. The only two years in the 11 shown in the table which abrogate those rough ground rules are 1964 and 1969, and the latter was a definitely unrepresentative year in many respects due to the retrenchment caused by the three-for-two stock split. So, it seems that for every dividend dollar Donnelley pays out it generally socks away the equivalent of two others ("the major part of earnings") for reinvestment in its business.

Figs. *H* and *I*—which reflect the same data in different form—show where the dollars Donnelley spends on itself come from, and how they are spent. The source of funds sections of the tabulations show that about 90 cents out of every dollar Donnelley takes in comes from its operations. Of each of those operational dollars earned, 60 cents comes from net after taxes, 35 cents from depreciation allowance and the other 5 cents is from deferred federal income taxes. Much of the "other sources" funds come from interest the company earns on the millions it has invested in federal, state and municipal securities.

For much of the decade 1964-73, about 85 percent of the funds Donnelley took in from operations and otherwise went into dividend and facilities expansion/improvement. Out of every $100 of funds expended during the interval, it paid stockholders about $20 in dividends and it spent about $65 on additions or improvements to land, or to buildings, or equipment. Another $5 or so went into the reacquisition of common stock and the other $10 was spent on debt reduction and other obligations. (How that $65 going into l/b/e was being apportioned is shown in Fig. J and is discussed in the next major segment of this study.)

While the foregoing generalizations applied loosely for much of the period, the changing of markets and tightening of the economy which began to be felt in earnest toward the end of 1970 began to make deep inroads into the investment patterns. Donnelley's loss of Look and Life in '71 and '72 and the worsening of the economy in those years began to show up in disruptions in the disbursement formulae: both the dividends and the l/b/e sectors began to suffer as inventory and receivables became increasingly expensive. The deepening of that trend-pattern in 1974 resulted in the lowest dividend rato in eleven years and (*proportionately*) the second-lowest allotment of dollars for l/b/e. The 1974 switch to LIFO inventory accounting was apparently a lot less of a drain on disbursement funds than was the cost of financing an inordinately sharp increase in receivables. The effect of rocketing paper prices permeates this later data.

Between Figs. H and I almost as much can be seen of the effects of the market and the economy on the commercial printing industry in general as on R. R. Donnelley & Sons Co. Inc.

An examination of Donnelley's allowances for depreciation over the period 1964-73 also reveals some interesting patterns—*Fig. J.*

Fig. G
Development of R. R. Donnelley's
Retained Earnings Fund, 1964-73

	Retained Earnings As of 1/1 ($ in 000s)	Net Income For Year ($ in 000s)	Stock Transactions Div'ds Pmts. ($ in 000s)	Stock Transactions Other Trans. ($ in 000s)	Amount Left to Reinvest ($ in 000s)	Retained Earnings At 12/31 ($ in 000s)	% Change Retained Earnings	Ratio Amt. Reinvested To Net Inc.
1964	$ 44,836	$ 17,297	$ 4,280	$ 8,890	$ 4,128	$ 48,964	9.21	23.8%
1965	48,964	20,486	5,798	0	14,688	63,652	30.00	71.70
1966	63,652	20,695	7,749	0	12,946	76,598	20.34	62.56
1967	76,598	22,093	7,754	0	14,339	90,937	18.72	64.90
1968	90,937	20,776	7,749	0	13,027	103,964	14.33	62.70
1969*	103,964	21,235	7,746	68,231	13,351*	49,222	(111.24)	(157.79)
1970	49,222	22,938	8,490	288	14,160	63,382	28.77	61.73
1971	63,382	24,382	8,474	19	15,979	79,271	25.07	65.17
1972	79,271	26,125	8,601	28	17,496	96,767	22.07	66.97
1973	96,767	31,109	0.089	172	22,192	118,959	22.93	71.34
Total	- - -	$227,136	$75,730	$77,628	$142,444	- - -	Av. 19.44	Av. 55.09%
1974	$118,959	28,778	10,211	18	18,549	137,508	15.59	64.46

*In 1969 there was a three-for-two stock split, as a result of which over $68 million was transferred from the retained earnings fund to the common stock equity account on the balance sheets. In all other years shown, the "amount left to reinvest" is that which is left over from the subtraction of the costs of stock transactions from the sum of columns 1 and 2 (retained earnings as of 1/1 plus net income). In 1969, $68,092,845 was transferred to common stock, and an additional $7,884,105 charged for other stock transactions, most notably the dividends figure shown. The $13,351,000 shown in the 1969 amount left to reinvest column is a hybrid figure in the sense that it represents subtraction of stock transaction costs *not including* the extraordinary expense of the $68 million transfer. All other data for the year are actual.

Fig. H
Percentage Record of a Decade of
Donnelley's Income and Expenditures

Source of Funds
(Sum of Cols. 1, 2 and 3 is 100% of Operating Funds; Sum of Cols. 4
and 5 is 100% of Funds from All Sources)

| | Provided from Operations | | | All Sources | |
| | (1) | (2) | (3) | (4) | (5) |
	Net Income +	Depre- ciation +	Defer'd Tax, I.C. =	% Total Funds Ops.	Other Sources
1964	60.17%	31.85%	7.98%	98.03	1.97%
1965	62.75	30.30	6.95	97.54	2.46
1966	61.49	32.15	6.36	98.22	1.78
1967	62.45	32.35	5.20	96.58	3.42
1968	58.20	34.84	6.96	95.48	4.52
1969	56.37	37.09	6.54	97.13	2.87
1970	56.76	38.92	4.32	80.83	19.17[1]
1971	56.91	45.53	(2.44)	80.21	19.79[2]
1972	58.76	38.53	2.71	80.77	19.23[3]
1973	61.54	34.33	4.13	88.57	11.43[4]
Av	59.54	35.59	4.87	91.34	
1974	56.62	37.62	5.76	88.20	11.80

[1] 15.78 of these percentage points came from sale of $7.9 million worth of state and municipal securities;

[2] 11.85 of these percentage points are from a $6.3 million increase in accounts payable, another 5.11 from a $2.7 million decrease in inventories;

[3] a $4.5 million increase in accts payable and accrued expenses accounted for 8.17 of these percentage points; a $4 million property sale for another 7.28;

[4] of this figure, 1.97 percentage points came from disposition of reacquired common stock and 7.85 from an increase in accounts payable and accrued expenses.

Disposition of Funds
(Sum of All Columns is 100%)

	Cash Div'ds	L/B/E Expend.	Reacqu'd Common St.	Red. in LT Debt	All Other
1964	16.36%	83.62%	– %	0.02%	– %
1965	19.81	69.98	–	6.84	3.37
1966	26.79	68.43	4.15	–	0.64
1967	21.90	74.02	3.02	1.06	–
1968	23.05	68.88	4.66	3.41	–
1969	15.62	57.31	4.93	1.84	20.30[1]
1970	30.30	63.65	5.87	0.18	–
1971	20.12	57.78	7.57	0.17	14.36[2]
1972	14.73	45.24	11.11	2.44	26.48[3]
1973	15.75	56.78	3.14	1.38	22.95[4]
Av	20.44%	64.57%	4.45%	1.73%	8.81%
1974	12.70	51.00	2.07	0.24	33.99[5]

[1] Of this figure, 20.22 percentage points are due to $10 million investment in state and municipal securities;

[2] 6.35 of these percentage points are due to an increase in payable federal income taxes, 6.52 to an increase in receivables;

[3] 25.85 of these percentage points represent an increase in receivables;

[4] 18.69 percentage points trace to increased inventories, 3.64 to an increase in receivables;

[5] 28.14 of these percentage points represent an increase of $22.6 million in receivables, another 3.11 to an increase in inventories and another 2 to a decrease in federal income taxes then currently payable (12/31/74).

Fig. I
Record of a Decade of Donnelley's Income, Expenditures

Source of Funds

	Net Income ($ in 000s)	Deprec.* Str.-Line ($ in 000s)	Defer.† Taxes ($ in 000s)	Prov. by Oper'ns. ($ in 000s)	Disp. of ‡ Reacq. St. ($ in 000s)	Net of All Other Inc. ($ in 000s)	Tot. All Sources ($ in 000s)
1964	$ 17,297	$ 9,155	$ 2,294	$ 28,746	$	$ 577	$ 29,323
1965	20,486	9,892	2,267	32,645		825	33,470
1966	20,695	10,822	2,140	33,657	375	132	34,164
1967	22,093	11,444	1,840	35,377	747	504	36,628
1968	20,776	12,439	2,485	35,700	1,402	289	37,391
1969	21,235	13,974	2,464	37,673	1,056	59	38,788
1970	22,938	15,731	1,747	40,416	1,116	8,471[1]	50,003
1971	24,382	19,505	(1,043)	42,844	891	9,677[2]	53,412
1972	26,125	17,129	1,207	44,461	993	9,593[3]	55,047
1973	31,109	17,356	2,089	50,554	1,123	5,399[4]	57,077
Total	$227,136	$137,447	$17,490	$382,073	$7,703	$35,526	$425,303
1974	28,778	19,116	2,925	50,819	1,221	5,575[5]	57,615

*An accelerated depreciation is used for income tax purposes.
†deferred federal income taxes and investment credit.
‡disposition of reacquired common stock.
NOTES:
[1] Includes $7,892,000 for sale of state and municipal securities, etc.;
[2] Includes income of $6,331,000 in accts. payable and accrued expenses plus decline of $2,732,000 in inventories;
[3] Includes $4,474,000 increase in accts payable and $4,007,000 from disposal of property;
[4] Mainly $4,479,000 increase in accts. payable and accrued expenses;
[5] Includes $4.9 million increase in accounts payable and accrued expenses.

Disposition of Funds

	Cash Div'ds ($ in 000s)	Expend's* on L/B/E ($ in 000s)	Red. in† L.T. Debt ($ in 000s)	Stock Reacqui. ($ in 000s)	Inc/Dec. Rec'bles ($ in 000s)	Inc/Dec. Invent's ($ in 000s)	Total‡ 'Other' ($ in 000s)	Total Dis. Funds ($ in 000s)
1964	$ 4,280	$ 22,679	$ 4	$ --	$	$	$	$ 26,963
1965	5,798	20,483	2,000	--			987[1]	29,268
1966	7,749	19,794	184	1,199				28,926
1967	7,754	26,205	374	1,069				35,402
1968	7,749	23,158	1,145	1,568				33,620
1969	7,746	28,417	912	2,446			10,065[2]	49,586
1970	8,490	17,834	50	1,644				28,018
1971	8,474	24,339	70	3,189	2,747		3,303[3]	42,122
1972	8,601	26,414	1,425	6,486	15,092	366		58,384
1973	9,089	32,761	797	1,812	2,098	10,784	355	57,696
Total	$75,730	$242,084	$6,961	$19,413	$19,937	$11,150	$14,710	$389,985
1974	10,211	41,018	190	1,668	22,630	2,502	2,208	80,427

*Expenditures on land, buildings and equipment.
†Reduction in long-term liabilities.
‡Mainly non-repetitive expenditures.
NOTES:
[1] Investment in Lakeside Bank;
[2] Including purchase of state and municipal securities worth $10,026,000;
[3] Includes $2,674,000 in decreased federal taxes, etc.

Fig. I-a
Fund Source/Disposition Summary

	Funds Source ($ in 000s)	Funds Dispos. ($ in 000s)	Net Change Work'g Cap. ($ in 000s)
1964	$29,323	$27,121	$ 2,202
1965	33,470	29,268	4,202
1966	34,164	28,926	5,238
1967	36,628	35,402	1,226
1968	37,391	33,620	3,771
1969	38,788	49,586	(10,798)
1970	50,003	28,019	21,984
1971	53,412	42,122	11,290
1972	55,047	58,384	(3,337)
1973	57,077	57,696	(619)
1974	57,615	80,427	(22,812)

Fig. J
Some Basic Data Relationships in Donnelley's Depreciation Policies

	Net Sales ($ in 000s)	Cost Sales ($ in 000s)	Gross Value of L/B/E[1] ($ in 000s)	Accum. Deprec. ($ in 000s)	Accum. Deprec. as % Gross L/B/E ($ in 000s)	Net Value of L/B/E ($ in 000s)
1964	$ 211,124	$ 162,276	$172,691	$ 73,323	42.46%	$ 99,368
1965	228,725	173,502	189,954	80,566	42.41	109,388
1966	247,921	191,289	208,522	90,495	43.40	118,027
1967	261,533	201,353	229,580	97,071	42.28	132.509
1968	272,905	210,474	248,469	105,892	42.62	142,577
1969	307,879	241,820	274,031	117,346	42.82	156,685
1970	331,163	261,233	288,472	130,046	45.08	158,424
1971	339,992	267,349	305,066	142,422	46.69	162,644
1972	353,565	276,689	292,547	124,625	42.60	167,922
1973	378,817	289,944	320,328	137,215	42.84	183,113
Total	$2,933,624	$2,275,929	+85.5%[2]	- - - -	43.32[3]	+84.3%[2]
1974	453,868	364,678	352,461	148,114	42.02	204,347

[1] Land, Buildings and Equipment;
[2] Percentage increase in values between 1964 and 1973;
[3] Average for the decade's percentages.

During the period shown Donnelley sold almost $3 billion worth of printing and complementary services. To earn that many sales dollars its factory costs alone were almost $2.3 billion. Over the decade net sales grew by almost 80 percent and the cost of those sales grew by 78.7 percent, while the gross and net values of the facilities it was using for all those activities grew by 85.5 and 84.3 percent, respectively. Evident in the closeness of the ranges of those percentages, and of the depreciation percentage, is the type of proportionate control Donnelley keeps over its operations.

How the LIFO inventory accounting change benefitted the company in relation to taxes is shown in *Fig. K*. The bite federal taxes took out of net income in 1974 was a full 5.8 percentage points less than the norm for the preceding decade and almost two percentage points less in relation to net sales for the year. In 1974, taxes were down to percentages that were the lowest for 11 years. (More about LIFO and its tax implications appears in subsequent discussion.)

Fig. K
How Taxes Donnelley Pays Relate to:

	Net Sales	Earn'gs Fr. Op'ns	Net* Income
1964	8.19%	52.41%	99.99%
1965	8.27	50.23	92.33
1966	7.71	51.40	92.34
1967	7.80	51.55	92.31
1968	8.39	56.41	110.22
1969	7.15	54.93	103.60
1970	6.64	52.26	95.91
1971	6.71	52.52	93.51
1972	6.90	52.35	93.40
1973	7.79	53.14	94.83
Av.	7.56	52.72	96.84
1974	5.77	52.99	91.04

*After taxes. In 1964, federal taxes came to $17,295,000 and net after taxes to $17,297,000.

R. R. Donnelley & Sons Co.
New York Stock Exchange
Common Share Prices, Ratios

Stock Prices

	High	Low	P/E Ratio
1964	$36	$20-7/8	27-20
1965	46¼	27½	29-21
1966	47	32-5/8	23
1967	50-1/8	29¼	28
1968	47¼	37¼	26
1969*	43½	37	23
1970	25¼	32	15
1971	26½	18-5/8	19
1972	28	18½	18
1973	27-3/8	17¾	17
1974	24-3/8	15¾	15

*Year of 3-for-2 stock split.

R. R. Donnelley: 20 Years
of Income, Equity Progress

	Net Income (000s)	Per Sh. Equity	Per Sh. Income
1954	$ 5,730	$ 2.86	$0.33
1955	6,600	3.20	.39
1956	7,581	3.83	.41
1957	8,092	3.93	.41
1958	8,057	4.15	.41
1959	9,180	4.69	.49
1960	10,114	5.07	.53
1961	10,167	5.43	.53
1962	12,484	5.91	.65
1963	14,272	6.44	.75
1964	17,297	7.08	.90
1965	20,486	7.86	1.06
1966	20,695	8.46	1.07
1967	22,093	9.18	1.14
1968	20,776	9.85	1.07
1969	21,235	10.48	1.10
1970	22,938	11.23	1.19
1971	24,382	11.97	1.27
1972	26,125	12.69	1.37
1973	31,109	13.93	1.64
1974	28,778	14.91	1.52

Land, Building, Equipment (L/B/E): Men, Managers

In any discussion of any company's policies relating to its investments in l/b/e, the type of data shown in *Fig. L* is essential and basic. It should be kept in mind that ratios which apply to operations the size of R. R. Donnelley & Sons are likely to be impracticable for other printers, for as the 1974 Ratio Study* puts it, "As a firm's size increases, so do the amounts of assets per employee," and "the larger the firm the more capital available to employ." Nevertheless, with such cautions considered, the relationships shown in *Fig. L* can be instructive to almost any printer, since some of them are relatively independent of size, or at least minimally dependent. An instance of the latter is the ten-year fluctuation in land values, which at a 183 percent increase far outstripped building and equipment value growth.

Fig. L
Value Relationships and Growth Data
for Donnelley's L/B/E[1]

($ in 000s)

	Land @ Cost	Bldgs. @ Cost	Ratio Land to Buildings	Equipment at Cost	Ratio Bldgs. to Equipment	Net Val. of L/B/E	Yr. to Yr. Growth in Net Val. of L/B/E	Net L/B/E as % Total Net Assets
1964	$3,402	$47,723	1:14.03	$121,567	1:2.38	$ 99,368	15.50%	56.32%
1965	3,796	50,647	1:13.34	135,511	1:2.49	109,388	10.08	56.37
1966	5,771	52,982	1: 9.18	149,768	1:2.55	118,027	7.90	54.09
1967	6,289	60,638	1: 9.64	162,653	1:2.43	132,509	12.27	56.95
1968	7,182	66,032	1: 9.19	175,256	1:2.39	142,577	7.60	56.46
1969	7,958	71,025	1: 8.93	195,048	1:2.47	156,685	9.90	57.69
1970	8,147	73,825	1: 9.06	206,500	1:2.52	158,424	1.11	55.18
1971	8,106	76,954	1: 9.49	220,006	1:2.59	162,644	2.66	53.62
1972	8,369	81,379	1: 9.72	202,798	1:2.26	167,686	3.25	52.53
1973	9,631	86,670	1: 8.99	224,026	1:2.33	183,113	9.05	52.72
	+183%[2]	+81.6%[2]	1:10.12[3]	+84.3%[2]	1:2.44[3]	84.3[2]	7.93%[3]	55.19%[3]
1974	9,780	99,295	1:10.15	243,368	1:2.45	204,347	11.60	55.01

[1] Land, buildings and equipment;
[2] Growth percentages, 1964-73;
[3] Average ratios for the decade.

The ratios of the values of land to values of buildings, and of buildings to equipment, are noteworthy for their steadiness. That is especially true of the ratio of building values to equipment values—averaging out to $1 investment in buildings for every $2.44 invested in equipment. It is true also of the relation between land and building values from 1966 through 1974, which, if figured for those years only instead of the entire ten years, would average out to $1 invested in land for every $9.37 in buildings.

The annual financial report on printer operations sponsored by Printing Industries of America.

While the rate of growth in the net value of l/b/e during the decade fluctuated far more widely than any of the other relationships shown in Fig. L, another noteworthy evidence of comparatively fixed ratio-setting is that between the net value of l/b/e and Donnelley's total net assets. Averaging just over 55 percent for the ten years, the widest variation in the period was between the high of 57.69 percent in 1969 and the low of 52.53 percent in 1972.

As Fig. L shows, despite the fact that Donnelley spent over $41 million in calendar year 1974 for expansion/improvement purchases, and that the sum was the largest it had spent in more than a decade, no commensurate dislocation occurred in the basic relationships of net value of l/b/e to total net assets, nor in the rather rigidly-structured ratios of the values of land to buildings, and of buildings to equipment.

Donnelley Personnel Policies

Manning R. R. Donnelley & Sons Co.'s $352,461,000 worth of facilities (gross) were, at the close of 1974, some 11,600 souls. About 6000 had been working for the company ten years or more; 2150 for 25 years or more. As *Fig. M* shows, the high tide of Donnelley's workforce complement came in 1970, when some 13,200 people were employed. By 1973 that figure had dropped by almost 2000, a drop which represents a loss of about 600 jobs a year following the 1971 and 1972 closings, respectively, of *Look* and *Life*. The reversal of the downtrend in jobs is apparently in good part due to a recovery in the company's magazine printing sector, for in its 1974 annual report Donnelley declares that "in absolute volume, these *(Look, Life)* losses have been largely offset by the substantial growth in special interest magazines."

Fig. M.
A Decade of Donnelley
Manpower Statistics

	Total Force	10-Yr. Veterans	25-Yr. Veterans
1964	10,880	4700	1300
1965	11,000	5000	1450
1966	12,000	5100	1560
1967	12,220	5400	1760
1968	12,030	5400	1745
1969	12,810	5500	1742
1970	13,200	5900	1845
1971	12,500	5900	2020
1972	11,800	5830	2140
1973	11,300	5700	2150
1974	11,600	6000	2150

A notable thing about *Fig. M* is the way it confirms the soundness of the company's personnel policies. While fewer people are employed now than in 1966, the number of ten-year veterans has grown by almost 18

percent and the number of 25-year veterans by almost 38 percent. Obviously, people who earn the option to stay, stay. Non-union, 110 years old,
Donnelley continues to maintain an up-to-the-minute expertise based on
responsiveness to employee needs. For instance, last year, recognizing that
"like everyone else our employees were affected by inflation, for the first
time in over 25 years we had a special company-wide wage increase, in
addition to regular annual adjustments and benefit improvements." That
increase was effectuated even though company management knew that its
changeover to a LIFO inventory accounting system was going to necessitate
its explaining to stockholders that net income and thus income per share
were down for 1974. Actually, the company went further with its infla-
tion-compensation: it also "provided improved benefits for the more than
1500 retired members of our Retirement Benefit Plan."

The RBP covers substantially all employees over age 30 who meet
service requirements. They receive an annual retirement benefit credit of
$60 for each year of service after 1969, for which no contribution is made
by the employee. All those eligible who elect to participate on a contribu-
tory basis contribute 2.5 percent of compensation in excess of $5400 per
year, for which they receive an additional annual retirement benefit computed at the rate of 2.125 percent on compensation in excess of $5400.
Costs of the plan charged to operations in 1974 were $5,475,000. Accord-
ing to Donnelley officials, no substantial changes had to be made in the plan
to meet requirements of the Employee Retirement Income Security Act of
1974, which went into effect for such plans at the end of 1975.

A stock option plan for management employees in which the company would match 70 percent of the participant's contribution (as opposed
to the 50 percent company contribution made before) was drafted for
stockholders' approval in March 1975. If approved, the portion of the
company's match which exceeds 50 percent will be paid in cash to "offset
in whole or in part the required withholding from the participant's earnings
of income tax on the entire company matching contribution." The number
of Plan participants who have elected to purchase shares during its nine-
year life through 1974 has ranged from 63 percent to 75 percent of those
eligible. The number of eligible officers, directors and employees, as of
January 1, 1975, was about 1100; if the increase in matching contribution
by the company is implemented, the plan could cost Donnelley in 1975 a
maximum of $1,102,000. *Note that Donnelley thus considers almost one in
ten employees to be VIPS.*

An employee program of which Donnelley is particularly proud is its
apprentice training program. According to its 1972 annual report, the
company had graduated more than 1100 employees from the "widely
copied" program in its 60 years. The report also pointed out that Nicholas
Vander Kloot, who had been with the firm 48 years and was retiring then
as a director and senior vice president, had been one of the company's
apprentice trainees.

Management,
Marketing

Since 1971, Donnelley has been operating with three semi-autonomous groups serving three major markets: books, publications, and catalogs and directories. The three product-oriented organizations specialize in specific market areas to "provide better job engineering to serve customer requirements and maximize equipment and facility design and utilization." Before the 1971 reorganization, four groups directed the company's affairs: general management (at the top), manufacturing management, sales management, and staff management. Now each of the three new groups has its own management, manufacturing facilities and sales and customer service organization. Centralized Donnelley corporate staff groups (in such areas as engineering, research and development, personnel, finance, purchasing, and marketing services) "in addition to serving general management also serve the needs of all groups and function as a catalyst in the coordination and interchange of information . . ."

Atop the Donnelley management superstructure today is Gaylord Donnelley, 64, who was to retire as board chairman May 31 to become chairman of the executive committee. He will continue as a director. In his 43 years with the company, he has served as an officer for 28. Next in line comes Charles W. Lake, Jr., president, aged 56, who has served as an officer of the company for over 20 years and is also a director. Others in the upper reaches of general management include Robert C. Fields, 54, a director and executive vice president, to whom the three group vice presidents report. They are: Charles C. Bronson, book group; Gordon R. Ewing, 61, catalog and directory group; Herbert R. Gotzes, 48, publications group. Completing the general management executive roster is Oscar R. Daum Jr., 54, senior vice president, administration. Staff officers include Louis L. Ackerman, vice president; Robert L. Crowe, vice president and secretary; John E. Dabbert, vice president, corporate manufacturing staff; Charles C. Haffner III, vice president and treasurer; John C. Kingery, vice president; Robert H. Lutz, vice president, administration and Arthur C. Prine Jr., and John B. Schwemm, respectively vice president and director of relations services and vice president and general counsel.

Two semi-retired executives who wield considerable clout in the Donnelley organization are Elliott Donnelley and Charles C. Haffner Jr. Elliott Donnelley, a brother of Gaylord, retired from the active lists in 1968, although his title then—vice chairman of the board—has been maintained under his directorship listing. Charles C. Haffner Jr., is a director as well as chairman of the company's finance committee. He too has held the latter title for over a decade.

Principal stockholders in the R. R. Donnelley & Sons Co. are the Donnelley borthers, their wives and dependents, and the Northern Trust Co.

Fig. N. would seem to imply that the depth of control of the company exercised by the Donnelley family has been slipping lately, but a closer look dispels that notion. While the two principal family stockowners held or controlled directly more than 26 percent of the outstanding common in 1968, and hold "only" 17.6 percent today, the number of shares outstanding grew by 46 percent in the interim. A 17.6 percent control of almost 19 million shares compares very favorably with a 26 percent control of 13 million. While the ownership spread of the outstanding common dropped numerically almost 20 percent between 1968 and 1974, the job of marshalling enough shares to directly out-vote the brothers Donnelley remained substantially unchanged. It would have taken some 3,360,000 shares then and it would take some 3,350,000 shares now—but that effort would heavily engage the Northern Trust Co., trustee for some 2.2 million shares, many of them for Donnelleys, and the Haffners, who are related and influential stockholders.

Charles C. Haffner III, vice president and treasurer, is Gaylord Donnelley's newphew. With his father, C. C., Jr., the Haffners in 1975 owned, or controlled or had in trust total common stock holdings amounting to 1.66 percent of outstanding shares. No other top echelon officers are related to the Donnelleys. The only other officer whose common stock holdings even approach the tenths of a percent is President Charles W. Lake Jr., whose listed 51,771 shares (in his name and beneficiaries) amounted in January 1975 to about 0.27 percent of all shares outstanding. No directors, other than the Donnelleys, Haffners and Lake, own anything like a tenth of a percent.

Elliott and Gaylord Donnelley, together with C. C. Haffner III, are associates of each other "within the meaning of the SEC Act of 1934," according to filed ownership information. Additionally, "Charles C. Haffner Jr. and Charles C. Haffner III, may be deemed associates within the meaning of the Act, also."

Fig. N
A Look at Major Ownership Interests
in R. R. Donnelley & Sons Co. Inc.

	Common Shares Outstanding	% Ownership Gaylord D[1]	% Ownership Elliott D[1]	% Ownership North. Trust	Total % Own'shp.	Number of Stockholders
1968	12,911,859	16.9%	9.2%	12.8%	38.9%	9300
1969	12,907,317[2]	16.1	8.3	15.0	39.4	8800
1970	19,294,297	15.1	8.5	13.4	37.0	8900
1971	19,273,707	14.8	8.3	12.6	35.7	8700
1972	19,162,170	14.8	8.3	12.6	33.3	8300
1973	18,972,190	12.0	7.3	12.1	31.4	7700
1974	18,893,363	11.4	7.3	11.2	29.9	7500
1975	18,870,367	10.4	7.2	11.7	29.3	n.a.

[1] Including holdings for wives and dependents;
[2] The year of a three-for-two share stock split.

All things considered—in view of the forementioned Donnelley-Haffner-Northern Trust relationships, the considerable dispersion of common shares among key employees and directors, and the performance of the company and its stock during these latter years of economic stress and market mayhem—the Donnelley clan dominance of R. R. Donnelley & Sons Co. Inc., would seem virtually impregnable. A "safe" margin for any successful raid would probably be much closer to six million shares than to five million. That would involve such frightfully expensive shenanigans that in the foreseeable future the chances of any cabal forming to plan a coup are as unlikely as chances of casual romance between Golda Meier and the Shah of Iran.

Fig. Na indicates the renumeration paid in 1974 by the company and its subsidiary to each director and each of its three highest-paid officers whose direct aggregate remuneration from R. R. Donnelley exceeded $40,000. Incidentally, such remuneration paid to all the company's officers and directors as a group—61 in all—in 1974 totaled $3,959,665. The income levels shown in *Na* are proportionately well in line with income earned by other top-level printing industry executives (see Printing Impressions, August 1974, page 8).

Fig. Na

1974 Remuneration of Directors and Officers
of R. R. Donnelley & Sons Co. Inc.

(Amounts in terms of salaries, fees and incentive compensation paid during the year to each director and each of three highest paid officers whose direct remuneration—aggregate—exceeded $40,000 for such year)

Officer	Title	Salary, Etc.*
Elliott Donnelley	Director**	$ 46,000
Gaylord Donnelley	Chairman of the Board	194,092
Robert C. Fields	Director and Group Vice President	164,550
Charles C. Haffner, Jr.	Director**	63,604
Charles C. Haffner III	Director, Vice President, Treasurer	71,241
Chalres W. Lake, Jr.	Director and President	194,091

*Exclusive of deferred compensation and company contribution under the stock purchase plan.
**Messrs Elliott Donnelley and Charles C. Haffner Jr. also serve the company on a consultant basis.

Donnelley's Markets, Clientele

In 1964 approximately 76 percent of Donnelley's sales were made to the company's 15 largest customers. Work for Time Inc. (*Time, Life, Fortune, Sports Illustrated,* etc.) then accounted for approximately 26 percent of sales, or about $55 million. In that year, the company printed and bound more than 1000 different telephone directories, but as *Fig. O* shows the magazine sector far outshone the others as an income producer. Magazines accounted for 42.6 percent of sales, books for 23.8 percent and catalogs for 19.5 percent. At 8.3 percent of sales, directories were second from last as moneymakers, with "other" (general commercial printing) on the bottom of the heap, pulling 5.8 percent. (Incidentally, in 1964 Donnelley began printing and binding *The New Yorker* and *Scientific American.* Both are still customers.)

When the record for 1974 was tabulated, it revealed marked changes in the income priority order. Magazines, at 28.1 percent of sales, had dropped to second place, edged out by 28.3 percent for catalogs. Books were still producing 23.8 percent of sales but directories had jumped from 8.3 percent of sales in 1964 to 15.6 percent in 1974. General commercial printing had dropped from 5.8 percent to 4.2 percent.

Fig. O

Product/Sales Breakdowns for R. R. Donnelley & Sons Co., Inc.

(Paper costs subtracted from sales before percentages computed.)

	1964	1969	1970	1971	1972	1973	64-73[1]	1974[3]
Magazines	42.6%	40.1%	39.6%	39.5%	35.5%	28.4%	- 33.3%[2]	28.1%
Catalogs	19.5	23.0	23.1	24.6	26.4	27.0	+ 38.5	28.3
Books	23.8	21.6	22.3	20.1	20.9	23.3	- 2.1	23.8
Directories	8.3	11.2	11.4	12.6	13.4	17.2	+107.2	15.6
Other	5.8	4.1	3.6	3.2	3.8	4.1	- 29.3	4.2

[1] Percentage change for decade.

[2] Loss of Look Magazine account in 1971 and of Life Magazine account in 1972 are primarily accountable for this drop.

[3] Presstime data shows first ascendancy of catalog volume to first place in recent history. Donnelley furnishes much of the paper it prints on—in 1974, such paper was used for about one-third of total output.

Between 1971 and 1973 some fairly sharp reordering of priorities took place. Magazines fell from 39.5 percent of sales to 28.4 percent. Catalogs went from 24.6 percent to 27.0 percent of sales; books from 20.1 to 23.3; directories from 12.6 to 17.2, and "other" from 3.2 to 4.1 percent. The push on telephone directory sales over the years since 1964 had seen production volume quintuple—in 1973 the company was producing some 5000 directories, the bulk of them for Western Electric, which had thereby become Donnelley's largest customer, accounting for some 12 percent of over-all sales, or about $45.5 million.

Of more than 1000 customers (see *Fig. P*) in 1973, the ten largest contributed 51 percent of sales. Next to Western Electric, Sears and Time Inc., are the "big names" but Sears' contribution is less than 10 percent and Time's is in the 8 percent area (before it folded, the annual sales contribution of *Life* alone was that). In sum, its three largest customers in 1973 contributed toward Donnelley's annual sales only about 3 percent more than Time Inc., alone contributed in 1964.

The rise of catalog production since 1964 was steady but relatively restrained until the *Look* and *Life* debacles. In 1964 catalog sales amounted to about $41 million; by 1973 they were contributing $102 million in sales. Of that latter-year sales figure, Sears Roebuck, the company's largest catalog account, contributed about $35 million.

According to Donnelley's 1974 annual report, while many of the catalogs it produces are delivered through the mail, "an ever-increasing number in the form of preprinted inserts are being distributed as special tabloid sections of newspapers." Says the report: "A majority of this work is currently printed by the gravure process, which provides a unique capability of faithfully reproducing full color merchandise on lower cost papers. Shorter run catalogs, however, are generally printed by web offset utilizing the glossier machine-coated papers." Other reasons cited for the upsurge in catalog sales are increased use of credit and development of the catalog showroom, "which provides economical merchandising through convenient warehouse pick-up services for catalog customers." Donnelley's catalog production is being done at the Warsaw, Chicago, Mattoon, Glasgow, Old Saybrook, Lancaster and Willard plants, to which will be added the output of the Gallatin plant. The latter, slated to start up this year, Donnelley calls its "new catalog module."

Fig. P
A Smattering of R. R. Donnelley's 1973 Accounts
(Taken from 1973 Annual Report and exclusive of trade books,
textbooks, bibles, telephone directories.
Note: this does not purport to be inclusive.)

Magazines
Air Classics
Appraisal Journal
Boating
Car & Driver
Carte Blanche
Children's Playmate
Color Photography
Cycle World
Ducks Unlimited
Esquire*
Family Circle*
Family Health
Farm Journal*
Fishing
Flying
Glamour*
Green America
Horticulture
Horse & Horseman
Hospital Practice
Industrial Distributor
Instrument Flying
Locker Room Talk
Logos

Mademoiselle*
Management Accounting
Management Development
Medical Insight
Medical World News
Modern Bride
Motorboat
National Geographic*
Nation's Business*
Needlework & Crafts
Newsweek*
New Woman
New Yorker*
Nursing
Physician's World
Popular Photography*
Product Engineering
Psychiatric Annals
Sail
Salt Water Sportsman
Scientific American*
Sesame Street
Sharing
Shopper's Voice

Simplicity Sewing Book*
Simply Tailoring
Snow Mobiling
Special Interest Autos
Sports Illustrated*
Stereo World
Sunset*
Surgery, Gynecology &
    Obstetrics
The Investing Professional
Time*
The Times of Israel
Top & Op
Travel Scene
U.S. News & World
    Report*
V.I.P. Playboy Club
    Magazine
Yachting
Your Church

*Mass-circulation, major
  publications

Financial Printing
Allied Chemical
Arthur Andersen & Co.
Ashland Oil
Baxter Laboratories
CNA Income Shares
Central & Southwest Corp.
Central Telephone Co.
Combined Insurance Co.
    of America
Continental Illinois

A. B. Dick Co.
Jack Eckerd Corp.
Harris Bancorp
HFC
Honeywell
Illinois Tool Works
Inland Steel
Iowa Electric Light &
    Power
McGraw-Edison

Northern Illinois Gas
Northern Trust Co.
Panama Canal Co.
Public Service Co. of
    Illinois
RCA
Rockwell International
Santa Fe Industries
Skill
United Cities Gas Co.

Catalogs and Buyers Guides
Altman's
Ambassador Catalog
Car & Driver Buyers Guide
Caron's Fall Specials
Culligan's Catalog
1974 Dodge Style
Electronics Buyers Guide
Equipto Catalog
Europe Charter Tour Book
Fabrizaar
Fisher Scientific Co.
Flying Annual & Pilots
    Buyers Guide
Freund Can Co.
Gates Belt & Hose
    Specifications
GCA Precision Scientific
Gordon's
Grey Rock
Harris Vegetable & Steel
    Catalog
Hemmings Motor News

Interstate Nurseries
Kelly Bros. Garden Guide
MacDonald Incentive Co.,
    E.F.
Mostow Co. Catalog
Northwestern Golf
    Manufacturers
Oldsmobile 1974 Catalog
Oldsmobile Trailering
J. Packard Ltd.
Park's Flower Book
J. C. Penney Catalog
Photography Annual
Photography, Directory
    & Buying Guide
Plymouth's Catalog
Radio Shack
Raleigh Belair Catalog
Remington
Roaman's
Sears, Roebuck & Co.
Skiers' Directory

Stereo Directory & Buyer
    Guide
Sturbridge Yankee
    Workshop
Sunset House
Teledyne Post
Telex TWX Directory
    & Buyers Guide
Top Value Stamps
Travel Planner/Hotel,
    Motel Guide
TWA Flight Shop Gift
    Catalog
Warner Consumer Buying
    Service
Weisfeld's Jewelers
Western Auto Supply
Western Motels Travel
    Guide
Wilson's
Williamsburg Reproductions
Worldwide Tour Guide

Fig. P (Continued)

Catalogs and Buyers Guides (Continued)

Directories, Reference Books, and Encyclopedias

American Bar Association
  Directory
American Heritage
  Dictionary
Avis Worldwide Directory
Buyers' Guide & Product
  Directory of Asia
  Manufacturers
Chemical Engineers
  Handbook
Chicago Street Address
  Directory
Classified List, Foreign &
  Domestic Corps.
Compton's Encyclopedia
  Series & Yearbook
Directory of Post Offices
Dun & Bradstreet's
  Reference Book

Ebony Pictorial History of
  Black America
Encyclopedia Britannica
  Series & Yearbook
Funk & Wagnal's
  Comprehensive Int.
  Dictionary
General Statutes of
  Connecticut
Gould Medical Dictionary
Handbook of Chemistry
  & Physics
Libraries & Information
  Centers
Moody's Municipal
  Government Manual
McGraw-Hill Encyclopedia
  of World History

Official Airline Guide
Paperbound Books in Print
Physician's Desk Reference
Popular Mechanics Do-It-
  Yourself Yearbook
Standard & Poor's Stock
  Market Encyclopedia
Teachers' Guide
Webster's Atlas & Zip
  Code Directory
West Point Register of
  Graduates
World Book Series &
  Dictionary
Young Students
  Encyclopedia

While the sales contribution percentages of Donnelley's magazine printing sector have dropped by one-third since 1964, it would be premature to predict their continuing decline. For instance, the company has invested heavily recently in printing facilities for special-interest, realatively short-run magazines (Donnelley's market researchers reportedly had forecast the decline of the mass-circulation giants as early as the mid-Sixties). With the start-up by Time Inc., of its strapping new weekly, People, Donnelley's Old Saybrook, Conn., plant got a timely reprieve—it having been the hardest hit when Life magazine folded. Besides that new People account, the Chicago giant has recently added some other impressively blue-ribbon titles to its magazine output—Glamour, Mademoiselle, U.S. News & World Report, and Newsweek's New York and New England editions. According to Donnelley's 1974 annual report, the volume lost through the demise of Look and Life has since been "largely offset by the substantial growth in special interest magazines." As mentioned before, magazines are printed and bound in Chicago, Mattoon, Glasgow, Lancaster and Old Saybrook. Glasgow produces web offset special interest magazines. Additional web offset magazine presses are being installed in Chicago, Lancaster East and Old Saybrook.

The company's book output emphasizes reference works but ranges the field. Next to reference books come elementary and high school textbooks, direct mail books for book clubs, religious books and, more recently, college textbooks, professional books, ficton and non-fiction books. While a majority are hardbound, an increasing percentage consists of higher quality paperbound books. Says the 1974 annual report: "There was a substantial increase in the volume of elementary and high school textbooks produced during 1974, requiring additional printing and binding capacity. The company also is making capital expenditures to meet the trend toward more specialized shorter-run books." For this purpose Crawfordsville's facilities are being expanded "to serve the college textbook, professional, religious and general trade book segments which require smaller printing and binding runs." The Crawfordsville and Willard plants are mainly used for book production.

In addition to its telephone directory production, the Chicago colossus produces airline guides, financial references, professional and scientific handbooks, legal tomes on rulings and statutes and references for schools, industry and associations. Its main directory plants are the Dwight and Lancaster ones, which serve the Mid-Atlantic and midwest portions of the country. Other directories are produced at Crawfordsville and Willard. Donnelley is currently involved in shifting composition done for directories from hot metal to computerized phototypesetting in its Electronic Graphics division and in a new composition facility which was started up in Elgin, Ill., in 1974.

A major area of its general—"other"—printing interests is that done for the financial community. During the past two years Donnelley has supplemented the financial printing activities of its Chicago plant with fruits of a foray into the Wall Street market. It opened an office in the heart of that district and connected it electronically with a newly-installed, specially-equipped financial printing "module" at Lancaster-East.

Management Efficiency, Methods

Many of the significant data relating the efficiency of R. R. Donnelley & Sons Co. to that of the industry at large appear in a study complementary to this. The data in that study are mostly concerned with Return on Investment (ROI) and they measure Donnelley against selected industry norms as reflected in the 1974 PIA Ratio Study mentioned earlier in this section. As stated previously, Donnelley fares beautifully in terms of ultimate performance ratios when compared to those industry norms.

Another way to get a "relative fix" on a company is to assess its reactions to those broad-based, general economic influences—such as inflation and recession—over which it has no control.

One of the leading lights at the January Economic Summit Conference for printers, sponsored in Chicago by Printing Industries of America, was Gerald Paul Hillman, an economist with the famed McKinsey & Co., management consultants. Let's examine some of the points he made at that meeting vis-a-vis recent Donnelley moves.

"Fake profit generation (in times of inflation) through inventory accumulation can be avoided only if firms switch to a LIFO system, by which the latest cost is matched to the latest price, or to a still hypothetical NIFO (next in-first out) system, by which anticipated costs for raw materials would be matched to the latest finished product price," said Hillman. "Printing firms must decide whether or not their share price might stay the same despite a change in their earnings multiple in a switch from FIFO to LIFO or, especially, to NIFO. If the capital markets would support such a change, it would help printing companies to preserve corporate resources by reducing taxation. The ability to predict raw material prices, however, will be a critical requirement for making such a system work. *The main point here is that rapid inflation may require a change from cost estimation to cost prediction.*"

Donnelley's 1974 switch to LIFO was probably a minor factor in its P/E ratio's 2-point drop in that year as opposed to 1973, but it was just as probably a major factor in the 2-percentage-point drop in the year's ratio of federal taxes to net sales and the 3.8-percentage-point drop in their ratio to net income (Fig. K). As is demonstrated in the aforementioned complementary study on Donnelley ROI performance, the Chicago giant is a very conservatively managed company. Consequently it was not using a FIFO inventory accounting system, which would have made the switch quite costly, but an average cost system, which softened the transition. Here's how the company's annual report announced the switch and its price:

"This change in the method of accounting for inventories had the effect of reducing net income for the year 1974 by $7.3 million or 39 cents per share below that which would have been reported using the previous inventory method. For this type of accounting change there is no cumulative effect on retained earnings as of December 31, 1973. LIFO inventories at December 31, 1974, were $58,970,000. Under the average cost method of accounting, inventories would have been $14,580,000 higher . . ."

Thus, while Donnelley might have been expected to have made the move from average cost to LIFO, its conservative bent would have indicated just as logically that it would not have taken the more venturesome route and gone from average cost to NIFO. However, considering that it supplies paper at cost to print anywhere from one-fifth to one-third of its output, and considering that paper is by far its major material cost, it would seem a good bet that behind the scenes the company's slide rules are busy on pilot plans for figuring how "anticipated costs for raw materials would be matched to the latest finished product price." The goad is there for Donnelley in spades, for as its 1974 annual report says, "in 1974 . . . we carried more paper in inventory to meet our customers' needs than has been the case in prior years." That factor, plus the "substantially higher prices" it paid for its paper "account in large part for the relatively large effect on net income caused by the change to LIFO . . ."

Another thing worth noting about Donnelley and its inventories is the relationship of that type of asset to sales. (See *Fig. Q*) In 1973, the company's inventories amounted to 7.94 percent of that year's sales, which Barron's praised last December as "relatively high" turnover. While that 1973 figure was down almost a percentage point for 1974—to 7.06—the average figure for the decade 1964-73 was 5.87 percent.

To return to Gerald Paul Hillman at the Summit Conference:

"The industry's excellent record of capital intensification is matched by the poor capital valuation practices employed . . . Rapid inflation will necessitate changes in these practices. Most of the industry's capital investment is being depreciated on a straight-line basis. This accounting convention artificially inflates profits in a period of rapid inflation. . . Straight-line depreciation does not reflect real replacement costs and, therefore, represents a form of capital consumption. In effect, price-insensitive accounting means that a printing company may be devouring its capital to maintain the appearance of viability. To guarantee that internal reserves for future capital spending are maintained, printing companies may continue to report straight-line depreciation for tax purposes while developing a real replacement cost depreciation basis for costing purposes."

Donnelley has been doing that for years. For income tax purposes it uses an accelerated method of computing depreciation on items of plant and equipment, at the same time making straight-line charges for financial reporting. As the rote notes to financial statements now put it: "For financial reporting, the company and its subsidiary generally use the straight line method of computing depreciation over the estimated economic lives. Accelerated depreciation methods are used for income tax purposes, and provision is made for the resulting deferred taxes . . . Investment tax credits are being reflected in earnings over the depreciable lives of the applicable assets. "The portion of the credit attributable to future years has been set out on the balance sheet as deferred investment credit." As the foregoing Figs. H and J attest, Donnelley has been far from coy in its depreciation. allowances. Annually, depreciation charges constitute about one-third of the funds it spends (*Fig. H.*), most of the rest coming from net income. Annually, anywhere from a half to two-thirds or more of those funds is spent on l/b/e. Each year Donnelley converts its gross evaluation of l/b/e to a net evaluation by charging the gross figure a depreciation percentage of over 42 percent (*Fig. J*). It would be hard to see how the Chicago colossus could be "devouring its capital" at those rates, inflation or no.

Fig. Q
Donnelley's Inventory
Relationships

	As % of Current Assets	As % of Total Assets	As % of Net Sales
1964	13.39%	5.77%	4.83%
1965	10.97	4.94	4.42
1966	14.21	6.38	5.61
1967	16.67	7.03	6.25
1968	15.35	6.53	6.05
1969	18.02	6.78	5.98
1970	17.47	7.55	6.55
1971	13.92	6.25	5.57
1972	13.35	6.04	5.46
1973	19.01	8.66	7.94
Av.	15.24	6.60	5.87
1974	19.56	8.63	7.06

Again to Mr. Hillman: "The printing industry is famous for passing on its productivity gains to its customers in the form of reduced price quotes. In other words, in their basic business operations printing companies tend to absorb the cost of technological innovation in order to stay competitive . . . Some absorption of the cost of technological innovation may continue to be necessary . . . (but) In the future, productivity gains may have to be retained as a corporate reserve for investment in a fast-changing technology."

Donnelley is not exempt from the productivity-pass-along charge. This is from its 1974 annual report: "In prior years we were largely successful in offsetting modest increases in wages, services and materials mainly by increased productivity, with the balance accounted for by slightly increased prices. In 1974, this picture changed. Thanks to effective cost control, our manufacturing costs increased less than 10 percent during the year. However, the prices of most of our supplies, materials and energy have had significantly higher increases." It would come as no surprise to any minimally well-informed Donnelley-watcher to discover that (a) its customers received a price-hike quite soon after the 1974 productivity-vs.-inflation trade-off ratio was formulated and (b) productivity pass-along practices are under review.

"The printing industry has always been well-known for relatively permissive and relaxed supplier-printer-customer credit arrangements," said Hillman. "In a time of rapid inflation, however, everyone tries to hasten cash payments to themselves and delay them to others. Discounts and rebates disappear; credit costs are made explicit and high and penalties for late payment grow in severity. The printing industry may soon be forced to fight for cash."

A look at *Fig. R* shows what happened to the company last year in terms of collection days for receivables. While the 1974 increase in such days was somewhat over eight days (about a 13 percent jump), the 1974 experience is actually some 19 days worse than the norm for the decade preceding (a 38 percent jump in severity) and the difference between '74 and '64 is a startling 28 days (about 67 percent) slower. Except for that "tilt" year 1969, the rise in collection days was inexorable but at least partially controllable. The reins slipped in 1972, tightened a bit in 1973 but seem to have gotten away again in 1974.

Fig. R
Collection Days of Receivables
for R. R. Donnelley*

1964	— 41.41 days
1965	— 46.42
1966	— 42.75
1967	— 45.95
1968	— 47.45
1969	— 56.78
1970	— 47.66
1971	— 49.37
1972	— 63.06
1973	— 60.88
Av.	50.18
1974	— 69.01

*Each year's accounts receivable divided by net sales, with the resulting quotient multiplied by 365 —the formula used in the PIA Ratio Study series.

As to the side-effects of that growth in collection days for receivables, the current assets section of *Fig. S* shows that the value of receivables jumped in 1974 by about 12.5 percentage points over the 1973 figure. In that same section, it can be seen that the value of securities dropped by about the same number of percentage points. A look at *Fig. T* will put dollar values on those shifts in percentages.

With resources like Donnelley's, the connection it has with Lakeside Bank, *Fig. U*, and the almost ludicrously minimal long-term debt load it carries (Fig. G), it will take quite a crunch over quite a while to make the company panic over a cash flow or liquidity problem.

We close this portion of our Donnelley commentary with some additional observations about Fig. S, which is in itself a prime demonstrator of the company's management techniques:

Fig. S
Review of Donnelley Assets,
Liabilities Relationships

Composition of Current Assets

% Cur. Assets/ Total Assets		Cash	(a) Rec's	(b) Sec's	(c) Inven.	Pre'd Expens
43.12%	1964	11.01%	31.48%	42.50%	13.39%	1.62%
42.54	1965	9.03	31.58	47.09	10.97	1.33
44.85	1966	9.60	29.67	45.12	14.21	1.40
42.16	1967	7.69	33.56	40.88	16.67	1.20
42.57	1968	7.29	33.00	42.95	15.35	1.41
37.62	1969	7.89	46.87	25.68	18.02	1.54
43.20	1970	6.30	34.86	40.65	17.47	0.72
44.88	1971	7.59	33.79	44.00	13.92	0.70
45.24	1972	6.36	42.24	37.71	13.35	0.34
45.57	1973	6.94	39.92	33.94	19.01	0.19
43.18	Av's	7.97	35.70	40.05	15.24	1.05
44.11	1974	5.94	52.36	21.46	19.56(d)	0.68

NOTES: (a) receivables; (b) US, state and municipal securities, at cost approximating market; (c) inventories at average cost less related billings and deposits; last column, prepaid expenses; (d) inventories at cost, less progress billings, according to new LIFO cost recording system.

Composition of Current Liabilities

Accts. Payable	Accru. Comp.	Other Accru.	Fed Inc. Taxes		% Cur. Liab./ Total Liabil's
(1)27.93%	16.01%	16.01%	32.38%	1964	11.55%
(2)28.37	25.03	16.92	29.68	1965	11.66
35.47	26.33	20.79	17.41	1966	14.99
30.62	27.01	20.01	22.36	1967	13.64
32.16	29.47	19.56	18.81	1968	14.79
30.93	29.29	23.93	15.85	1969	15.77
24.11	30.95	25.18	19.77	1970	14.87
26.14	31.94	29.48	12.44	1971	15.29
26.08	30.74	31.58	11.60	1972	15.95
32.20	30.45	25.86	11.49	1973	16.12
29.40	28.49	22.93	19.18	Av's	14.46
29.14	36.18	26.49	8.20	1974	15.97

NOTES: (1) Total Current Liabilities (TCL) for 1964 were reduced by value of US gov't securities held ($9.8 million). (2) TCL for 1965 reduced by $9.6 million representing value of US securities. The percentages shown for these two yrs. disregard those reductions and relate only to the individual percentages each of the four quantities bear to the sum of the four, as in the eight succeeding relationships.

Fig. T

Donnelley's "Quick Assets,"*

1966 through 1974

	Cash	US Gov't Securities[1]	State/Mun. Securities[1]	State/Munic. Approx. Mkt.[2]	Rec's
1966	$ 9,394	$44,155	$	$	$20,035
1967	7,547	40,100			32,927
1968	7,839	46,171			35,477
1969	8,061	26,339		10,026	47,892
1970	7,819	42,966	7,450	2,134	43,244
1971	10,336	51,118	8,764	1,443	45,991
1972	9,796	46,916	7,619	4,593	61,083
1973	10,977	44,039	9,675	3,015	63,181
1974	9,727	22,468	12,697		85,811

*Cash or near-cash items;
[1] These securities carried under current assets and valued at cost plus accrued interest;
[2] these securities listed under "other assets" and valued at cost. However, both are listed as marketable securities in Donnelley's annual Consolidated Statements of Changes in Financial Position.

Fig. U

R. R. Donnelley's Investments in

its Lakeside Bank, "at underlying

book value."

($ in 000s)

1966	$ 987	70(1)
1967	1,000	70%
1968	1,016	70
1969	1,037	70
1970	1,141	72
1971	1,179	71
1972	1,204	69
1973	1,327	58
1974	1,546	63

Note: First year of operation.

To study Fig. S, and many of the other data tables in this review, it might simplify things to consider various elements in biological terms. For instance, let's consider total assets and total liabilities genus-level data; current assets and current liabilities species-level data; items such as cash and accounts payable subspecies data. Fig. S is a prime example of how Donnelley keeps its relationships between genus levels and species levels stable while manipulating the sub-species items, using them as shock absorbers to compensate for unpredictable "bumps" from a year's roadbed in a way that assures the "main frame" a relatively smooth ride, according to a master plan.

Fig. S shows that the genus-species relationship between total assets and current assets from 1964 through 1974 has—except for that three-for-two stock split year 1969—been held quite steady, with current assets hovering at about 43 percent of total assets. On the like liabilities level, the interval has seen current liabilities fluctuate narrowly at a mean of about 15 percent of total liabilities (the years 1964 and 1965 being "tilt" for the reasons given in the notes to the table). At the sub-species level of current assets, relatively wide variations can be noted in all five item-categories, especially in the first three and especially for 1974. Last year receivables zoomed by $22 million and federal securities holdings dropped by that amount (See *Fig. T*), yet those movements and others less severe among the other "shock absorbers" combined to produce minimal effect on the ratio of current assets to total assets. In like manner, the current liabilities sub-species components last year absorbed a 6 percentage-point gain in accrued compensation and a 3 percentage-point drop in federal taxes while maintaining the current liabilities/total liabilities ratio within one percentage point or so of the established pattern. The drop in the magnitude of 1974 federal taxes as a current liabilities factor is dramatic in terms of proportion. Since 1971, year of the Look Magazine loss and of more than a 7-point drop, tax percentages have been falling steadily, but losses of key accounts have been strong contributing factors. That 1974 drop of 3.3 percentage points from the 1973 tax ratio is proportionately comparable to the 1971 drop of 7 points, but this time the reduction was purposefully engineered. While management attention to the tax aspects of its business has been obviously constant, the latter-years success of reduction efforts seems extraordinary, even allowing for incidental assistance such as the losses mentioned. Disregarding the admittedly hybrid percentages shown for the years 1964 and 1965, the 1974 figure represents about a 60 percent reduction from a mean for the years '66 through '70.

A final note about the data in the tables for this part of our study. In some instances there may be some minor variances in percentages or other data due to use of figures for one year which appeared in another year's annual report. A case in point: in the 1973 annual report, Donnelley's working capital figure was reported as $102,305,000 while in the 1974 annual report that same figure was revised upward to $105,318,000. An effort was made to keep to the figures that were reported first for a year—to use, in this case, the 1973 figures reported in the 1973 annual report.

Aside from such variances, any other data problems would be due to failure of our double-checking systems to detect them. In addition to those tables which are keyed into the text we recommend also study of those which relate net income to net sales on a $1-to-x ratio rather than a percentage ratio, and the table which reports how Donnelley progressed on a year-by-year basis in terms of percentage of growth (or shrinkage) over the year before.

Where Donnelley's Managers Keep Their Profit Keys

An idea of how efficiently R. R. Donnelley & Sons Co. is managed can be drawn in part from comparison of its operating costs with those of the commercial printing industry at large, and particularly those printers who most nearly approximate it in size—what might loosely be called the giant's "peer group." Figures for such a peer group, and for the industry at large, can be taken from the authoritative Ratio Study published annually by Printing Industries of America. All the non-Donnelley comparative data herein will be from the 1974 PIA Ratio Study, which is based on 1973 statistics.

In assessing the following analyses one prime fact should be kept ever in mind: in America's commercial printing industry R. R. Donnelley & Sons Co. is really a "world unto itself." It has no eyeball-to-eyeball rivals in terms of size. Its plant acreage and annual sales are approximately twice those of its nearest competitor. Its annual sales are anywhere from ten to 20 times greater than those of the companies which make up the median bulk of the closest peer group the Ratio Study considers: printers with "Over $10 Million in Sales."

Despite those qualifications as to size, the comparative analysis of Donnelley's operating data with those of the industry is both critically valid and informative. For instance, the giant company's repute as a superlative example of production efficiency is assumed by most to also imply that it enjoys production cost-advantages not available to others. The data appears to refute that assumption. Indications are far stronger that the admiration of the industry should go instead to those who manage Donnelley's administrative and selling operations. Here is why:

Factory cost of product (which Donnelley calls "cost of sales") was 76.53 percent of net sales for the subject company in 1973. The Ratio Study's "All Firms" percentage was 80.26; the total "Profit Leader" community (identified as those who clear 8 percent or over before taxes) registered a 75.53 percentage. In the Sales Over $10 Million category, the Profit Leaders' segment spent 77.68 percent of sales as factory cost of product while the average percentage for the grouping was 83.73 percent.

Donnelley was thus a bit over 1 percent more efficient than the elite among its peer group in keeping total production costs down, although it was 1 percent less efficient than the average for the whole Profit Leader community. Since Donnelley's is an individual figure and the others are composites, it seems self-evident that there are a number of firms contributing to the composites for all groups that spend less for factory cost of product than Donnelley does, and thus are more efficient in that respect.

Gross Profit as a percentage of net sales was 23.46 percent for R. R. Donnelley in 1973. For the industry—All Firms—it was 19.74 percent; for the Profit Leaders at large, 24.47 percent. The elite of the Over $10 Million Sales club came in at 22.32 while the figure for the whole club was 16.27.

Administrative and Selling Expenses for Donnelley amounted to 8.81 percent of sales in 1973. For Profit Leaders in the Ratio Study's universe, such expenses amounted to 13.52 percent; for All Firms, 14.27 percent. Profit Leaders in the Over $10 Million category registered 11.73 percent while the category itself averaged 10.39 percent.

It is obviously at the administrative and selling expenses phase of the operating cycle that there occurs the first strong indicator of superiority of system or technique on Donnelley's part. It would be entirely too glib to say that the sort of advantages Donnelley enjoys by virtue of tremendous single-account sales were largely responsible for that favorable Administrative/Selling indicator. Four major product-types accounted for the bulk of Donnelley's 1973 sales. The largest, magazines, amounted to 28.4 percent of income; the smallest, directories, accounted for 17.2 percent. The loss of Look magazine (1971) and Life (1972) went far toward leveling single-account dominance.

Income from operations was 14.65 percent of sales for R. R. Donnelley in 1973. The composite figure for All Firms was 5.47 percent and that for all Profit Leaders 10.95 percent. In the Over $10 Million category, the Profit Leaders percentage was 10.59; the average for the category, 5.88. Thus Donnelley seems almost half again as efficient at squeezing essence from its sales dollars as are the bulk of the elite of the largest firms as well as the smaller ones.

Other Income, Other Expense for Donnelley was a small honey pot in 1973—at 1.34 percent of sales it added to net income as much of a hypo as an additional $15 million in sales would have done. For most Ratio Study printers, this is a category of "income" that results in a drain, since "other" expenses exceed whatever extra cash is earned in excess of sales. For the All Firms universe, other expenses resulted in a loss of 0.44 percent of earnings from operations; for the profit Leader universe, other income exceeded expenses enough to add 0.13 percent of sales to the net income total. Among Donnelley's peers, however, the average for All Firms diminished earnings from operations by 0.71 percent and it reduced such earnings for the elite of the group—the Profit Leaders—0.19 percent.

Fig. I

Operating Costs as Percentages of Net Sales

R. R. Donnelley & Sons Co. Inc.

(Donnelley data compared with those for "All Firms" in the 1974 PIA Ratio Study)

	Cost of Sales		Gross Profit		Admin/Sell Exp.		Earnings from Ops.		Other Income*		Net Before Taxes	
	Donnel. %	All %	Donnel. %	All %	Donnel. %	All %	Donnel. %	All %	Donnel. %	All %	Donnel. %	All %
1964	76.86	77.95	23.14	22.05	7.51	16.29	15.63	5.76	0.75	(0.20)	16.38	5.56
1965	75.86	78.02	24.14	21.98	7.68	15.88	16.46	6.10	0.76	(0.04)	17.22	6.06
1966	77.16	78.80	22.84	21.20	7.84	15.00	15.00	6.20	1.06	(0.07)	16.06	6.27
1967	76.99	79.78	23.01	20.22	7.88	14.72	15.13	5.50	1.12	(0.20)	16.25	5.30
1968	77.12	80.18	22.88	19.82	8.00	14.50	14.88	5.32	1.13	(0.18)	16.01	5.14
1969	78.54	80.21	21.46	19.79	8.45	14.13	13.01	5.66	1.03	(0.34)	14.04	5.32
1970	78.88	78.99	21.12	21.01	8.40	15.74	12.72	5.27	1.07	(0.58)	13.79	4.69
1971	78.63	79.96	21.37	20.04	8.60	15.15	12.77	4.89	1.11	(0.55)	13.88	4.34
1972	78.26	80.72	21.74	19.28	8.56	14.07	13.18	5.21	1.11	(0.39)	14.29	4.82
1973	76.53	80.26	23.46	19.74	8.81	14.27	14.65	5.47	1.34	(0.44)	16.00	5.03
Av.	77.47	79.49	22.53	20.51	8.18	14.96	14.35	5.54	1.05	(0.30)	15.39	5.25
1974	80.35	N.a.	19.65	N.a.	8.76	N.a.	10.89	N.a.	1.22	N.a.	12.11	N.a.

*Less other expense.

Donnelley's "other income, other expense" posting gathers much of its sweetness from a pretty prodigious purse-full of government securities. For instance, in 1973 its holdings in federal, state and municipal securities were valued at $56,728,332 worth. Such holdings fell below $40 million only once in the past decade—1969's securities were worth a little over $36 million.

As *Fig. I* shows, those securities, plus other income-earning properties and activities have averaged over 1 percent of net sales for the past decade. Considering Donnelley's total net sales for the period, and the rate at which it can capitalize on those sales in terms of net income, over the past ten years that 1 percent in "other income" has posted earnings equivalent to over $30 million in additional net sales.

Net Income Before Taxes was 16.00 percent of net sales for Donnelley in 1973. For All Firms it was 5.03 percent; for the Profit Leaders, over-all, it was 11.08 percent. For the Over $10 Million Sales group, the All Firms average percentage was 5.17 and for the group's Profit Leaders it was 10.40.

In Summary: From the foregoing—plus supporting data in *Fig. I*—it seems clear that it is not its custom-engineered machines or super-secret know-how as much as its administrative and selling management's expertise—plus those comfortable investments—that make Donnelley's Operating Statement shine among those of other industry factors, peers or no.

Balance Sheet Dynamics

"The Balance Sheet is the dynamic factor in the evaluation of your company," the 1974 Ratio Study tells its readers. "If your Balance Sheet does not show the proper make-up and relationships, *regardless of profit*, your business will falter." That phrase we italicized *could* well give Donnelley chills, but we doubt it will, for sundry reasons which will be developed herein. Let's see how R. R. Donnelley & Sons Co.'s Balance Sheet data fit the industry's patterns as revealed in the 1974 PIA Ratio Study and what may be concluded as a result.

Comparative analysis of the subject's Balance Sheet with industry norms shows most conspicuously that—relative to the industry at large—Donnelley is inordinately heavily capitalized in all respects. Being undisputed king of commercial printerdom, twice the size of its nearest competitor, that will come as a surprise to those "in the know" only in the matter of degree. Those who have studied the PIA Ratios have known from the beginning that "Profit Leaders possess more assets and net worth per employee," and have a considerably stronger financial base than the mass of printers. As the 1974 Study puts it, "as a firm's size increases, so do the amounts of assets per employee. For example, the assets-per-employee ratio in the Under $250,000 Sales class is $9515; in the Over $10 Million class it is $20,906. The larger the firm the more capital available to employ." Keep the foregoing in mind while reading the following:

Sales as a percentage of Gross Assets was 78.18 in Donnelley's 1973 ledger and 124.40 percent for All Firms. For the Profit Leaders overall, the percentage was 125.77.

Sales as a percentage of Net Assets was 109.07 for Donnelley and 175.70 for all Firms. For the Profit Leader universe it was 172.62.

Sales as a percentage of Gross Plant (before depreciation/amortization) was 118.26 for Donnelley. It was 204.03 percent for All Firms and 213.78 percent for the Profit Leaders.

Sales as a percentage of Current Assets was 239 percent for Donnelley; 327 percent for All Firms and 323 percent for the Profit Leaders.

Sales as a percentage of Working Capital was 370.28 for Donnelley; 644.75 percent for All Firms and 541.97 percent for the Profit Leaders.

The import of that comparative data could be expressed just as meaningfully as follows:

Whereas it took the industry at large $1 worth of gross assets to produce approximately $1.26 worth of sales in 1973, it took Donnelley $1 worth of gross assets to produce only 78¢ worth of sales.

While it only took the industry $1 worth of net assets to produce about $1.76 worth of sales, it took Donnelley that much to produce only $1.09 in sales.

Where $1 worth of gross plant investment produced some $2.04 worth of sales for the industry at large in 1973, for Donnelley's $1 the yield was only $1.18.

Where annual sales were almost 3.3 times the value of current assets for the All Firms universe in 1973, for Donnelley they were abut 2.4 times as large.

While for the industry the ratio of working capital to sales was about 1-to-6, for Donnelley it was less than 1-to-4.

Those relative proportions are not at all peculiar to Donnelley's 1973 experience. As *Fig. II* shows, the relationship of the five factors examined above to Donnelley's sales figures for each of the years of the 1964-73 decade has remained relatively stable.

The natural reaction to the foregoing-despite the preface about size/capitalization ratios—will be something on the order of "Something's wrong here! How the hell could an outfit like Donnelley show up *that* far out of line?" We can only suggest that, however logical those doubts, they be tested by the incredulous.

In 1973, Donnelley's sales were $378,816,871. Its gross assets (total current assets, plus other assets, plus property, plant and equipment, at cost, before depreciation) were worth $484,524,623. Dividing sales by gross assets and multiplying by 100 to give a percentage can only yield 78.18. The company's net assets (the above less $137,215,141 depreciation) were valued at $347,309,482. Divide the later figure into sales, adjust for percent, and you get a comparatively paltry 109.07. Gross plant in 1973

Fig. II
A Decade of Donnelley Sales/Asset Ratios

	Sales % Gr. Assets	Sales % Net Assets	Sales % Gr. Plant	Sales % Cur. Assets	Sales % Work'g Cap.
1964	84.52	119.64	122.26	274.44	378.92
1965	83.29	117.87	120.41	277.07	381.72
1966	80.31	113.62	118.89	253.30	380.50
1967	79.31	112.40	113.92	266.60	393.97
1968	76.14	108.08	109.83	253.88	389.01
1969	79.15	113.39	124.63	301.29	518.70
1970	79.39	115.35	114.80	266.98	407.13
1971	76.06	112.11	114.45	249.80	378.83
1972	79.58	110.60	120.86	244.47	377.54
1973	78.18	109.07	118.26	239.33	370.28
Av.	79.59	113.21	117.83	262.72	297.66
1974	87.35	122.17	128.77	276.96	434.06

was valued at $320,328,169. Divide that into sales, do the percentage adjustment, and the inescapable result is 118.26 percent! Current assets were $158,281,892 for Connelley in 1973, and its working capital was $102,305,000. Double check those ratios to sales and you'll come up with 239.33 and 370.28 percent, respectively.

Another indication of how heavily capitalized R. R. Donnelley is in relation to the rest of the industry can be had by comparing its schedules of assets and sales per employee with those for the rest of the industry. (See Fig. III)

In 1973 R. R. Donnelley had 11,300 employees. Its investment (net assets) per employee came to $30,740. The Profit Leader segment of its peer group (the Over $10 Million Sales firms) had an assets to employee ratio fo $22,580 while All Firms in the group had a ratio of $20,900 per employee. The Ratio Study's All Firms universe averaged $17,300 in assets per employee while the total Profit Leader segment had assets of $19,350 per employee.

While it was to be expected that Donnelley's assets per employee would far outshadow even those for its peer group, it would also seem logical that sales per employee would, as a result, be commensurately greater. Given superior tools and resources—which Donnelley's ratio of assets per employee would imply—that expectation would only seem common sense. However:

Sales per employee for Donnelley in 1973 equated to $33,520, while for the Profit Leaders in its peer group they were $39,990 and for All Firms in that group, $33,830. Sales for the Ratio Study's universe of All Firms in 1973 equated to $30,400 per employee and for the Profit Leaders they came to $33,400.

Those 1973 relationships of Donnelley's vs. the industry at large and its peer group are not disporportionate; they apply in degree to data for other years as well. Again, what becomes of Donnelley's vaunted reputation for efficiency if it takes a Donnelley worker some $30,000 worth of tools and plant to produce sales equivalent to what it takes other printers about $20,000 to produce?

Automation has long been considered to be a Donnelley hallmark. Its engineering research efforts, highly budgeted toward an optimum attainment of precision through automation, are widely considered unique in the industry; its top-secret, proprietary machine modifications are a universal source of envy. Why then isn't there at least a far higher sales-per-employee ratio for Donnelley than for other firms? Shouldn't such production advantages be translatable into more output per employee?

The answers to those questions are most certainly not going to come from Donnelley if past is prologue, for Donnelley discusses operations only with God. Two possible explanations can be inferred from what we know, however: (1) Despite its automation the giant is so conservatively managed that it probably keeps on tap very comfortable manpower reserves, and (2) having been so long non-union the century-old behemoth probably has developed far more than most other commercial printers what might be termed a quasi-Japanese type of relationship with its workers—a tradition in which generations from the same families naturally gravitate toward its gates. Donnelley management repeatedly inserts into the company's annual reports notes about the high ratios of on-the-job seniority among its work-force. In the 1973 report, for instance, it was noted with obvious pride that 5700 of its 11,300 workers had been with the company over ten years and 2150 for 25 years or more. Those two foregoing assumptions might also explain the following:

Donnelley's net income before taxes per employee in 1973 was $5,360, while for Profit Leaders in its peer group the figure was $4,160 and for All Firms in that group it was a mere $1,750! For All Firms reporting to the 1974 Ratio Study on their 1973 experience, the average net income before taxes per employee was $1,530 and for the Profit Leaders in the full universe it was $3,700.

Since that differential in Donnelley's favor is so pronounced in the net income column, and proportionately so unfavorable in the assets and sales per employee columns, somewhere in between a powerful productivity factor must be intervening.

It's been seen in the foregoing that where Donnelley pulls away from the pack is in the administrative-and-selling costs area. It seems reasonable then to conclude that the synergism at work for the company exists in the relationships between sales and production, and sales and administration. The amount of waste or of lost motion in those interrelationships must be infinitesimal in comparison with the industry at large, for how else could lower sales per assets—and relatively so-so sales per employee—translate themselves into much higher *income* per employee?

Returning to the stricture quoted at the opening of this section, it would appear that Donnelley manages to thrive on a type of summitry economics that is neither available nor applicable to other printers.

Fig. III
How Selected Donnelley Asset and Operating Data Equate Per Employee

	Number Employees	Net Assets/ Employee	Net L/B/E* Employee	Gross L/B/E* Employee	Net Sales/ Employee	Net Before Tax/Empl.	Net After Tax/Empl.
1964	10,880	$16,200	$ 9,130	$15,870	$19,400	$3,180	$1,590
1965	11,000	17,640	9,940	17,270	20,790	3,580	1,860
1966	12,180	17,900	9,690	17,120	20,350	3,270	1,700
1967	12,220	19,040	10,840	18,790	21,400	3,480	1,810
1968	12,030	20,990	11,850	20,650	22,690	3,630	1,730
1969	12,810	21,200	12,230	21,390	24,030	3,370	1,660
1970	13,200	21,750	12,000	21,850	25,090	3,400	1,740
1971	12,500	24,260	13,000	24,400	27,200	3,770	1,950
1972	11,800	27,090	14,230	24,790	29,960	4,280	2,210
1973	11,300	30,740	16,200	28,350	33,520	5,360	2,750
1974	11,600	32,030	17,620	30,390	39,130	4,740	2,480

*Land, Buildings and Equipment.

Assets/Liabilities; Cash Flow

Conservatism as a hallmark of Donnelley fiscal management is strongly evident in its working capital relationships (*Fig. IV*).

The industry at large, as reflected in the 1974 Ratio Study (of 1973 data) registered a 2-to-1 relationship of current assets to current liabilities. The Profit Leaders in the Ratio Study stood at 2.3-to-1. Donnelley's was a comfortable 2.83-to-1, and that happened to be its second lowest relationship in 20 years! The lowest was 2.39-to-1, which occurred in 1969, the year a stock split gave holders of common shares three for two. Over the 1964-73 decade the current ratio has averaged 2.65-to-1; over the previous nine years, it averaged 4.42-to-1. (See Summary of Financial Statistics)

All Firms in the 1974 Ratio Study had a "quick assets" to current liabilities ratio of 1.3-to-1. (Quick assets are cash or near-cash items such as receivables and securities, the Study points out.) For the Profit Leaders of the Ratio's universe, the ratio was 1.5-to-1. For Donnelley it was 2.28-to-1. In 1972, the All Firms quick assets/current liabilities ratio was 1.3-to-1 and the Profit Leaders' was 1.7-to-1. Donnelley's was 2.45-to-1. (In that year Donnelley had lost the Life magazine account.) For the past decade, Donnelley's lowest quick assets ratio was 1.92-to-1; its highest was 3.17-to-1, and its average ratio was 2.53-to-1. (See *Fig. IV*)

As the Ratio Study says, this is the "acid test" of liquidity. Donnelley passes that test with a 50 percent margin over the Profit Leaders of the industry.

Cash flow is another new element in the 1974 Ratio Study. It is determined by dividing profit (earnings before income taxes) by working capital.

For all Firms in 1973, that ratio was 32.44 percent; for the Profit Leaders over-all, it was 60.07 percent. For Donnelley it was 59.24 percent. Over the past decade the cash flow ratio so determined averaged 60.9 for Donnelley, ranging from a high of 72.84 to a low of 52.57 percent (see *Fig. IV*).

Fig. IV
Donnelley Assets/Liabilities; Cash Flow

	Cur. Assets/ Cur. Liabils.	Quick Assets[1] Cur. Liabils.	Cash Flow[2]
1964	3.73 ° 1	3.17 ° 1	62.02%
1965	3.65 ° 1	3.15 ° 1	65.76
1966	2.99 ° 1	2.52 ° 1	61.09
1967	3.09 ° 1	2.54 ° 1	64.00
1968	2.88 ° 1	1.92 ° 1	62.23
1969	2.39 ° 1	2.40 ° 1	72.84
1970	2.60 ° 1	2.38 ° 1	55.25
1971	2.94 ° 1	2.51 ° 1	52.57
1972	2.84 ° 1	2.45 ° 1	53.98
1973	2.83 ° 1	2.28 ° 1	59.24
Av.	2.65 ° 1	2.53 ° 1	60.90
1974	2.76 ° 1	2.20 ° 1	52.58

[1]Cash or near cash items.
[2]Earnings before provision for income taxes ÷ working capital.

For a further look at how the Donnelley Balance Sheet ratios stand in their own right and—in the latest instance—vis-a-vis of those of their peer group's elite, we have prepared the data shown in Figs. V and VI.

Fig. V
Ratios for Assets;
Donnelley's and a Peer PL Contrast*

	1965	1967	1969	1971	1973	PPL'73
Cash	4.28%	3.24%	2.97%	3.41%	3.16%	3.13
Receivables	14.99	14.15	17.63	15.17	18.19	31.46
Inventories	5.22	7.03	6.78	6.25	8.66	20.15
Other Assets	18.06	17.74	10.24	20.06	15.66	3.12
Total Current	42.55	42.16	37.62	44.89	45.57	57.86
Land/Bldg./Equip.	97.89	98.67	100.89	100.60	92.23	73.24
Less Depreciation	41.52	41.72	43.20	46.96	39.50	34.89
Net Fixed Assets	56.37	56.95	57.69	53.64	52.73	38.35
Other	1.08	0.89	4.69	1.47	1.70	3.79
	100.00	100.00	100.00	100.00	100.00	100.00

*Source for the 'peer group Profit Leader contrast' PPL column is the 1974 PIA Ratio Study, the data in which covers 1973 performance.

Fig Va
Basic Assets Percentages
for years listed in 'Note':
Donnelley's vs. All Firms data

	Aver. Donn.	Aver. All Firms
Current Assets	42.56%	52.77%
Net Fixed Assets	55.47	42.30
Other Non-Current Assets	1.97	4.93

Note: Averages based on data for years 1965, 1967, 1969, 1971, 1973.

For the period covered in *Figs. V* and *VI*, the average percentages for the All Firms universe in respect to each of the main asset and liability segments are shown in *Figs. Va* and *VIa.* Inspection of all the schedules for the latter series reveals the basics of the sharp differences between Donnelley economics and the economics that apply to the rest of the commercial printing industry—hinting also, of course, at the disparity between even a median for the Over $10 Million Sales category and the actual data for the other printing giants in the proximity of $100 million sales.

In 1973, Donnelley's net income was 16.00 percent of sales. The All Firms average was 5.03 percent; the total Profit Leaders percentage was 11.08 percent. Among firms with Over $10 Million Sales, the average for All Firms was 5.17 and for Profit Leaders 10.40 percent.

Fig. VI

Ratios for Liabilities:

Donnelley's and a Peer PL Contrast*

	1965	1967	1969	1971	1973	PPL'73[1]
Accts/Notes Payable	4.71%	4.17%	4.88%	4.00%	5.19%	14.40%
Other Current Liabils.[2]	6.96	9.46	10.89	11.29	10.93	9.93
Total Current Liabils.	11.67	13.63	15.77	15.29	16.12	23.33
Longterm Liabilities[3]	10.09	9.89	9.53	8.73	7.93	10.74
Total Liabilities	21.76	23.52	25.30	24.02	24.05	35.07
Stockholders Equity	78.24	76.48	74.70	75.98	75.95	64.93
	100.00	100.00	100.00	100.00	100.00	100.00

[1] Ratios for Profit Leaders among 1973's Over $10 Million Sales group. Source: 1974 PIA Ratio Study.
[2] Includes accrued compensation and Federal income taxes.
[3] Includes deferred investment credit and deferred Federal income taxes.

Fig. VIa

Basic Liability Percentages for

the Years Listed in 'Notes':

Donnelley's vs. All Firms Data

	Aver. Donn.	Aver. All Firms
Current Liabils.	14.50%	25.08%
Longterm Liabils.	9.23	17.78
Total Liabilities	23.73	42.87
Shareholders Equity	76.27	56.80

Note: Averages based on data for years 1965, 1967, 1969, 1971, 1973, as per Figs. V and VI. 'All Firms' Liabilities averages do not total 100% because 'reserves not already included' (not available for Donnelley) not figured in. That data accounted for the 0.33% difference.

Investment Turnover   The second of the two ROI factors is the percentage for turnover on investment (TOI), achieved by dividing sales by gross assets. Here the Donnelley organization's capital structure—predictably—yields group of percentages at wide variance with data published in the Ratio Studies:

In 1970, Donnelley's turnover on investment was 79.39 percent; in other words, for every $100 invested in gross assets the company posted

$79.39 worth of sales. The All Firms percentage was 121.29, or $121.29 sales dollar for every $100 worth of gross assets; the total Profit Leader figure was 118.25 percent, or $118.25 worth of sales for every $100 in gross assets.

In 1972, Donnelley's investment turnover was 79.58 percent. The average for All Firms was 118.53 percent; for Profit Leaders 124.90 percent. In the ultra club—the Over $10 Million Sales firms—the average percentage was 104.20 while that for the Profit Leaders was 118.14.

In 1973, Donnelley's investment turnover was 78.18 percent. The All Firms average was 124.40 percent and the Profit Leaders, over-all, came in at 125.77 percent. The Over $10 Million club had an average All Firms percentage of 112.94; the club's Profit Leaders had an average of 131.32 percent.

The ROI Results

As mentioned above, the ROI formula requires multiplication of the income-as-a-percentage-of-sales factor by the investment-turnover factor (based on gross assets). Here is how that exercise turns out for Donnelley as compared with the Profit Leaders of its peer group:

In 1970, Donnelley's ROI was 10.95 percent; the peer Profit Leaders' 14.16.

In 1972, Donnelley's ROI was 11.37 percent; the peer Profit Leaders' 12.32.

In 1973 Donnelley's ROI was 12.51 percent; the peer Profit Leaders' 13.66.

Of course, the All Firms average percentages for the peer group were very considerably under Donnelley's. For 1970, 1972 an 1973, respectively, they were 5.91 percent, 5.45 percent and 5.84 percent.

There is no gainsaying the fact that the Chicago subject is a bit ROI-low compared with its closet Ratio Study peers but—be that as it may—the fact that, in view of its huge gross and net asset figures, Donnelley's ROI is even in the ballgame is of itself an accomplishment. Incidentally, as *Fig. VII* shows, over the decade 1964-73 Donnelley's ROI remained relatively stable, averaging 12.25 percent, with but two wide fluctuations— from the high of 14.35 in 1965 to the low of 10.59 in 1971. The same is true for the rest of the averages in Fig. VII; because the data-fluctuations are narrow the averages are closer to medians than most such figures tend to be.

What You Can Spy via ROI

Return on Investment (ROI), widely considered the best index of true profitability, needs neither introduction nor assessment here. No one denies it is a primary criterion for judging both over-all management efficiency and the efficiency of each of those activities which in concert determine the final, full verdict on managerial competence.

The 1974 PIA Ratio Study team enthusiastically endorses ROI, to which a whole section of the Study is devoted. In the section, this statement appears: "As the years pass it becomes increasingly evident that the printing industry—as a 'capital intense' industry—must adapt to the ROI concept." Here is how the ROI criteria apply to Donnelley vis-a-vis the rest of the industry.

The formula for ROI is income (net *before* taxes) divided by sales, multiplied by sales divided by assets. The assets figure used in *gross*, not net, assets. The first of the two ROI factors yields data on "income as a percentage of sales." The second of the factors reveals a company's annual "investment turnover." Their multiplication results in the basic ROI information.

To find income as a percentage of sales is to discover what to many authorities is the most important part of the ROI concept. While, as the Study says, "it's true that Profit Leaders generally show a higher investment turnover, *the real difference* is found in their income as a percentage of sales." Here's how Donnelley's data reflect on performance in terms of that "real difference:"

In 1970, Donnelley's net income before taxes was 13.79 percent of sales. For All Firms the percentage was 4.69 and for the total Profit Leader segment it was 12.10 percent. Donnelley's closest peer group in that year's Study was that doing $5 Million Sales or Over. In that group the average was 5.19 percent overall, and 11.96 percent for the Profit Leaders.

In 1972, Donnelley's income as a percentage of sales was 14.29. The All Firms average was 4.82 percent; the total Profit Leader group's average was 10.99 percent. The largest grouping in the Ratio Study covering that year was the Over $10 Million Sales group. The percentage there was an average 5.23 over-all, with 10.43 being average for the Profit Leaders.

R. R. Donnelley's Ratio
of Net Income* to
Net Sales, $/$

1964	$1	:	$12.21
1965	1	:	11.17
1966	1	:	11.98
1967	1	:	11.84
1968	1	:	13.14
1969	1	:	14.50
1970	1	:	14.44
1971	1	:	13.94
1972	1	:	13.53
1973	1	:	12.18
Av.	1	:	12.89
1974	1	:	15.77

*After Taxes

Net Asset ROIs

The 1974 Ratio Study takes two sightings on ROI—one based on gross assets and the other based on net assets. As explained in the Study, each has its peculiar advantage and its peculiar disadvantage: the gross assets ROI "prevents management from showing a good ROI with a plant that is obsolete because it always relates income to original investment." In this respect, the net assets approach is better because it "accurately indicates the true return on assets invested." However, the net assets ROI permits a management to continue to "look good" despite increasing obsolescence while the gross assets ROI prevents that distortion.

In 1973, Donnelley's net assets ROI was 17.45 percent; the figure for its peer group Profit Leaders was 18.42 and for the All Firms peer group the average percent was 8.37. In the Study's "universe," the All Firms net assets ROI was 8.83 and the Profit Leaders' 19.13 percent. *Fig. VII* shows the Donnelley average for net assets ROI for the 1964-73 decade as 17.36 percent and the related investment turnover average as 113.21 percent.

Fig. VII
Donnelley's ROI, 1964-1973

	Income as % age of Sales	Gross Assets TOI%*	Gross Assets ROI%	Net Assets TOI%	Net Assets ROI%
1964	16.42	84.52	13.84	119.64	19.60
1965	17.22	83.29	14.35	117.87	20.31
1966	16.06	80.31	12.90	113.62	18.25
1967	16.25	79.31	12.89	112.40	18.27
1968	16.01	76.14	12.18	108.08	17.29
1969	14.04	79.15	11.11	113.35	15.91
1970	13.79	79.39	10.95	115.35	15.20
1971	13.88	76.29	10.59	112.11	15.56
1972	14.29	79.58	11.37	110.60	15.80
1973	16.00	78.18	12.51	109.07	17.45
Av.	15.39	79.62	12.25	113.21	17.36
1974	15.60	81.35	13.63	122.17	19.06

*TOI equals turnover on investment.

ROI on Equity, Long-Term Debt

A measure of the profitability of a company in terms of assets financed by shareholders' equity is computed by dividing income (net before taxes) by shareholders' equity, which yields the ratio of return on that specific investment sector. For the All Firms and the Profit Leader universes in 1973, shareholders' equity ROI was 16.88 percent and 30.10 percent, respectively. For Donnelley it was 22.98 percent. (See *Fig. VIII*)

Fig. VIII
Donnelley's Equity/L.T.
Debt ROIs

	ROI Based on Shareholders' Eq.	ROI on Share Eq. Plus Longterm Debt
1964	25.29%	23.70%
1965	25.95	24.78
1966	24.28	23.28
1967	23.87	23.01
1968	22.89	22.25
1969	21.31	20.84
1970	21.05	20.62
1971	20.48	20.09
1972	20.84	20.58
1973	22.98	22.78
Av.	22.89	22.19
1974	19.50	19.36

How Major Donnelley
Operating Data Relate to Sales

	Cost of Sales	Gross Profit	Sell/Ad. Expense	Earnings Opera'ns	Pre-Tax Income	Post-Tax Income
1964	76.86%	23.14%	7.51%	15.63%	16.38%	8.19
1965	75.86	24.14	7.68	16.46	17.22	8.96
1966	77.16	22.84	7.85	15.00	16.06	8.35
1967	76.99	23.01	7.88	15.13	16.25	8.45
1968	77.12	22.88	8.00	14.88	16.01	7.61
1969	78.54	21.46	8.45	13.01	14.04	6.90
1970	78.88	21.12	8.40	12.72	13.79	6.93
1971	78.63	21.37	8.60	12.77	13.88	7.17
1972	78.26	21.74	8.56	13.18	14.29	7.39
1973	76.53	23.46	8.81	14.65	16.00	8.21
Av.	77.45	22.52	8.17	14.34	15.39	7.82
1974	80.35	19.65	8.76	10.89	12.11	6.34

How Donnelley Vital Statistics Changed,
Year-by-Year for the Decade 1964-1973, and for 1974
(All percentages plus except those in parenthesis)

	Net Sales	Net Income	Net Share	Stock Equity	Stock Eq/Shr.	Net L/B/E*	Work'g Capital
1964	14.66%	21.20%	20.00%	10.68%	9.94%	15.50%	4.12%
1965	8.34	18.44	17.77	11.01	11.02	10.08	7.54
1966	8.39	1.02	(0.94)	7.98	7.63	7.90	8.74
1967	5.49	6.67	6.54	8.55	8.51	12.27	1.88
1968	4.35	(5.96)	(6.14)	7.23	7.30	7.60	5.68
1969	12.82	2.21	2.80	6.32	6.40	9.90	(15.39)
1970	7.56	8.02	8.18	6.86	7.16	1.11	37.04
1971	2.67	6.30	6.72	6.28	6.59	2.66	10.34
1972	3.99	7.15	7.87	5.22	6.02	3.25	4.35
1973	7.14	19.08	19.71	8.80	9.77	9.05	9.24
Av.	7.54	8.42	8.44	7.89	8.03	7.93	7.35
1974	19.81	(7.49)	(7.32)	6.87	7.04	11.60	2.20

*Land, buildings, equipment

A final measure of ROI used in the Ratio Study is ROI on long-term debt and shareholders' equity, computed by dividing the sum of both into net before taxes. Says the Study: "We find that computing the ROI on the total of long-term debt equity and shareholders' equity has considerable value for two reasons: (1) Long-term debt financing is an alternative for shareholders' equity, and (2) shareholders' equity is often an alternative for long-term debt financing."

For All Firms and Profit Leaders, full study, the ROI based on shareholders' equity plus long-term debt was 12.26 and 25.40 percent, respectively, in 1973. For Donnelley it was 22.78. Note that for both ROIs 1973 firmly consolidated 1972's beginning reversal of a downtrend.

In Summary: Donnelley's ratios of income to sales ("the real difference")—averaging 15.39 percent for the 1964-73 decade—are almost as superior to industry Profit Leader norms for such data as its investment turnover ratios are inferior to those norms. The ROI result is something of a stand-off. While, in comparison to its peer group Profit Leaders, Donnelley stayed a bit on the low side of the ROI ratings through 1973, there is a noticeable trend in that respect: the difference between the percentage for the top Profit Leaders and Donnelley's was a good 3.22 percent in 1970, by 1972 that difference had been cut to 0.95 percent, and in 1973 the differential had held at 1.15 percent.

Donnelley's net assets ROI and gross assets ROI in 1972 and 1973 were close enough to Profit Leader norms to indicate that Donnelley is doing little that is unusual in respect to "trading up" or "trading down" on the value of its assets.

An interesting comparison exists between the Profit Leader ROIs for shareholders' equity and shareholders' equity plus long-term debt and those data for Donnelley. For the former, the respective ROIs (30.10 and 25.40 percent) differ by a healthy 4.70 percent. For Donnelley that percentage difference is only 0.20, due to its relatively empty long-term debt saddle.

Over the next few years, that debt policy is bound to pay very high dividends for Donnelley unless the prime rate topples. The Chicago champ's habit of paying-as-it-goes for the great majority of its plant and equipment expansions has not only been great training for the present. It has left it almost debt-free in an era of soaring costs and credit strangulation.

Crawfordsville Manufacturing Division prints encyclopedias, textbooks, Bibles and many other kinds of commercial printing.

Warsaw Manufacturing Division
one of many large
multi-color gravure presses.

Willard Manufacturing
Division—two large multi-color
web offset presses.

R. R. Donnelley & Sons Co., Inc.
2233 Martin Luther King Drive
Chicago, Illinois 60616

Arcata National Corporation

How Printer's Ink Came to Flow
from Forests of Redwood

Reported to be America's second largest printing organization,
Arcata National Corp., chalked up printing and
printed product sales of just under $200 million for
the fiscal year 1974. Major elements
in this nationwide printing combine include
such one-time leading independents as Kingsport (Tenn.) Press
and Halliday Lithograph of Hanover, Mass.

Arcata Graphics Inc.,
Buffalo division.

Kingsport Press'
$2 million warehouse and
distribution center has storage
space for 25 million books.

Arcata National Today

Ranking: Arcata National Corp. is reported to be the second largest printing organization in the United States, with printing and printed products sales for the fiscal year ending June 30, 1974 of $199,047,000. Its 15 plants are strung out from coast to coast, and they provide services ranging from typesetting and color separation through offset, gravure, and letterpress printing, including binding and mailing. Arcata's products include books, magazines, catalogs, directories and a full line of greeting cards.

Product Mix: Arcata's book production accounted for 40 percent of total corporate sales for the last fiscal year. Magazine production represents 15 percent of corporate revenues and makes it one of the top five periodical printers in the United States. Arcata's third largest segment is printed products, including greeting cards and gift wrap paper. Assorted commercial printing accounts for the balance of the product line.

More than 70 million hard cover books were produced last year at Kingsport Press alone, and Halliday Lithograph turned out over 30 million volumes. Periodicals printed by Arcata include *Reader's Digest, Newsweek, Time, TV Guide, Sports Illustrated, U.S. News and World Report, Penthouse* and *Money*. The commercial printing bag comprises annual reports, brochures, catalogs and promotional material.

Capital equipment includes two Cameron belt press book production systems (including the first installed in America; there are now only 12 such presses in the world), three cathode ray tube (CRT) phototypesetting systems, and more than 40 web offset presses. Commitments for new press and related equipment are estimated at $14 million in fiscal year 1975, which included provisions for the initial costs of a new $10 million book plant.

Organization

Arcata National Corporation, the parent organization, with headquarters in Menlo Park, California, is a publicly owned corporation. It is listed on the New York and Pacific Stock Exchanges under the symbol ACA. J. Frank Leach is president and chief executive officer, and G. Robert Evans serves as executive vice president and chief operating officer.

Arcata National is composed of 17 operating divisions organized in five groups. The Book Group, headquartered in Kingsport, Tennessee, is under the direction of Hugh Swaney and consists of two book manufacturing divisions—Kingsport Press and Halliday Lithograph—and a microfilm services division, Arcata Microfilm.

The Publications Group, under the leadership of Ed Jewett, is headquartered in Los Angeles. The group is composed of Graphic Press, Rotary Offset Printers, Arcata Graphics San Jose, Arcata Graphics Pacific Press, Arcata Graphics Buffalo and Perfect Bindery.

The Consumer Products Group was created in 1973 under the direction of Harry Earle to extend Arcata's capabilities into the development and sales of consumer printed products. Two companies—CharmCraft Publishers and Ridge Press—were acquired to initiate the new group.

The Industrial Products Division, headed by M. Walker Rast, provides specialized printed products for industrial and commercial markets. Its four operating components are Computer Printing Corp., Data Composition, Arcata Data Management, and Real Estate Data, Inc.

In addition to its printing operations, ANC, through its Arcata Redwood Co., is a leader in redwood timber management and lumber production. Byron B. Miller heads this activity.

Financial/Ownership

The following figures apply to the printing and printed products groups only, and the last three digits are excluded. Earnings are before interest and income taxes.

	1974	*1973*
Sales	$199,047	$175,146
Earnings	17,347	12,072
	1972	*1971*
Sales	$159,963	$156,705
Earnings	10,762	5,027
	1970	*1969*
Sales	$157,515	$148,608
Earnings	12,142	11,475
	1968	*1967*
Sales	$124,834	$106,553
Earnings	9,511	9,124

Arcata National Corp.'s outstanding 7.3 million common and dilutive common equivalent shares are owned by more than 6,000 stockholders, none of whom holds more than five percent of such outstanding shares. C. Davis Weyerhaeuser, with 285,075 shares as of December 31, 1974, is the largest single shareholder.

Since its reorganization into its present form, Arcata National has not published officer remuneration figures for the printing and printed products groups.

Book Group

Kingsport Press, Kingsport, Tenn., Hugh F. Swaney, president. 1.8 million sq. ft., 3,000 employees; manufactures annually more than 70 million Bibles, textbooks, encyclopedia and reference sets, and general trade books.

Halliday Lithograph, West Hanover, Mass., Fred Bristol, vice president. 240,000 sq. ft., 750 employees; offset printing and binding of short-run college textbooks, technical, professional and other books. About 80% in black and white.

Arcata Microfilm, Winston-Salem, N.C., B. Carl Jones, president. 400 employees in five plants coast to coast, who microfilm patients' records for hospitals. Total U.S. market is calculated to be $20 million. Arcata estimates that only about half of this market has been tapped. Competition consists primarily of small local and regional companies. An emerging companion business is microfilming x-ray records. Arcata estimates that less than one-quarter of this market has been tapped.

Publications Group

Arcata Graphics, Buffalo Division, Depew, New York, William R. Kumpf, vice president and general manager. 900,000 sq. ft., 1800 employees; produces nine million copies of *Reader's Digest* monthly, special interest publications, catalogs, *Harpers, Money, Golf Digest* and 350 million paperbacks a year.

Pacific Press Division, Los Angeles, James N. Shelton, vice president and general manager. 398,000 sq. ft., 600 employees; prints and binds magazines including *Newsweek, Sports Illustrated* and *Time,* plus catalogs and promotional material.

San Jose Division, San Jose, Calif., John F. O'Conner, vice president and division manager. 270,000 sq. ft., 300 employees; gravure printing of *TV Guide* for western distribution.

Graphic Press, Los Angeles, Peter K. Silk, executive vice president. 34,000 sq. ft., 150 employees in main and branch plants in Denver and San Francisco; web offset and sheetfed printing of over 80 special interest magazines.

Consumer Products Group

CharmCraft Publishers, Brooklyn, William M. Winship III, president. 172,000 sq. ft., 650 employees; manufactures greeting cards and affiliated products, with distribution facilities in Cleveland, Detroit, St. Louis, and Los Angeles.

Ridge Press, New York, N.Y., Kenneth G. Northrup, vice president. 35 employees producing special interest custom books under Ridge and Rutledge hallmarks.

Industrial Products Group

Computer Printing Corp., Buffalo, N.Y., Dale C. Dequaine, vice president. 30,000 sq. ft., 50 employees, customized continuous business forms for computer use.

Data Composition, San Francisco, Gary D. Willcuts, general manager. 8,000 sq. ft., 50 employees; computerized composition for telephone directories and *TV Guide.*

Arcata Data Management, Hawthorne, Calif., James E. Still, Jr., president. 300 employees producing illustrated parts catalogs and other technical documentation for aerospace and related industries.

Real Estate Data, Inc., Miami, Fla., Richard A. First, president. 300 employees compile and publish data such as property identification maps, aerial photography and ownership records for use by real estate brokers, appraisers, mortgagees, lending institutions, title companies, surveyors and government bodies.

Arcata Milestones

1964 Arcata Redwood Co., Arcata, Calif., a timber management and lumber processing firm, decides to diversify into other business areas to increase future earnings potential.

1965 Arcata Redwood Co. buys J. W. Clements Co., Buffalo, N.Y., and its Pacific Press Division (Los Angeles) and San Jose/Phillips & Van

Orden Division (San Francisco) for $13.5 million. (Founded 1879) Producers of periodicals, telephone directories, paperback books, and various commercial products.

1965 Computer Printing Corp., Buffalo, N.Y., formed in 1959, bought. Producer of continuous business forms for electronic data processing.

1967 Arcata National Corp. formed, with Arcata Redwood Co. as a division and J. W. Clement Co. as a subsidiary.

1967 Rotary Offset Printers, Anaheim, Calif., printers of shortrun, special interest magazines (5000 to 300,000 runs) bought.

1967 Graphic Press, Los Angeles, specialist in sheetfed litho color work and annual reports, bought.

1968 Arcata National goes public, sales at $95 million; net earnings $6 million.

1968 Decision reached to invest $15 million in three CIC (common impression cylinder) web offset presses.

1968 Arcata National forced to sell half its redwood holdings for government park land use.

1969 Halliday Lithograph Corp., West Hanover, Mass., purchased and merged. 275-man operation founded 1942, specializing in production of short-run, soft-cover books; 1968 sales $4,460,277.

1969 Kingsport Press, Kingsport, Tenn., purchased. Founded 1928; employed over 2500 in 1969; sales $34,929,492. Specialist in hard cover book manufacturing and distribution.

1970 Arcata National listed on New York Stock Exchange, with sales $176,000,000 and 7300 holders of eight million common shares.

1970 Arcata Graphics Corp. formed, Harry W. Earle Jr., president. Composed of: J. W. Clement, Buffalo; Pacific Press, Los Angeles and San Jose; Phillips & Van Orden, San Jose; San Francisco Graphic Press, Los Angeles; Rotary Offset Printers, Anaheim and Denver; Computer Printing Corp., Buffalo; Data Composition, San Francisco.

1971 Graphic Services Group formed, consisting of Arcata Graphics Corp., Kingsport Press Inc., and Halliday Lithograph. G. Robert Evans, president, Kingsport Press, named vice president, Arcata National, in charge of Graphic Services Group and president of Arcata Graphics Corp. Harry W. Earle Jr., named vice president/marketing; Hugh F. Swaney elected president of Kingsport Press. (Month: March)

1971 Government gave Arcata 10,500 acres of timberland as partial payment for 11,000 acres taken for park land use in 1968.

1971 Pacific Press Engraving, division of Arcata Graphics of Los Angeles, sold to AccuGraphics Corp. (Month: March)

1971 Arcata Graphics Corp. files suit for $5.1 million vs. Goss over performance of CIC presses (one of three ordered is rejected) at Buffalo. (Month: July)

1971 Arcata National establishes Information Services Group composed of Arcata Data Management, Arcata Microfilm, Arcata Research, Arcata Real Estate Data. (Month: June)

1971 Arcata National discontinues unprofitable operations in Information Services Group for net loss $10.5 million.

1972 Arcata National Graphic Services Group files another suit vs. Goss, this one for $4.1 million on two operating CIC presses at Buffalo. (Month: Jan.)

1972 Time Inc. discontinues publication of Western edition of Life magazine, which was printed in Arcata Graphic subsidiary. (Month: Feb.)

1972 Arcata National reports nine months sales $160 million vs nine month 1971 sales $136 million: earnings 1972 period $2.9 million vs. net loss $2.6 million for 1971 period. (April)

1972 Robert O. Dehlendorf II, Arcata National president and chief operating officer since 1965, resigns for personal reasons. Succeeded by J. Frank Leach, 51, former executive vice president and chief operating officer of Bunker-Ramo Corp. (June)

1972 Arcata National posts fiscal '72 sales $210 million, earnings, from continuing operations of per share 81 cents vs. 1971 sales $187 million, earnings per share of 34 cents (Graphic Services Group's contribution in 1972, sales $144,591,000; earnings $11,679,000.)

1972 William M. Winship III, formerly vice president of sales, McCall Printing Corp., joins Graphic Services Group as vice president of national sales. (September)

1972 Graphic Services Group management control tightened by forming two organizations: Arcata Graphics—East and Arcata Graphics—West. East consists of Computer Printing Corp., Buffalo divisions; West consists of Pacific Press and Graphic Press, Los Angeles; Rotary Offset Printers, Anaheim, Denver, San Francisco and San Jose divisions.

1973 Arcata Chairman John Pascoe, in reporting on fiscal 1972, hails 106 percent rise in pretax earnings; Group reports "strong progress made with CIC press program . . . Several promising printing contracts for catalog and special interest publications were signed in the last half of the year (fiscal 1972) for production on these presses."

1973 Arcata National sells off all of its telephone interconnect subsidiaries. Operation of these affiliates had resulted in a loss of $3.2 million in fiscal 1973.

1974 Arcata Chairman John Pascoe reports earnings of $10.4 million on net sales of $234 million in fiscal 1974, as compared with $4.9 million on $209 million in sales the previous year. Earnings were up to $1.40 a share and dividends doubled over 1973. CharmCraft Publishers, a manufacturer and distributor of greeting cards, and Ridge Press, a custom producer of illustrated luxury books, were acquired. They marked ANC's initial entry into the lucrative consumer printed products market.

Arcata Up Late in 1964, Arcata Redwood Co. decided to diversify into the communications industry. The first major step was the acquisition, in 1965, of J. W. Clement Co. of Buffalo, N.Y. Founded in 1879, J. W. Clement ranked sixth among independent printers in the country, with $80 million in annual sales and 1.3 million square feet of plant space in Buffalo, Los Angeles and the San Jose/San Francisco areas. In 1967, as acquisitions continued, the name of the parent company was changed from Arcata Redwood Co. to Arcata National Corp.

The next major acquisition was the 1969 purchase of Kingsport Press, Kingsport, Tenn., a $36 million-a-year manufacturer of hard-cover books operating in 1.2 million square feet of floor space. By 1972, sales by Arcata Graphics amounted to $144.6 million, 69 percent of total Arcata National sales. Much of that growth derived from acquisitions.

The peak year 1969 also saw the acquisition of Halliday Lithograph Corp., West Hanover, Mass., and the allocation of $15 million for a "technically advanced offset press program." Harry W. Earle, Jr. was elected president of the J. W. Clement subsidiary; G. Robert Evans was elected president, Kingsport Press; three other subsidiaries got new presidents: Butler Data Systems (Richard S. Moore); Arcata Redwood (Byron B. Miller) and Arcata Data Communications (Don G. Thomson).

Chief architect of the Arcata growth-by-acquisition program was Robert O. Dehlendorf II, co-founder and former vice president and treasurer of Microwave Electronics Corp. of Menlo Park. After its acquisition, he became president of J. W. Clement while retaining his vice presidency of Arcata Redwood. Dehlendorf was named president of the newly named Arcata National Corp. in 1967. He became chief executive officer of Arcata in 1968, a position he held until June, 1972. (During his stewardship, Arcata National's sales increased from $8 million to $210 million. Earnings, from continuing operations, grew from 48¢ per share to $1.30 per share.)

In 1969, the graphics organization consisted of J. W. Clement Co., Kingsport Press and Halliday Lithograph Corp. as subsidiaries and the following as divisions or subsidiaries: Clement-Buffalo, W. B. Burgard as vice president and general manager; San Jose Division, Robert L. Laird, vice president and general manager; Computer Printing Corp., Buffalo, R. W. Brouse, Jr., vice president and general manager; Graphic Press, Los Angeles, James F. Johnson, president; Pacific Press Division, Los Angeles, R. H. Johns, vice president, marketing; Rotary Offset Printers, Anaheim, Calif., Evert S. Peterson, president. (Arcata National's other subsidiaries in addition to Butler and Arcata Redwood were Atlantic Microfilm Corp., Brand Rating Research Corp., and Microfilm Business Systems Co.)

In fiscal 1970, many changes were made in Arcata National and in its graphic arts circles: J. W. Clement subsidiary was renamed Arcata Graphics, Harry W. Earle, Jr., president; Computer Printing had a new vice president, general manager (Willis W. Lund); M. W. Rast came from U.S. Gypsum as vice president, operations, Buffalo Division; Pacific Press Div. got a new vice president, general manager (Lindsay S. Livengood); Rotary Offset Printers had a new president, Keith R. Cutting. (Butler Data Systems was renamed Arcata Data Management; Atlantic Microfilm was renamed Arcata Microfilm; Brand Rating Research was renamed Arcata Research. Real Estate Directories, Inc. had been acquired; Arcata Investment had been formed to help minority businesses and Arcata Management to advise them; Communications Management and Continental Communications Construction had been acquired, as had Arcata Communications. Four non-graphics subsidiary and divisional heads had rolled; seven new ones had appeared.)

In fiscal 1971, G. Robert Evans was promoted from president of Kingsport Press to over-all command of a new "Graphic Services Group" composed of Arcata Graphics Corp., Kingsport Press and Halliday Lithograph. He also became a corporate vice president of Arcata National.

Arcata
Down

It was in fiscal 1971, with the recession still bottoming, that the Arcata steamroller crashed into an entirely unforeseeable obstacle. In the previous fiscal period it had invested $15 million in three huge, custom-made CIC web presses. Arcata found its startup costs heavier than it had budgeted, and reportedly could not achieve planned output; it rejected one press. Resulting litigation entailed damage suits by Arcata of $5.1 million. At the same time, "record performance by Arcata Real Estate Data was·more than offset by losses at Arcata Microfilm and Arcata Data Management," reported President Dehlendorf.

For the first time in Arcata National's short, peppery history a net loss was experienced, a loss of $10.5 million, equivalent to $1.72 a share. Arcata Microfilm and Arcata Data Management were "sharply curtailed" and other information service companies sold. One new company was being added at year-end: Knight, Gladieux & Smith, consultants in computer information systems and environmental controls.

Arcata
Up Again

"I am pleased to note that the fiscal year ended June 30, 1972, was a year of noteworthy earnings recovery. The year was also one of significant management transition."

Thus Chairman John J. Pascoe introduced his annual report for Arcata National, which posted for the Graphic Services Group earnings of $11.7 million, up 106 percent from 1971 and sales of $144.6 million, up $7.8 million from 1971.

"The significant management transition" statement referred primarily to the replacement of President Robert O. Dehlendorf II by J. Frank Leach, 51, former executive vice president of Bunker-Ramo Corp. John M. Lille, whose chief executive officer role was added to that of the new president, had also resigned. Arcata Communications had gotten a new chief, Charles F. Smith, to replace Don G. Thomson. Other new arrivals were the corporation's treasurer, George B. James; its secretary and general counsel, Robert A. Ferris, and two other divisional heads.

Actually, of a 1971 corporate executive lineup of 12 men, only five remained on Arcata National's new eight-man team.

The reversal of 1971's trend was clearly not the work of the new corporate lineup, however, since Dehlendorf was able to report at the end of the second quarter of 1972, "earnings of $1.9 million to date compared with a net loss of $3 million after extraordinary items last year. . . ."

Goals,
Formulas

"We are now a company in two basic businesses, printing and printed products and redwood lumber, where we have depth of management experience, technical experience and strength and reputation in the marketplace. We see the opportunity to not only grow our book and publications printing businesses profitably, but also to build upon our strengths in the graphic arts by logical extensions into printed products through out Consumer Products and Industrial Products Groups.

"I think it is also important to recognize that the earnings and rate of earnings growth from our printing groups are now strong enough that, coupled with the elimination of the discontinued operations no longer bleeding us, we can begin to implement a plan to reduce the cut rate of Arcata Redwood to achieve sustained yield."

These words, delivered by J. Frank Leach, president and chief executive officer of Arcata National Corp., to the Security Analysts of San Francisco on November 7, 1974, sum up the leadership philosophy and orientation of the company. Much has been accomplished in the last two years to put Arcata squarely and soundly into the printing business, which now accounts for the bulk of its sales and profits.

The fundamental goal of growth through acquisitions in the printing business, now being carried forward by Leach, was first enunciated by his predecessor as president, Robert O. Dehlendorf II. While Dehlendorf's growth strategy was based on acquisitions, the firms he purchased quickly showed appreciable gains in operations. For instance, his 1965 purchase of J. W. Clement—for an astonishingly "reasonable" $13.5 million in cash—brought into Arcata National's fold a $40 million a year firm with a history dating back, at that time, for 85 years. By 1970, its sales had exceeded $80 million. When he bought the 47-year-old mamoth book operation—Kingsport Press—in 1969, its sales were $35 million. They have since been raised to $45 million. (The Kingsport purchase, incidentally, involved a stock exchange of one Kingsport common share for 0.4 Arcata National Common and 0.25 of an AN convertible preferred.)

The Clement and Kingsport components now provide over 83 percent of AN's graphic arts sales.

Acquisition Planning/ Recruiting

Acquisitions made by Arcata National under the Dehlendorf reign (which account for 90 percent of corporate history to date) have been either of the filler type (to round out existing entities) or of the "stepout" type (into new fields).

Step-out acquisitions under Dehlendorf were planned as follows: "We first conceptualize the new area into which we want to move to broaden our basic capabilities. We then search the nation for a person with the background and experience required. Once aboard, that person is responsible for developing a detailed five-year plan for his yet non-existent activity, including potential acquisition candidates. With board approval, he alone becomes responsible for implementation of the plan."

Dehlendorf's success with this philosophy, expressed before the New York Society of Security Analysts, was mixed.

It seems to have worked quite well with the Graphic Services Group, not too well with other units created according to plan in the late Sixties. Of the many subsidiaries and divisions formed between then and 1972, the only one which remains substantially intact unit-wise is Graphic Services.

In the course of those later years, as the foregoing accounts testify, the attrition among top executives recruited to form the step-out organizations was notably high. It was different, however, in the Graphic Services Group, where attrition was comparable to that among executive ranks in peer operations during the recession, and where promotions within the Group and into corporate posts have been par, at least.

Under the new Leach administration, the company reportedly will continue to be growth-oriented, both from expansion of present operations and through acquisitions of businesses related to present Arcata National operations.

Executive Promotion/ Motivation

"To the maximum extent possible, we promote from within, and by our non-threatening but demanding involvement approach to management have been generally successful in retaining and re-motivating management of acquired companies.

"When we do go outside for a key operating manager, we often seek persons outside the industry, believing strongly in the need to avoid the 'NIH' (not invented here) syndrome, and to bring to bear the broadened scope which multi-industry experience affords."

So former President Robert O. Dehlendorf declared at the height of his rule.

While it seems that high office promotions from within the Graphic Services Group were frequent, there could be at least as good a case made for the opposite viewpoint—that, in the early years anyway, the inward-looking recruitment eye was no more searching than the outward-looking one. Arcata Graphics top management has a strong McCall alumni flavor as well as a touch of Donnelley and assorted other printing giants. As for top-top graphics leadership, G. Robert Evans is a U.S. Gypsum alumnus put in charge of a Kingsport Press operation by no means visibly bereft of promotable material. When Dehlendorf himself was succeeded by Leach, that was again a case of "shopping outside" for a top executive with no graphic arts experience to run a corporation essentially graphic arts oriented and possessing an experienced corps of graphic arts executive types.

Reportedly, a key consideration in Leach's selection as Dehlendorf's successor was the need for an executive with strong operating experience in the electronics industry to help solve the major and growing problem with Arcata Communications, the rapidly expanding but unprofitable venture into the telephone interconnect business. Leach and his team wrestled with the Arcata Communications problem for a year before deciding that the best solution was divestiture. They concluded that the capital investment for research and development and manufacturing facilities required to stay competitively in the interconnect business was too great for the risk involved. (Announcement of final arrangements for sale of most of Arcata Communications to General Dynamics was made early in June, 1973.)

It should be noted here that most recent promotions (1972-73) have come from within the Graphic Services Group.

*Present
Graphic
Management*

The fact that the Arcata superstructure is composed entirely of professionals whose accomplishments are their sole warrants was emphasized by Evans as another Arcata strength. "None of our top people are 'family seated,' " he pointed out. "As for management continuity, we require each operating unit chief to submit written plans for development of personnel toward management rank and succession."

Each month the Group holds management meetings for the heads of all Graphic Services operating unit chieftains. The meetings are slated so as to take place at major facilities on alternate months. All present are expected to return and report on decisions to at least the two highest management levels within their own units.

Each operating unit is expected to evolve its own annual operating plans aimed at achieveing goals approved by top management. Each unit must also formulate five-year plans.

Arcata's San Jose division.

In 1975 Kingsport Press
installed its second Cameron
book production system
which produces books in
a continuous high-speed operation,
beginning with a roll of paper
and culminating in a carton
of books ready for shipment.

Arcata's Computer Printing Corp. division,
a six-part form is produced by collating
six pre-printed webs of carbon paper.

Arcata Publications Group,
Perfect Bindery, Inc. division
provides adhesive binding
capabilities to serve the
short-run, fast turnaround market.

Arcata National Corporation
2750 Sand Hill Road
Menlo Park, California 94025

60

Wallace Business Forms, Inc.

*How Wallace Scores
as a Profit Leader
in Business Forms*

Wallace Business Forms Inc.,
Corporate Headquarters,
Hillside, Illinois.

Wallace's Gastonia, North Carolina
manufacturing plant.

Wallace's Luray, Virginia
business forms production plant.

Wallace Business Forms' fiscal 1974 sales were $55.7 million, up about 36 percent from 1973's figure of $40.9 million; net per share, at $2.04, was up a shade less than 38 percent over 1973's $1.48.

Ross B. Whitney, chairman of the company's executive committee, credits the increases to continuing demand and to improved productivity both in the business forms field, which represents 75 percent of the firm's business, and in the production of catalogs, a specialty of the Wallace Press Division which generates 20 percent of the company's income. The remaining 5 percent comes from the Visible Computer Supply Corp., a wholly-owned subsidiary which markets computer-related accessory hardward, ranging from files and collators to other items. This is done primarily through direct mail merchandising.

Since the organization has reported its financial details publicly, some 15 years, it has shown uninterrupted growth in both sales and net income. Sales in the period 1964-74 nearly trebled (they were $19 million in 1964) as net per share has done. It took Wallace 56 years to reach the $20 million mark, five more to reach $30 million, four to top $40 million and only one more to explode the $50 million barrier.

Wallace considers itself about number five in business forms volume, but number two in profit ratio.

Dividends have been paid Wallace stockholders every year since 1933, and in January 1974 the company announced its second increase in 12 months to an annual rate of 49 cents per share, quarterly. Whitney told a 1974 meeting of the New York Society of Security Analysts, "Historically, Wallace has maintained a policy of keeping its dividend payout rate at approximately 30 percent of net income.

"Our goal," Whitney said in late 1974," is to equal or exceed the profit ratio of the Number One company (Moore). We would have a very long way to go to equal their volume!"

Wallace Business Forms Inc.
Stock Price History—FY74/73

	Price		P/E*	
Quarter Ended	High	Low	High	Low
January 31, 1974	$18.75	$14.00	8.6	6.5
July 31, 1974	$24.375	$18.125	13.9	10.3
April 30, 1974	$20.25	$14.00	12.5	8.6
October 31, 1974	$19.875	$14.375	9.7	7.0
January 31, 1974	$20.25	$14.75	13.2	9.6
October 31, 1973	$20.875	$18.00	14.1	12.2
July 31, 1973	$20.875	$14.75	14.7	10.4
April 30, 1973	$25.00	$21.00	18.1	15.2
January 31, 1973	$26.00	$23.25	20.0	17.9
October 31, 1972	$23.875	$21.00	19.3	16.9

*Earnings in 1974 quarters adjusted for LIFO (last in, first out).

Explained President Theodore Dimitriou: "We can't be as big. Our manufacturing units are as good or better, however. And we take the time and training necessary, select the manpower to penetrate the market, design our equipment for maximum productivity, and make the necessary capital investment to approach their profit ratio."

Not any one thing, but all things contribute to the solidity of the company, according to Whitney. He points out that the momentum comes from cooperation and pride between business, manufacturing and sales.

Morale Building;
Productivity

The Company operates by objectives, with each worker involved in setting objectives for the next year. Members of the staff participate in each year's budgeting with the goals in mind. Each one reviews his goals and makes revisions. Areas of strategic and high priorities are marked out, as for example the earnings of $2.04 per share. Then each supervisor figures what is necessary on his part to attain that goal. Key managers then share this with their subordinates, and so from top to middle management the objectives are formalized, and shared with all levels of employees.

Along with the goals are bonuses contingent on meeting those objectives, and wherever possible the goals are quantitative. For example, one goal has been waste reduction by x percent. The performance is constantly checked, and comparisons are made with the goal a figure (after taxes) in dollars and cents. Each periodic report to management includes how well the department has come along in meeting its objectives.

Another part of the employee relations program which results in improved productivity is the program of home visits with employees.

In most of the plants a line management representative meets with each employee in the employee's home, usually once a year. There, on the employee's home ground, they discuss the individual's objectives as they relate to corporate plans. The result, Whitney feels, is the development of an understanding which translates into dedication and productivity.

Wallace, has, according to Dimitriou, "the highest ratio of productivity per employee" in the industry.

The fact that there is no union in the Business Forms Division is another indication of the good labor relations which lead to greater productivity.

"We pay better than union scale, we teach managers to treat people humanely, and we make an effort to communicate with them," explained Whitney. "The personal contact, the opportunity they have to ask questions and the home visit program all have helped us to improve productivity each year," he said.

An employee morale survey taken regularly in the plant assures, as Whitney puts it, "that we're not stubbing our toe. We find things that need to be changed at different locations. Generally, the survey is reassuring. We also share the results with the employees, highlighting the things that will be revised, and giving them an opportunity to comment."

Productivity is also the key to success of the Business Forms Division's highly-trained sales force. Extensive college recruiting each year, followed by classroom study at corporate headquarters in Hillside, a southwest Chicago suburb, and field training, all help develop sales personnel adept at direct selling, contract sales and other forms of marketing business forms.

In fiscal 1973 this program resulted in what is believed to be the highest average output per salesman in the industry—$244,000.

"The most important factor in our sales training program," Dimitriou emphasizes, "is that we teach our sales representatives that their first responsibility is to listen to the customer in order to understand his needs. The second factor is that the sales force is confident of the manufacturing operation's flexibility in meeting the customer's particular requirements. This, of course, has been proven through performance."

Wallace does its recruiting of salesmen by going to the leading colleges. Last year, for example, it recruited at more than 100 colleges and hired the top talent available.

"These men and women are trained not only at our sales offices, but also in our manufacturing plants and with our forms designers," Whitney told the New York Security Analysts. "They know just about everything there is to know about forms design, usage, and production—and they can bring that knowledge to bear on sales calls."

Their high productivity level, he pointed out, reflects "our commitment to investing in plants and equipment which can improve productivity. Capital investment per employee in 1973 was at an industry high of $18,778, and our ratio of capital expenditures to sales also is the highest in the industry. The relatively broad geographical siting of our plants, each with complete capabilities, enables us to serve our customers efficiently and profitably."

Plants;
Products
Wallace's Business Forms Division manufactures its products at five plants in Chicago and Clinton, Ill.; Luray, Va.; Gastonia, N.C.; and Marlin, Texas.

The Marlin plant was dedicated only a year or so ago and is already manufacturing at a profit, reported Dimitriou. "We have shifted some planned overload from our midwest region plants to Marlin, but anticipate this to be an intermediate term procedure, both because of growing southwestern demand and because of other market growth plans which involved Marlin."

Ground was broken in May 1974 for a plant in Osage, Iowa, a planned 80,000-square-foot facility which will cost approximately $3.5 million, and to be financed through revenue bonds.

The Wallace Press Division operates from the Hillside headquarters, while Visible Computer Supply Corp. is in nearby Westchester, Ill., another Chicago suburb.

What business forms does Wallace manufacture?

Dimitriou divides business forms into four categories: continuous forms, unit sets, sales books and register forms.

"The first two categories represent approximately 95 percent of industry sales, and continuous forms represent the largest and fastest growing segment. These forms include custom printed forms such as invoices, purchase orders and payroll checks. Continuous stock forms are used generally for internal purposes and are sold almost as a commodity item. Unit sets, approximately 34 percent of the total forms market, are used for source information activities or at the point of sale. These, too, can be custom-designed or sold as stock items."

Wallace's president told the analysts, "The International Business Forms Institute (IBFI) estimates that for calendar year 1973 the business forms industry achieved total sales of approximately $1.6 billion, growing at approximately a 16 percent rate. Five firms, including Wallace, control approximately 55 percent of the market."

He added that more than 80 percent of Wallace's Business Forms Division sales currently are related to computer usage. In 1973 it is estimated that there were 60,000 on-line general purpose computers in the United States, with 450,000 terminals—all using hard-copy impact printers which need business forms to complete their jobs.

Wallace is so closely linked to the computer industry that we asked, "Are you going to pin your whole future on the computer market? If not, how will you diversify?"

Whitney's answer was to quote a report from Arthur D. Little, from information available from the computer industry as well as from IBFI indicating that computer growth is seen to be 12 to 14 percent by 1980. They're also looking ahead to the explosion of the minicomputer, which has seen as much as 50 percent growth in one year.

"This will enable smaller businesses to use the computer. We'll be training our sales force to make sales to this branch of the computer industry," he said.

Wallace also has the potential of growing 17 to 18 percent of the industry's total growing in the business computer field, and with the recent acquisition of Municiple Forms and Systems Inc. of Durham, N.C. by an exchange of stock, it expects to tap a new market, that of tax forms and related supplies for small businesses.

Municipal Forms, with sales for fiscal year ended September 30, 1973, of $800,000, sells to accountants and on a direct-to-the customer basis.

This market of small businesses is expected to use mini-computers for billing, invoicing, receivable recording and output of operational data—all hard copy functions. That's why the acquisition of Muncipal Forms, with a growth rate of approximately 15 percent over the past five years, is so important to Wallace's future.

Municipal Forms has a branch in Columbia, Mo.

Other areas for market exapnsion include the international market.

"We are beginning to investigate opportunities in Europe, Japan and South America for a method of profitable participation," Dimitriou told the analysts.

"Most likely," he continued, "this will be through a technical assistance program or joint-venture. We aren't committed to any timetable, however, and will not commit ourselves until we are reasonably confident that sufficient economic stability and market maturity has been achieved to make our entry profitable on a long-term basis."

Plans for the next two or three years include expansion in the United States. The firm plans to add at least two new business forms plants; one in the East and one on the Pacific Coast. But there's no timetable for this expansion.

Pacific Coast marketing responsibilities have been assigned to the sales organization with headquarters in Marlin, Texas. In addition to continued expansion of all the southwest region, these men will be working to achieve sufficient penetration of the West Coast to make plant development profitable. The Marlin plant will serve as the base plant for Pacific expansion, which is the primary reason for taking Midwest overload responsibilities off Marlin and building the Osage plant for spring 1975 completion, it was explained.

Industry analysts are projecting that the business forms industry will grow at an 8 to 11 percent annual rate to approximately $3 billion in sales by 1980. Wallace executives believe that their organization has the potential of exceeding that level.

The firm's current growth, the fastest of any period in its history, gives reason for this conclusion. For the six-month period ended January 31, 1974, net sales of $25.1 million were 27 percent over the comparable period of last year. Net income in this year's first half increased 34 percent to $1.675 million or 92 cents per share.

"During this most recent cycle of increases, Wallace, like most of our competitors has been able to significantly reduce the discounting factor previously so prevalent in our industry," Whitney told the New York analysts. "We have been able to pass-through cost increases, particularly in the most dramatic area—paper. Finally, we have been able to increase our prices, and recently effected an approximate 10 percent increase on most of our larger volume products. In effect," Whitney concluded, "between 25 and 35 percent of sales increase can be directly related to inflation. This leaves an actual rate in the 15 to 20 percent range, which we believe is acceptable, both in current terms and as a continuously realizable objective."

Basic Operating Data
for Wallace Business Forms

	Net Sales (000)	Net Income (000)	Share Earnings*	Dividend Per Share*	Working Capital (000)	Long-Term Debt (000)
1974	$55,719	$3,700	$2.04	$.4950	$8,334	$5,212
1973	40,850	2,686	1.48*	.4125	7,794	2,128
1972	36,055	2,243	1.24	.40	7,134	2,544
1971	33,736	2,162	1.20	.40	6,031	2,960
1970	32,516	2,079	1.15	.35	4,697	1,876
1969	29,339	1,865	1.05	.35	5,129	600
1968	26,032	1,625	.92	.35	4,050	- -
1967	24,418	1,571	.90	.312	3,338	- -
1966	23,405	1,342	.78	.30	4,313	588
1965	21,556	1,217	.73	.205	3,522	650
1964	19,027	837	.57	.175	3,589	2,300
1963	17,528	737	.45	.175	3,011	2,400
1962	14,229	626	.38	.175	2,627	2,422
1961	11,966	574	.70	.175	2,994	- -

*Adjusted for 2-for-1 stock split, July 1965 and November 1970, and based upon average number of shares outstanding during each year.

Marketing Methods

Wallace uses two basic marketing methods with independent marketing organizations. Contract sales, which account for approximately 40 percent of annual volume of business forms, is a particularly effective method for this company. It began back in 1923, and grew in this field as it sold to large customers and warehoused the forms for them.

Sales representatives, explained Dimitriou, work directly with contract customers to give them unique service—primarily through upgrading forms systems while reducing total cost. There are benefits to Wallace from having a high volume of contract business: it provides relative stability, and more important, enables the firm to plan for facilities expansion with maximum efficiency based on accurate demand anticipation. In the end they have improved return on investment.

The direct sales force calls on customers as well as serves them through direct mail and dealer sales of tax and standard body forms. Sales to this market, the smaller users of forms, would be impossible on either a direct or contract sales basis, and costs would be prohibitive.

To do the printing of business forms, Wallace has 12 continuous and unit set, single web wet litho presses, and 34 dry litho units as well as two dry litho collator presses. There are 16 standard roll diameter continuous collators and four jumbo collators and seven standard-roll-diameter unit set collators. A jumbo collator is on order.

Wallace Press

What about the Wallace Press? It is said to operate out of one of the most modern plants in the printing industry. Producing catalogs, directories and manuals, this division recently installed a Hantscho multiple-web, high-speed press. This is in addition to two Miehle webfed presses and a four-color perfecter press in the plant.

Presswork, typesetting and composition are all handled there, with computer composition being the key to growth. Some 25 percent of the total printing is generated by the computer and comes through the computer with new automated equipment. As many as 21,000 plates are made annually in the Hillside operation. Much of their publication is for the burgeoning automotive after-parts industry and business has been increased by the expanding trend of shopping at home or from the office for many products displayed in catalogs. This plant operates five days a week on three shifts.

Wallace has built on the principle of locating its plants where labor is available, and training them on the scene, rather than transferring personnel.

Wallace engineers design most of the equipment and systems utilized at the various plants. While the total research and development budget in terms of the expense ratio is low, explained Whitney and Dimitriou, compared to some companies, this doesn't tell the whole story. Many of the projects are farmed out to plants and don't show up in the profit statement.

"One of our best improvements," they said, "showed up on a third shift in Clinton. Then one of our supervisors tried a new method which we ended up patenting."

They also have more formal programs and the formal corporate budget for R & D in 1974 was four times what it was in 1973.

"We work with the Technical Association of the Pulp & Paper Industry (TAPPI) in its round robins on paper, work with chemical and product development committees there, and screen ideas from the field, as well as working with manufacturers of some of our equipment," Whitney said.

In meeting its objectives outlined each year as the budget is set up and goals outlined, Wallace uses computer analysis to review operations. A regular report is prepared detailing profit and loss by salesman, district, product, contract, customer, job and manufacturing plant. Immediate adjustments can be made where deficiencies from carefully prepared budgets occur.

Bulletin: Continental Carbon Joins the Wallace Fold

"I would like to discuss Continental Carbon Paper Mfg. Co., which we acquired as of December 31, 1974. This was a purchase transaction, involving approximately 78,000 shares of Wallace stock and assumption of a mortgage and cash totaling more $350,000. Continental had sales for the 12 months ended December 31, exceeding $4.5 million, primarily in carbon paper and carbon ink. The latter area is of primary importance to us, as carbon ink is in demand and Continental has the capability of becoming the largest supplier of carbon ink in the United States. The company also has excellent research facilities with capable chemists, which will enable Continental to expand its market. We are committed to that objective."—
T. M. Dimitriou, at Chicago Investment Analysts Meeting, February 2, 1975

Wallace Milestones

1908 Founded by W. F. Wallace, Sr., when he exchanged a farm in Niles Center, Ill., a Chicago suburb, for a printing business. With two small handfed presses first year sales were $7,720.

1923 Wallace hits first $1 million sales mark by adapting two basic ideas: concentration of sales on contract printing for large customers, providing warehousing and off-the-shelf service, and using offset printing, with early presses which printed from the original litho stone. "Type-less printing" was advertised and the process was used for street address directories.

1929 Western Electric, one of Wallace's prime clients, asked the firm to go into the production of continuous and snap-apart forms. By the time of the founder's death in 1954, forms accounted for about half of the output of the firm, which than had annual sales of $5 million.

1952 W. F. Wallace, Jr. became chief executive officer, and inherited a company whose equipment averaged 28 years in age, and a workforce of some 34 persons. He started rebuilding the company from scratch in 1954.

1959 Ross Whitney became vice president of marketing. By this time Wallace had broadened his customer base, hired an engineering staff, and began expanding toward the 43 sales offices and 110 salesmen on the staff today.

1961 Wallace Business Forms, Inc. became publicly held with the sale of 184,435 common shares in September, 1960, in the company's first public offering. President W. F. Wallace noted that the company had plants located in Chicago and Clinton, Ill., and that it employed approximately 650 personnel. In October, 1960, ground was broken for a 21,000 sq. ft. addition to the Clinton, Ill., plant. The Clinton plant was originally constructed in 1958. A 2% stock dividend was paid on July 31, 1961.

1962 On March 17, the company purchased 80% of the outstanding stock of Standard Business Forms, Inc., Gastonia, N.C., for $2,402,358. On July 31, a new single story, air-conditioned, humidity-controlled building in Gastonia was completed, and the Standard Business Forms operation was transferred to the new plant. The expanded facilities were large enough to permit a 50% increase in production.

1963 Wallace Business Forms, Inc. was adopted as the new corporate name to better reflect the company's principal business. The annual report noted a 50% increase in business forms sales. In June, Wallace acquired the remaining outstanding stock of Standard Business Forms, Inc., which was then liquidated and its operations continued as a division of Wallace.

1964 Sales reached $19 million for the first time in the company's history. On March 31, Consolidated Business Systems Division and Consolidated Business Systems of North Carolina, Inc., were purchased from Diebold, Inc. for $997,000. These two plants were in New Brunswick, N.J., and Durham, N.C.

1965 The annual dividend was increased from 35 cents per share to 60 cents per share. The stockholders approved a two-for-one split. The number of shares of authorized stock was increased from 750,000 to 1,000,000. Par value was halved from $10 per share to $5 per share. Sales reached $21,556,000 to pass the $20 million mark for the first time. W. F. Wallace was elected chairman of the board of directors and chief executive officer; Ross Whitney was elected president.

1966 Site was purchased in Luray, Va., for a new manufacturing plant to replace the New Brunswick facility and provide for much needed expanded capacity. A second expansion of an additional 40,000 sq. ft. was begun in Clinton.

1967 Luray plant was opened late in the year. Durham plant was closed, and operations were moved to Gastonia. Despite Luray startup expenses and closing costs in New Brunswick and Durham, net income increased 17%.

Ross Whitney was elected chief executive officer as well as president.

1968 Third expansion was completed in Clinton. Number of stockholders increased to 3,000 following the second public offering of 247,627 shares.

1969 Company broke ground in Hillside, Ill., for the new Wallace Press Division plant and corporate office building. Sales reached $29,339,000.

1970 Annual sales ($32.5 million) passed the $30 million mark for the first time. Capital spending ($4.1 million) also was a record high. Profit reached a new peak for the ninth consecutive year.

Expansion projects were begun in Clinton (fourth) and Luray (first). Visible Computer Supply Corporation was acquired.

1971 In early 1971, Wallace purchased the business forms operations of a small southwestern forms manufacturer, and moved production equipment to a temporary manufacturing facility in Marlin, Tex.

Wallace common stock was split two-for-one on November 9, and was listed on the New York Stock Exchange, effective Feb. 1. Ticker symbol: WF.

A 26,000 sq. ft. addition was built at Wallace's Clinton, Ill., plant; an addition aggregating 46,000 sq. ft. was completed at the Luray, Va. plant, and renovation of the Chicago plant began in the third quarter.

1972 Plans were made for groundbreaking for a permanent plant in Marlin, Tex. An audit committee was appointed on the board of directors.

1973 Record sales of $40.85 million were achieved, a 13% increase from the $36.06 million reported in fiscal 1972. Net income of $2.69 million or $1.48 per share represented the 12th consecutive annual increase. The Marlin, Tex., plant was completed in July.

As a result of the record earnings increase and strengthened financial position of the company, the directors voted in July to increase the annual dividend rate to 45 cents per common share, to be paid at the quarterly rate of 11¼ cents per share.

1974 Record sales in excess of $55 million were recorded during fiscal 1974. Municipal Forms and Systems, Inc., and Continental Carbon Paper Mfg. Co. were acquired. Groundbreaking took place for a new business forms plant in Osage, Iowa; and dividend payments were increased three times during fiscal 1974 to 55 cents per share annual rate.

Wallace Business Forms, Inc.
4600 West Roosevelt Road
Hillside, Illinois 60162

Each of Wallace's five
business forms manufacturing plants
is equipped to meet
almost every production requirement.

At a cost of $1 million,
the Wallace Press Division recently
installed a high-speed,
four-color web catalog press,
the most expensive machinery investment
in Wallace's history.
It enlarges to a substantial
degree the printing need the
Wallace Press Division can meet.

J. L. Clark Manufacturing Co.

*Metal Decoration
Makes Challenging,
Magnificent Litho*

Inspecting a flat sheet of metal,
just off one of Clark's
high-speed offset lithography presses.

J. L. Clark's corporate headquarters
and principal plant in
Rockford, Illinois.
The corporate office building
is at center right.

In growing from a small hardware store to a huge conglomerate, the J. L. Clark Mfg. Co. followed the basic American formula for success. It kept producing something that the public needed. And it did so efficiently and artistically. In 1974 its annual sales volume exceeded $60 million.

Headquartered in Rockford, Ill., Clark specialized in producing metal and plastic containers. You find their products everywhere. The exotic-looking spice can in your kitchen may have been produced by Clark, or the ornamental tobacco can in the den. The bandage box in the bathroom, the cosmetic container in the bedroom, and even the wax can in the garage may have been designed and lithographed by the J. L. Clark Mfg. Co.

Especially fascinating to printers are the metal containers produced by the company. These are examples of lithography at its finest—intricate designs on 150-line screens permanently preserved on a sheet metal base. They offer a challenge to those lithographers who still regard metal decoration as a form of printing too far off the beaten path.

All this began in the 1890s when a Rockford hardware merchant, J. L. Clark, designed an improved flue stopper with a folded cross-wire fastener which became a success. The company still manufacturers the Gem flue stopper and other proprietary items, but now produces more than 2,500 different sizes and shapes of lithographed and fabricated containers. And that line is constantly changing and expanding.

While the main plant is still in Rockford, Ill., where J. L. Clark founded the company in 1904, other plants and divisions have sprung up in Downers Grove, Bedford Park and Chicago, Ill.; College Park and Havre de Grace, Md., where a $3 million facility was opened in 1972; Lancaster, Pa. (2); Morgan Hill, Calif.; Wabash, Ind.; Waverly, Ohio, and Toronto, Canada.

Net sales for 1974, the company's 70th year, were $69.2 million, compared to $56.1 million, an increase of more than 50 percent over 1973 earnings of $3.6 million. As of November 30, 1974, there were 1,880 shareholders owning 1,278,563 shares of stock, and 2,050 employees. Capital expenditures in 1974 amounted to $3.6 million compared to $1.6 million for the previous year.

A trio of experienced business veterans have been guiding the company through its years of steady growth. They are: Russell C. Gibson, Chairman of the Board; Roland E. Palmer, President, and William O. Nelson, Executive Vice President. Other key members of the current executive line-up are: R. LaVerne Ax, Vice President—Manufacturing; Richard W. Malmgren, Vice President—Market Development; Harold A. Acker, Treasurer and Assistant Secretary; Avery O. Gage, Secretary, and Vernon E. Zumhagen, Controller.

"Our growth," said Mr. Gibson, "is due primarily to our activities as specialists in custom metal decorating—lithography on metal, embossing, and custom production of lithographed containers." He attributes the company's success to these three things:

1. A creative combination of marketing with research and development;
2. Flexible management thinking, and
3. Company pride.

On the basis of its $69 million sales volume, J. L. Clark Mfg. Co. is the nation's sixth largest metal decorator, and metal decorating is virtually identical with lithographic printing. What is different are the customer list and the product lines.

Approximately half of Clark's sales consist of containers. These are lithographed metal, combination metal and plastic, and blow-molded plastic containers. Another 20 percent of the sales is comprised of metal packaging specialties, such as spools for wire and adhesive tape, dispensers for razor blades, and outer shells for dry-cell batteries. Other products include metal and paper tubes, molded plastic industrial components, and decorated houseware items such as wastebaskets and canisters.

A few of Clark's important clients are Avon Products, Colgate-Palmolive, Gillette, Johnson & Johnson, Lever Brothers, Kraftco, McCormick & Co., 3M and other household names. In 1973 alone, Clark produced more than 1,000 different types and sizes of containers and metal packaging specialties for its customers.

Clark produces outer shells for batteries of Ray-O-Vac, Inc. and Union Carbide Corp.; spice cans for C. F. Sauer Co.; collapsible tubes for Vick Chemical Co., and insulating tubing for Western Electric telephone equipment.

Clark salesmen are trained in all aspects of the company's manufacturing processes and consequently are well qualified to consult with customers and prospects concerning the details of their particular requirements.

Expansion Through Acquisition

J. L. Clark has made eight acquisitions since 1955, all in fields related or complementary to metal lithography and packaging. Most acquisitions were made for cash, although the most recent involved stock.

Clark has a continuing interest in acquisitions, primarily in packaging and in related fields.

Three-Year Financial Highlights
(Dollars in Thousands)

Years Ended November 30	1974	1973	1972	1971
Working capital	$16,129.0	$13,169.1	$12,878.0	$ 9,104.9
Cash and securities	8,646.8	5,916.8	6,526.9	4,590.5
Receivables	6,035.8	4,691.5	4,131.7	2,476.4
Inventory	10,355.5	7,822.2	6,231.4	4,988.8
Current assets	25,706.4	18,813.8	17,107.5	12,199.2
Current liabilities	9,577.8	5,644.7	4,229.4	3,094.3
Plants and equipment	14,302.4	12,379.1	12,835.0	11,849.0
Long term debt	5,336.1	2,794.0	2,883.0	3,170.0
Shareholders' equity	25,002.6	22,979.9	22,997.0	21,193.0
Cash dividends declared (J. L. Clark shares only)	1,213.0	1,129.0	1,030.0	786.3
Shares outstanding	1,278,563	1,364.7	1,455.3	1,451.1
Number of shareholders	1,880	1,898	1,983	1,960

Ten-Year Financial Review
(Dollars in Thousands Except Per-Share Data)

Years Ended November 30	1974	1973	1972	1971	1970	1969	1968	1967	1966	1965	1964
Net sales	$69,218	$56,087	$49,756	$48,812	$49,430	$49,846	$43,857	$38,682	$38,150	$33,024	$29,548
Operating profit	10,720	6,945	6,159	5,325	4,962	5,389	4,111	3,582	4,126	2,876	2,535
Earnings before income taxes	11,017	7,215	6,296	5,396	4,725	5,238	3,771	3,494	4,176	2,930	2,525
Provision for income taxes	5,640	3,650	3,145	2,735	2,443	2,795	1,946	1,669	2,016	1,396	1,249
Net earnings	5,377	3,565	3,151	2,661	2,282	2,443	1,825	1,825	2,160	1,534	1,276
Per average shares	4.09	2.52	2.15	1.83	1.57	1.69	1.37	1.20	1.42	1.01	.84
Dividends per share	.93	.80	.74$\frac{1}{10}$	.69$\frac{1}{3}$	.66$\frac{2}{3}$	.60	.53$\frac{1}{3}$	.51$\frac{2}{3}$	.46$\frac{2}{3}$	.43$\frac{1}{3}$	.40
Number of employees	2,050	2,206	1,935	2,029	2,295	2,570	2,738	2,434	2,250	1,932	1,917
Shareholders equity per share	19.56	16.84	15.80	14.61	13.21	12.25	11.16	10.52	9.78	8.77	8.12

Prior acquisitions have enabled Clark to geographically expand its markets. With plants in California, Pennsylvania, Maryland, Canada, Indiana, Ohio, and Illinois, the company is able to give better service because production facilities are near present and prospective customers.

The principal acquisitions have been the Atlas Tube Co., the Metal Working Division of Federal Tin & Paper Co., Baltimore; and the Liberty Can and Sign Co., Lancaster, Pa.

Atlas, now a Clark division, fabricates and lithographs metal tubes for a variety of consumer and commercial products. The plant is in Downers Grove, Ill.

The Liberty Can and Sign Co., Clark's first acquisition, is now the Lancaster Division. It manufactures and lithographs metal containers much like the products turned out in the main plant in Rockford. Containers are also produced in Clark's new plant in Havre de Grace, Maryland. Two acquisitions were made in the plastics field primarily to acquire plastic technology.

The company does metal lithography at its plants in Rockford, Lancaster, Havre de Grace, and Downers Grove. The Morgan Hill plant fabricates containers from flat sheets lithographed in the Rockford plant.

Clark's housewares division, which was augmented in 1968 by the acquisition of Peoria Metal Specialty, makes a line of lithographed metal wastebaskets, canister sets, trays, and bread boxes.

Stone Industrial Corp., which Clark acquired in 1972, is a manufacturer of small-diameter, spiral-wound paper tubes, plastic tubes, drinking straws, and filters for various industrial applications. In mid-1974, the company purchased a 168,000 sq. ft. building in Lancaster, Pa. (its second site there), into which it consolidated the Filter Division of Stone and the Platt Division from College Park and Baltimore, Md., respectively, into what is now the Paper Products Division.

At the beginning of 1973 Clark acquired the Ritchie Paperboard Packaging Division of Stone Container Corp., a manufacturer of quality containers for the toy, drug, cosmetic, specialty food, and hardware industries. It specializes in composite containers which combine paper with either foil or plastic film, or with both, in the creation of anything from oil cans to body powder boxes, from planters to boxes for playing cards.

The acquisition of Ritchie brought to Clark such customers as Korex Co., Sovereign Oil Co., William Underwood Co., Playskool, Inc., Coty, Inc., Gerber Foods, Hindu Incense Mfg. Co., Tootsie Roll Industries, and Kaukauna Dairy Co. Early in 1975, Clark moved the Ritchie Division from its former Chicago location into a new 135,000 sq. ft. manufacturing building in Bedford Park, Ill.

Among the products developed by Clark during 1973-1974 were the Wild Cricket table lighter for Gillette; metal containers for the international coffee line of General Foods; colorful tobacco humidors for the Skallorna label of American Tobacco Co.; reusable containers for Hallmark; and a new series of antique cans for a number of food manufacturers.

Lithographing On Metal

Clark installed its first lithographic press in 1925, when plate production was changed from hand-transfer to photo-composing. The Rockford and Lancaster plants have creative and mechanical art departments and camera facilities for color separation, multiple step-and-repeat work, and plate production.

All artwork and plate procedures for lithography, whether commercial or metal-decorating, are the same. The difference starts when the plate moves into the pressroom.

The plates for both end products are basically the same, but metal-decorating presses must be of heavier construction than commercial presses. Whereas inks printed on paper dry by oxidation, metal decorating inks are baked in the metal. For this reason, all printed work goes through long ovens for drying.

Generally, fine screens can be printed on metal as on paper. The industry standard is 133-line, but J. L. Clark uses 150-line screen on its metals.

While paper can come in a variety of colors, metal does not. This means that metals must first be coated with special synthetic paints. These can range from alkyds to acrylics to epoxies to vinyls, depending on the requirements of the job. Inks must dry well and be scratch-resistant.

About 70 percent of Clark's production involves what is called "black plate" (steel), 20 percent is tin plate, which is actually steel with an electrolytic deposit of tin, and 10 percent is aluminum. The amount of aluminum used is on the increase.

When a printer buys paper, he must consider weight and finish. When Clark buys metal for lithography, it must consider weight, finish and temper. The nature of the product to be packed is also important, for Clark has to design and specify an interior lacquer and an exterior varnish for the containers that will hold that product.

Harold Lee, Clark's director of lithography, says that the company maintains more than 5000 ink formulas, each of which has been developed to precise specifications.

Clark does all of its own color matching and whenever possible tries to sell a customer on a straight color. Clark's ink lab turns to 15 basic colors and black in mixing ink to meet a customer's specifications.

Metal sheets are decorated on presses which are connected to conveyor ovens. Decorated sheets are then cut to size on shearing equipment. This is followed by fabrication on punch presses, can-forming and can-closing equipment and other specialized machinery. The Rockford plant has six coating lines, and eight single and two-color press lines with 29x36″ and 35x36″ presses. Precision operation is essential, since metal is so much more expensive than paper. Even a 1/32″ waste sliver can create a sizable cost problem.

The plastics division has four automatic screen printers, numerous hand screen tables, automatic hotstamping turntables, and other heavy-duty and hand-operated hot stampers. The division is fully equipped to do anything in the finishing line—hot stamping, screen printing, rotogravure wood graining, and vacuum metalizing.

Marketing Concepts

Clark spends about $2 million a year on selling, advertising, market research, product development, and promotion. One of its most famous promotion activities is its annual Masterpiece letterholder calendar. Each year this features the reproduction of outstanding works of art from the Chicago Art Institute, and is distributed to customers and prospects.

The Clark approach to marketing accounts for a good part of the company's considerable success. As William O. Nelson, Clark's executive vice president and former director of marketing, puts it, "We are structured to respond and adjust to the changes in graphics, convenience features and product protection required in packaging. We work closely with the customer and call in our research and development and visual design departments to work on the customer's problems. The visual department is told to disregard manufacturing problems and concentrate on designing what is the ideal package, structurally and graphically, for the market. The job of the R & D departments is to work on the technical aspects of the container. In this way we evolve the ideal goals from both ends, and then work towards the most economical, practical solution that is best suited to the customer."

Board Chairman Gibson illustrates the Clark concept with this instance: "We thought for some years that we ought to be in the aerosol business, but we didn't want to be just another maker of aerosol cans. We wanted to get into aerosol with a one-piece can, for without a seam, we can decorate all around. We're metal decorators, and with the seamless can we can best project our capabilities . . ."

Clark's first aerosol was a purse size container for women's cosmetic products and personal deodorants. While only one instance, this demonstrates that the uncovering of the market must come first before any profitable production can begin.

Most of Clark's work is custom made to a customer's size, color and design specifications. Such custom work is about 95 percent of Clark's container business, again demonstrating the important role that marketing and uncovering the needs and interests of the customer's customer plays in Clark's marketing strategy.

This manifold approach to metal decorating as a function-filling operation, and not as a passive "sell 'em what we got" has resulted in an enormous variety of products. Clark turns out packaging items of such things as razor blades, bandages, tape, pipe tobacco, lotions, hair dressings, and other cosmetics, glues, typewriter ribbons, flashlight batteries, spices, chesse dips, water colors, toothpaste and polishes.

Clark's orders range from as little as 5000 containers to more than ten million. "We are not necessarily looking for large runs that some of the larger companies need," Nelson says, "therefore we do spend more time developing the unique and unusual approach to packaging through lithography."

The company is obviously riding the consumer-field trend to self-service selling. This has created a need for a package that strongly projects a product's image and for uniformity in design and color for a variety of products under a single brand.

A Special Need: Control

Both production, in the person of Harold Lee, and top management in Gibson, Palmer and Nelson, speak of the need for color control, and for uniform quality, as important factors in Clark's sales success.

In the spice field, in which Clark produces more than half of the containers used in the United States, color control is especially essential.

"With some of our spice customers, we furnish the containers for a broad range of spices that are displayed in marketplaces throughout the nation," Nelson said. "Therefore the colors must be the same whether the can is on the supermarket shelf in Boston, Dallas, or Seattle. We feel we have the control and quality which results in the necessary consistency."

On some jobs there are as many as 30 or 40 quality-control checks—on others as few as five. The number of checks is determined by the complexity of the job and the number of prints required.

Some checks are made against dimensional tolerances and others are for craftsmanship. Clark not only has to check for tolerances in color register, but also for mechanical tolerances which will affect the later fabrication processes.

Clark also seeks consistency in the operation of the finished package itself. The company feels it must control all containers within a run so that they will open with the degree of ease or convenience a customer desires. "Control over coverfits on items such as cookie and cracker cans, and spice and cosmetic boxes gives them a consistency in the marketplace that eliminates complaints from customers."

Research:
Sales,
Technical

Clark spends about 1 percent of its sales dollars on research and development. This includes research into new types of packaging, improvements on present packaging, and development of new packaging closures.

Several years ago Clark intensified its market research activities and established that responsibility as a fulltime position.

"We felt that we needed to get a better fix on what was coming along in the next five or ten years," William O. Nelson adds, "and to do this we had to beef up our market research activities."

Market research and survey activities have been extended to include all aspects of packaging. "We are developing packaging machinery to furnish complete units to our customers, including items we do not manufacture, so that we can offer a complete packaging service."

While the extruded aluminum aerosol containers were the most recent product of Clark's research development, the company is working on setting up production lines for the manufacture of individual foodpack items of aluminum with an easy-open top. Clark was also the developer of the lift-tab closures on aluminum containers for dips, cheeses, and other dairy products.

The company has been particularly successful in combining metal and plastic in containers for consumer products. This is evident in Clark's spice containers, nearly all of which now involve plastic tops with various convenience closures.

Pollution has become a subject of national concern in the printing industry. In recent years Clark converted all its heating and oven equipment in all its plants to the use of gas. An incinerator unit which Clark developed and installed on one of its lighographing ovens is successfully removing all odors normally emitted when certain materials are being used. Six additional units were installed in 1971. More will be added over the next few years to completely control odor emissions in all Clark plants.

J.L. Clark Manufacturing Co.
2300 Sixth Street
Rockford, Illinois 61101

(From left to right)
Russell C. Gibson, Chairman
of the Board, Roland Palmer,
President, and William O. Nelson,
Executive Vice President,
discuss applications of
several new Clark products.

A collection of Clark Products.

82

W. A. Krueger Co.

Krueger Flexes
Sturdy Sinews
at Forty Plus

Krueger's Phoenix, Arizona plant.

Printing plant in New Berlin, Wisconsin.

Synopsis In July 1934, William A. Krueger established W. A. Krueger Co. as a four-man operation in a 4,000 sq. ft. shop in Milwaukee. Their product was lithography, and in their first year they sold $16,000 worth. In three critical respects, Krueger's action was a remarkable profession of faith: it was a proclamation of confidence in a process almost universally scorned by the reigning experts of printing; it required breaking his bonds to a comfortable family printing business; and it was timed for one of the harshest years of the deepest depression in American history. In addition, there was not the slightest reason to believe that economic relief was in sight, nor that a technological breakthrough in lithography—then an admittedly imprecise process—was imminent.

That beginning only seems the more incredible when studied in the hindsight perspective of the intervening 40 plus years—years which have so resoundingly vindicated William Krueger's judgment. As examination of the company's sales curve shows, it took almost two decades of plodding before the Krueger's rocket countdown began to simmer, and during those decades it must have taken many extra doses of faith to hold fast to a lithographic formula while all around letterpress peers began taking wing.

Today, W. A. Krueger Co. is a $70 million-a-year organization, one of the country's top ten printing manufacturers, employing over 1,800 people and registering a capital worth in excess of $50 million. Now headquartered in Scottsdale, Ariz., it has large printing plants in Brookfield and New Berlin, Wis.; Phoenix, Ariz; Jonesboro, Ark.; Senatobia, Miss.; and Pasadena, Calif. A smaller plant in Woburn, Mass. has preparatory and composition equipment only, whereas all the others have large roll feed presses, bindery, and preparatory equipment.

In addition, Krueger has a wholly-owned subsidiary in Watford, England, where it does much of its typesetting. During the 10 years from 1964 to 1974, the company's sales increased well over 400 percent—from $16.2 million to $69.0 million.

The first significant milestone in the company's history had a long-range effect but did little to promote its immediate financial well-being. It came in 1940, when Krueger technicians, working with Eastman Kodak researchers, developed Krueger's soon-to-be famous Micro-Color (trademark) process. In that year, the company's sales were $110,640. They rose to about $250,000 in fiscal 1944, then reached the million-dollar mark in the middle of fiscal 1949. Those sales doubled in the fiscal 1950-52 period as the result of the next big Krueger coup: its 1950 winning of the contract to print the color sections of *Arizona Highways*, which was then a 100,000-circulation magazine beginning to achieve fame. Micro-Color, of course, was a crucial factor in swinging that sale.

The biggest managerial move of Krueger's mid-history came in 1957, when—with sales at $4.45 million—the company went public on the over-the-counter market. It was the first of many small, privately-held printing companies to take that capital route. Much of the proceeds of its initial offering went into the construction of what was to become the company's hub plant in Brookfield, Wis., to which site it moved from downtown Milwaukee in 1958.

In late 1958, Krueger made another of its crucial decisions: this time it was to enter the el-hi textbook market. To do that the company installed its first web offset press at Brookfield and in 1960 began selling web offset signatures for textbook printing. At about the same time, it began acquisition negotiations with the Tyler Printing Co., Phoenix, the company which had been printing *Arizona Highways'* black-and-white signatures since 1950. That merger—completed in 1961—strengthened Krueger substantially in magazines, its then primary market, while consolidating production of the bellwether magazine which for over a decade had been growing into a major account. Not incidentally, it put the whole job of printing the account where it belonged—back in Arizona.

While the aforementioned arrangements were being finalized, Krueger's marketeers were coming to a basic conclusion: the only way to make money in the book market was to produce the whole product, not just those Micro-Color signatures. Accordingly, in July 1962, management concluded negotiations for the purchase of Brock & Rankin, a major Chicago bookbinding concern founded in 1892.

In the years whose sales refelect these acquisitions and basic marketing decisions—1960 through 1963—Krueger's consolidated sales went from approximately $5.5 million to almost $14 million. In the next year, fiscal 1964, they took another appreciable leap, rising almost 13 percent to $16.2 million.

In 1964, Krueger was 30 years old. It was a solid success, of course, but there was nothing in its sales history, as reflected in its annual results, that augered anything unusual, growth-wise. Between 1934 and 1944 the sales curve was relatively flat—even though it showed a twelve-fold increase in the latter year's sales over those of the first year. Nor was the second decade too unlike the first. True, sales had again multiplied by about the same factor, but they had also done that for a lot of printing firms who were not destined for top-ten stardom.

It was its third decade that marked Kruger as a "Big Time" contender. Between fiscal 1954 and 1957, sales increased by nearly $2 million—almost as much as in the previous 20 years. In the next four years they rose another $2.5 million, then in the subsequent three (1962, 1963, 1964), they shot from $7 million to over $16 million. That $9 million increase was equivalent to the total growth registered over the company's first 28 years of existence. Most of that sales increase, of course, traced to the consolidation into the parent company's of the sales of two subsidiaries—Brock & Rankin and Tyler.

The next great leap ahead came in 1968 when Krueger won an 11-year contract to print 350,000 issues a week of McGraw-Hill's *Business Week.* The order represented all of the magazine's circulation except the 14 eastern states, and it amounted then to about ten percent of the company's total sales. To produce the magazine, Krueger built another plant in Brookfield, 116,000 sq. ft., and launched itself heavily into web offset.

After that came, in rapid succession, a sequence of events that doubled company sales in five years. That growth occurred despite a 14-week strike in Krueger's Wisconsin plants and the worst recession in 20 years. Most notably, those years saw the sale of Brock & Rankin (1971), the opening (1972) of a major plant in Jonesboro, Ark., and the planning of another in Senatobia, Miss. Both the latter plants were conceived as big guns in the Krueger arsenal—both are primarily periodical manufacturing facilities. Senatobia, which went on stream in January of 1974, is equipped to specialize in the web offset production of short-run publications—those in the 5,000 to 35,000 circulation areas.

Early in 1975, Krueger acquired a modern 50,000 sq. ft. printing plant in Pasadena, Calif., belonging to Ambassador College, one of the many arms of The Worldwide Church of God. Now being printed under the Krueger flag at Pasadena and Senatobia are two million copies of the organization's publication entitled *Plain Truth*, together with other requirements of Ambassador College.

For most of W. A. Krueger Co.'s first 30 years, top management was the preserve of a triumvirate. Chief among them was William A. Krueger, founder and for the past 20 plus years chairman and then chairman emeritus. Robert A. Klaus, who served 13 years as president before becoming chairman in 1970, was next in seniority. The third figure was Harry Quadracci, who served most of those early decades as executive vice president, with production as his main responsibility.

The tenure of Robert C. Matthews as president began in late 1970, one of the worst years of that recession period. His regime has seen the introduction of a number of substantive changes in operating techniques and has already proven itself by substantially increasing company sales despite the lingering malaise in the general economy and the intensive competitive infighting in the printing market which has prevailed during most of his stewardship to date.

Marketing   When in 1943 W. A. Krueger Co. perfected its trademarked Micro-Color concept for lithographic color printing, its produce was mostly commercial printing and its annual sales were $198,860. By the time the decade was over, product emphasis had shifted markedly toward periodical printing, and sales had risen to $1,143,500.

Krueger's development as a major magazine producer began in that period, with the contract to print all the magazines of Ideals Publishing Co.—an account the company still has among its recently reported 370 active customers. What nailed down the trend toward periodical production, however, is generally conceded to have been the 1950 acquisition of the contract to print the color sections of *Arizona Highways*, another account still on Krueger's books. The growth of *Arizona Highways* is substantially coincident with Krueger's own. From a 1950 magazine with 100,000 circulation, it has grown into a nationally celebrated publication with 500,000 monthly readers and a Christmas season distribution of 800,000. In the years since 1950, Krueger and its bellwether periodical account have cooperated not only in the development of improved methods for periodical production but also in the evolution of new sales promotion and marketing techniques—with color printing a main theme.

When Krueger went public in 1957 total lithographic sales were estimated at $1.25 billion. The company's publication work accounted for 53.4 percent of its $4,454,423 sales for that year, commercial and industrial printing for the rest. All its publication work was covered by contract. Its two above-mentioned major accounts contributed 28 percent of the company's total sales; two other publication accounts contributed another 12.25 percent. Twenty-two commercial customers accounted for about 26 percent of the rest. (Other large periodical customers included the *American Investor*, published by American Stock Exchange; *Banking*, the official publication of the American Bankers Association, and *Together*, the Methodist Church's official publication, which had a monthly circulation then of 950,000.)

In 1957, sales offices were maintained in Chicago, New York and Milwaukee. While most (57 percent) of the sales income was still earned in the Wisconsin market, the rest came from a growing number of new, national accounts. The company chose its sales force from college ranks, paid them primarily on a salary basis, did its own sales training. It advertised mainly in publications in the advertising field and via direct mail. It operated a publications department which conducted market surveys for its accounts and planned circulation campaigns in both subscription renewal and newsstand sales. It acted as an advertising counsel for customers who needed advice on evaluation of products and on promotion tactics for print, radio and TV marketing. Services also included creation of sales manuals, point-of-purchase displays, etc.

Krueger's move into web offset began in 1958, when it occupied its then brand-new Brookfield, Wis., plant, built largely with proceeds from its first public stock offering. In that year management set in motion its plan to become a supplier to the el-hi textbook market through sales of web offset signatures for textbook printing. Company marketeers quickly decided, however, that the way to make money in the book market was to produce the whole book, so in mid-1962 Krueger's management bought Brock & Rankin of Chicago, a large case-binding concern founded in 1892. Book manufacturing sales rapidly overtook periodical sales until in 1964-65 they accounted for 40 percent of that year's $18 million sales total, while magazine printing had dropped to 25 percent. General commercial printing amounted to 35 percent. (It was to be almost ten years before periodical production would resume its ascendancy as chief income earner.)

By 1965, Krueger had also grown in many other ways. Twenty-five salesmen working out of six sales offices (Boston, Chicago, New York, Los Angeles, Phoenix and Brookfield) sold the products manufactured by 800 people in four plants. It had over 500 active customers, the four biggest of which contributed more than 25 percent of its sales. It was producing some 30 magazines and its two biggest magazine customers contributed 13 percent of sales. No commercial printing customers accounted for more than 2 percent of income. Whereas the company ranked about 25th among the leading producers of lithography in America the year it went public, by 1965 it had risen to somewhere between the 12th and 15th.

The main thrust of its growth between the late '50s and mid-'60s was generated by Krueger's increased emphasis on web offset, which in turn dictated that periodical production would remain an integral and major source of income. During that period the company bought Tyler Printing Co. of Phoenix (in 1961), which was co-producer of *Arizona Highways*, and started an aggressive marketing campaign to convert business and specialty publications—as well as long run work such as catalogs and annual reports—to web offset production. In pursuit of that goal it extended its customer services well beyond those of 1957.

The company now also offered publishers cost analysis projections for prospective as well as for existing magazines and it extended professional help with design, layout and even editorial assistance. It maintained a library of over 4,000 full-color photographs for use on magazine covers or internally; its subscription services were fully computerized; its distribution operations for magazines and direct mail were as sophisticated as any in the industry. (As President Robert A. Klaus put it in his 1963 annual report message: "Your company is fortunate in being geared to the rapidly-growing demand for web lithographic production, as sales for sheetfed lithography continue to remain depressed . . . Extremely heavy booking on our web manufacturing facilities extends into the spring of 1964 on a three-shift production basis.")

In 1968, Krueger landed the biggest contract in its entire sales history—the job of printing the western and midwestern run of *Business Week*, calling for a minimum production of 350,000 copies a week for 11 years. Alone, the contract amounted to a full 10 percent of that year's annual sales. To provide for its fulfillment, a new plant addition was built in Brookfield and $4.8 million was raised to pay for construction, equipment and other expenses. Total production capacity was expanded by almost 50 percent.

When the *Business Week* contract bloomed, textbook sales were beginning a period of decline. While in fiscal 1967 they had accounted for 46.5 percent of total sales ($28.8 million), in 1968 they had dropped to 38.1 percent of that year's $30 million sales. Whereas magazines had accounted for 30 percent of total 1967 sales, they accounted for 33.4 percent of 1968 sales. (The main cause of the book sales drop was a sharp reduction in federal aid to education, and thus to textbook purchases.)

Krueger's active customer rolls in 1968 stood at about 350, reflecting the increased emphasis on the larger-order clientele that goes with a web offset orientation. Its five big book publishing customers accounted for about 24 percent of total sales. The five principal magazine accounts contributed about 19 percent of total sales. (In 1968, Krueger was printing 53 magazines, almost 10 percent more than in 1967.) While its roster of commercial printing customers included many very large firms, none accounted for as much as 3 percent of total commercial sales. The company still ranked about 15th among America's lithographic giants, despite its $30 million annual sales and its production that year of 17 million books. (Also in 1968, the company produced its first major web offset annual report job—a million-copy run for General Electric.)

With the textbook market fading, Krueger's marketeers turned from el-hi textbooks to more promising prospects. By October of 1970, President Klaus could report to stockholders that "notable advances have been made in our book division, with production orders for 3.5 million books for Time-Life and three-quarters of a million books for Rockville House . . . We have also entered the encyclopedia market with the production of a 20-volume set for publication by Encyclopedia Britannica." While that lateral adjustment in book sales was taking place, however, the general economic recession was striking at the magazine base of company sales, cutting page production appreciably and even affecting sheetfed volume. Still, two new magazine accounts were acquired from the American Medical Association (soon to be a major boon), plus several new titles from McGraw-Hill and another big one—Dun & Bradstreet's *Dun's Review.*

Volume potentials during 1971 continued to be unpredictable, but Krueger managed to more than hold its own, in both magazine and book sales. On March 3, 1971, new President Robert Matthews was able to report that, while the market remained "soft," Krueger had during the preceding quarter signed term contracts to print the weekly *Journal of the American Medical Association,* two Putnam Publishing Co. magazines—*Food Processing* and *Chemical Processing*—*Jack & Jill, Golden Magazine* and, for the W. Clement Stone Organization, *Success Unlimited.* In addition, the company had won contracts to produce two major external company organs—Gulf Oil's *Orange Disc* and Union Oil's *Seventy-Six*—and it had landed the job to produce the newly revived *Saturday Evening Post.*

The big plum of the year, however, was the American Medical Association's *Journal,* a weekly said to rival the *Business Week* account in over-all size. (Incidentally, the *Journal* was first produced by Krueger when, as president Matthews put it, "due to a potential labor interruption at another company's plant, we were requested to produce it for ten weeks" during fiscal 1971's fourth quarter, ended June 30. At the same time, Krueger also "assisted *Newsweek* for eight weeks by printing a 64-page late form and binding approximately 500,000 copies.")

Book division sales progress during fiscal and calendar 1971 was similarly impressive (Krueger converted in 1971 to a calendar year for its accounting). A 16-volume *Encyclopedia of Cooking* series was produced for Meredith Publishing, as was Time's multi-volume Wilderness Series set—also new sets including a 12-volume *Atlas of Today's World* and a 16-volume *Illustrated Volume of Nature,* both by Rockville House. In the last half of the calendar year, long-term contracts were signed with Time-Life Books calling for one new book every seven weeks for five years, and for American Heritage Publishing Co.'s and Horizons' on-going series of case-bound magazines. As with the story of the year's magazine sales experience, the really outstanding bit of new book contract news was announced last by Matthews, thus:

"We recently were awarded what may be the largest single educational order ever placed, covering one million kindergarten and elementary school kits to be produced in the next 18 months for the Boston Educational Research Corp. and for their publishers and distributors, J. B. Lippincott & Co."

During the 1971 calendar year, two new sales offices were opened—one in Dallas and one in San Francisco.

By 1972, sales were at $52 million. Magazine production was again paramount (42.7 percent of 1971 sales, as against 34.7 for books and 22.6 for commercial work). The company still had approximately 350 active accounts, with the ten largest now providing 40 percent of sales volume, none accounting for more than ten percent. Now, however, Krueger ranked itself among the country's top ten producers of magazines, books and general printing, with a total of over 1,400 employees in America and Watford, England.

During calendar 1972, the new Jonesboro, Ark., "medical printing facility" created expressly to produce magazines for the American Medical Association came on-stream satisfactorily and, forthwith, another brand-new feather in the Krueger marketing cap sprouted—the Short Run Magazine Group (about which more later).

In his report for first-quarter 1973, president Matthews reported—in a review of his then two-year-old stewardship—that "we have made significant progress in magazine contracts." He declared that in the two years past the total number of such contracts had grown from 49 to 66. "It (magazine production) now represents 41.4 percent of our increased total volume." New accounts included the *Harvard Business Review*. There were cancellations, too—Woodall's *Trailer Travel* (which Matthews reported was being re-wooed), the color sections for two magazines of Petersen Publishing, and *Modern Maturity*.

The trend away from el-hi textbooks continued and that toward direct mail and subscription books gathered steam. New prime accounts which had been signed on in the two-year period included *Reader's Digest* (For *The World Around Us* series); *U. S. News & World Report* (for a new two-volume history set), the Dreyfus Fund, "and others." Despite the sales growth emphasis, however, Matthews noted that volume was definitely second to bottom-line policing:

"We are determined," he said, "not to accept work, especially for overtime hours, if the pricing is not at least at levels we consider reasonable . . . We will accept a diminishing rate of volume increases with an acceleration in the ratio of earnings to sales."

Another comment in that progress report—almost an afterthought, it would seem—reintroduced the Short Run Magazine Group: "A year ago we disclosed we were entering a new field with a specialized short-run magazine plant to be built in Senatobia, Miss. This plant is now a reality and it went live in mid-December, producing the January issues of 16 magazines . . ."

"The marketing plan for this specialized plant is to increase the number of titles produced on a monthly basis until reaching its capacity at approximately 100 monthly magazines early in 1975 . . . As is the case in all new plants located in areas new to the graphic arts field, startup problems, to a degree, are being experienced."

Matthews issued that statement in early March of 1974. By the end of the year's first quarter, very shortly later, he had cause to rue the restraint with which he had viewed Senatobia's startup problems. When he next "came on the air," it was to report that "unfortunately now, only two months after the plant started production, it is obvious that our planned time and cost goals cannot be reached and that additional costs of starting up this new plant will adversely impact earnings in 1974. Most of the causes for delay were happenings of the times. The first was a delayed building, followed by extremely poor and incomplete deliveries of basic mechanical and electronic equipment . . .

"Much more significant, however," Matthews added, "is the fact that further contracts were by necessity delayed until these late deliveries and missing parts situations were overcome . . . These delays of accepting contracts will materially affect the volume (and operating results) to be generated in this plant, which has rather high fixed expenses as a basic part of its concept."

For all the problems with getting Senatobia fully operational, however, Matthews is not about to regret the idea. In answer to a question at the April 25, 1974 annual meeting of Krueger stockholders—the question being "if there's overcapacity in printing now, why Senatobia?"—the company president replied:

"Business opportunities arise and disappear very quickly and those able to grasp them have an opportunity for profit. We were well situated from a volume point of view, from a capacity point of view, and from a product mix point of view. Then suddenly a market appeared which posed the opportunity to earn returns on investment much greater than those normally achievable in an on-going contractual printing business.

"This market was made up of specialized, short-run magazines for which the printing equipment has formerly been flatbed letterpresses which are no longer made, and frankly are just wearing out. There was a demand on these publishers to convert to offset for their ads.

"This type of magazine is not desirable in a magazine manufacturing plant such as the Krueger plant, the Donnelley plant and so forth. We don't want those short runs. We can't handle them. They crucify our cost sheets.

"So the idea was conceived for our Senatobia operation. These magazines were sitting there and the only place they could go was to the trade shops in the cities. The trade shop was capable of manufacturing them, but that's only half the battle. A trade shop didn't know how to distribute them, get them into the mail. The publishers were suffering to a great degree.

"Therefore we had the concept of a very specialized plant to do a very specialized type of operation—one kind of magazine, one size of magazine, one grade of paper. This would allow for maximum efficiency with almost a pure production line and would provide an opportunity to earn a return on investment far superior to anything we have ever done before.

"But the time had to be then. Since plans for our Senatobia plant were announced, the comments from our competitors have been 'we knew it, but we didn't move fast enough—you beat us to it.' "

Then Matthews added: *"When we decide to go into a new product line, it must bring a return higher than anything we have had in the company before ... The Senatobia plan calls for a return on investment significantly above anything now achieved in the other Krueger plants—or, as a matter of fact, in the industry's plants."*

Production   In 1934, W. A. Krueger Co. employed four men in a 4,000 sq. ft. plant in downtown Milwaukee. By 1973, it was employing some 2,000 people in five plants whose total floor space exceeded 800,000 sq. ft.

Between 1934 and 1939, progress was steady. In the latter year, 48 employees produced $89,800 worth of lithography. (If today that sales figure for that workforce seems preposterous, it would help to consider that in 1939 you could buy a brand-new Chevrolet for $800.)

In 1940, working with technicians from Eastman Kodak Co., Krueger's craftsmen developed a proprietary method of handling color separations which the company registered as "Micro-Color." Ever since, the Micro-Color trademark has been featured on Krueger stationery and corporate literature. In its impact upon the company's fortunes in terms of identity and pride, and thus on consequent sales directions and effectiveness, the breakthrough proved to be the single most powerful springboard for all Krueger's subsequent growth history.

By 1950, the year the company landed its bellwether contract to print the color sections of *Arizona Highways*, it was employing 148 people and its volume had just broken the million-dollar barrier ($1,143,500 in 1949). In the post-Micro-Color decade, therefore, the workforce had trebled while sales had soared over 1,000 percent (from 1940's $110,640). The *Arizona Highways* contract, largely landed thanks to the Micro-Color influence, worked a synergistic transformation on Krueger: from then on publication printing, and later illustrated book printing, rapidly became its paramount activities. Prior to 1950, about 80 percent of its work was in commercial and industrial printing; by 1957 the year of the company's next great milestone (its going public), publication work accounted for 53.4 percent of that year's $4,454,423 sales.

When Krueger took the public ownership plunge, it was employing 250 people, including 120 lithographers, 70 "artisans and specialists," and the rest in nonproduction posts. It was located in a 65,000 sq. ft. plant in downtown Milwaukee and leasing 20,000 additional sq. ft. in a nearby warehouse. It was working three shifts, its equipment included "numerous one-color, two-color and four-color high speed press units (with each type of press in pairs)" and doing its own color separations and platemaking "which is believed to be unusual in the lithographic industry," said the stock prospectus. The prospectus also announced that the company planned to install and test web press equipment in the immediate future.

What Krueger badly needed in 1957 was more space. The proceeds of the sale of its shares were to help build a 135,000 sq. ft., one-story, air-conditioned plant in suburban Brookfield, where the company had prepared a 5.5 acre plot for it. At the time, Krueger ranked about 20th in size amongst American firms engaged solely in lithography; its sales per mechanical employee were $22,000 while the industry average was

$14,000; sales for the year before had increased over 30 percent while the workforce had been increased only 15 percent; the original management (Krueger, Klaus and Quadracci) was still at the helm.

By 1960, Krueger was on-line with its first web offset press, an eight-unit machine, and had begun producing web signatures for the textbook industry as well as for periodicals. In the following year, Krueger bought Tyler Printing Co., Phoenix, Ariz., the other prime printing contractor for *Arizona Highways*, and began preparations to produce the entire magazine there. In 1962, having decided that the money in book manufacture lay mainly in the production of the whole book, Krueger bought Brock & Rankin, the Chicago case-binding concern.

In 1965, with sales at $17.8 million and four plants—one in Brookfield, Wis., two in Chicago and one in Phoenix—Krueger ranked 12th and 15th among the country's high-volume producers of color lithography and the printing and binding of books and magazines. It had more than 800 employees, working in 500,000 sq. ft. of manufacturing facilities, and its "product mix" in terms of dollar-volume was: magazines, 25 percent; books, 40 percent; other products (catalogs, annual reports, etc.) 35 percent. Of its 800 employees, over 650 were in production. Its Brookfield plant had been expanded to 190,000 sq. ft.; its two Brock & Rankin plants totaled over 250,000 sq. ft., and the Tyler operation in Phoenix occupied 35,000 sq. ft. in its new 50,000 sq. ft. plant.

Three offset webs, 36″ and 38″ four- and five-unit presses, were operating in Brookfield and Phoenix by 1965, with a fourth (an ATF 54″ web with a 42″ cutoff) scheduled for installation completion by the end of the year. "Generally, the web press equipment is operated three shifts per day and ... approximately six days per week," said Krueger's 1965 prospectus.) The company also had 11 sheetfed presses, eight of them multi-color, ranging in size from 14x20″ to 52-3/4x77″. It was operating those five days a week on a three-shift basis. At Brookfield three bindery lines were capable of producing 19,000 soft-bound magazines and pamphlets an hour and a perfect binder with a 9000 unit/hour capacity was on order. Phoenix was similarly equipped for soft binding. Brock & Rankin facilities included three automated bindery lines, each capable of producing 35 hard-cover books a minute or about 6,000 per hour. A fourth line with a 75-book/minute capacity was on order.

By 1966, another web offset press had been installed, bringing the total then to five, which total was boosted to seven by the end of fiscal 1967. At that time, June 30, 1967, textbooks accounted for 45 percent of sales, magazines having dropped to 30 percent.

The year 1968 was an epochal one for Krueger production-wise as well as in terms of sales: it landed an 11-year contract to print 350,000 copies a week of the midwestern and western editions of *Business Week*. The company committed itself to a major expansion program, primarily to handle the new account—a program that by the end of the fiscal year (June 30) had expanded production capacity by 20 percent, and would expand it by a full 50 percent when all planned additions to plant and equipment were fully emplaced. A 116,000 sq. ft. addition to the main periodical production plant in Brookfield was constructed mainly for the *Business Week* workload, and a 200,000 sq. ft. plant begun in New Berlin, Wis., in 1967 was rushed to completion in 1968. Close to $3 million in new equipment was installed in both new premises.

In 1968, the company was employing about 1,200 full-time personnel, 875 of them production workers. By late August, eight web offset presses were operating in the company's plants and three more were being built; sheetfed presses had been cut to seven multi-colors, ranging from 22x29″ to 52-3/4x77″. Brookfield was binding 650,000 magazines a day and Phoenix 180,000; the Chicago and New Berlin binderies were tooling up for 130,000 books daily. All was great in '68.

But in the second half of the following year events took a sudden turn from sunshine to shadow. Just when upward momentum seemed strongest, the company suffered the first work stoppage in its history—a 14-week walkout affecting its Wisconsin division, where 286 members of what was then the Lithographers & Photoengravers International Union (LPIU) went on strike. Despite the fact that the rest of the 905-employee contingent kept the division operating, losses were heavy. Physical growth ground to a standstill.

No sooner had Krueger's management begun to recover from the 1969 strike than the bottom started to fall out of the printing market as a result of the then-worsening recession. Stymied in expansion efforts by prevailing market conditions, Krueger officials turned their attentions inward. They entered into a research program with Sun Chemical Co., McGraw-Hill Publishing Co. and Blandin Paper Co. Known as the Suncure Program, it concerned ultra-violet (UV) printing techniques and was pursued with high optimism ("We are very fortunate to be partners in this endeavor, which we believe will be fully successful in a comparatively short time," President Klaus predicted in October of 1970"). Lack of progress in the program or more pressing necessities must have intervened shortly for no more was heard about it.

Another 1970 preoccupation was production streamlining and automation.

Besides extending its electronic data processing capabilities and computerizing 90 percent of its composition, Krueger also computerized the exposure controls for its process cameras, automated its Misomatic plate-making equipment and its web press controls, and scheduled a four-phase program for its engineering department. The program called for revision of standards, the improving of pre-press preparatory methods and establishment of both time and cost-saving innovations.

A final development of latter 1970 was the election (October 20) of Robert C. Matthews as president of Krueger to succeed Robert A. Klaus, who became the chairman. In one of his first reports (December 31, 1970), president Matthews was able to announce results of the above-mentioned production "belt tightening" campaign:

"Plant labor, both direct and indirect, in addition to a 13 percent reduction at New Berlin, was reduced approximately 4 percent over-all in the other plants. Supervisory personnel were upgraded and major programs were introduced and implemented covering waste control and cost reduction procedures."

By June 30, 1971 magazine production had replaced books as Krueger's major product, the sales ratio being 42.7 percent to 34.7 percent, respectively, with 22.6 percent of sales represented by commercial printing production. The company's magazine products included *Business Week, Arizona Highways, Dun's Review, Jack and Jill* and the *Journal of the American Medical Association.* Its book products were predominantly secondary and elementary textbooks and some college texts. It was also producing the hardbound American Heritage magazines and set books for Encyclopedia Britannica, Time-Life, Inc. and Meredith Publishing Co. Commercial products remained mainly catalogs and advertising printing. Approximately 1,400 full-time people were employed, 1,100 in production. Total plant area occupied was 750,000 sq. ft., of which 630,000 was owned, the rest leased.

During the first half of that calendar year—1971—while advertising declined and severe price deterioration set in, Krueger still kept up its steady although slackened growth in sales volume. Those months also saw the book field continuing in its steep slump, leaving the Brock & Rankin subsidiary in Chicago in a tenuous position. "Should this continue," reported president Matthews, "we shall have to consider alternative courses of manufacturing to preserve profitability." The condition did continue, so on August 30 the subsidiary entered into agreement with Krueger's sales vice president, John E. Hilton, to sell him "certain of its assets, including the name Brock & Rankin," and to sublease its premises to him. The transaction was closed September 30 and Krueger withdrew from Chicago and consolidated all its book manufacutring at New Berlin.

The big news bombshell of 1971 was broken by Matthews almost as an afterthought. At the October 25 annual meeting, he reported that, contingent on its establishing a separate printing facility for the purpose, Krueger had been offered the contract to print four magazines for the American Medical Association. He disclosed that consequent plans had been developed for the erection of such a facility in Jonesboro, Ark., on a 31-acre site donated by the city for the project. In addition, the city was to issue $5 million in municipal bonds to help finance the project while the Arkansas Educational Development Office would "undertake complete training of the necessary people" in the University of Arkansas' School of Printing, which grants four-year B.S. degrees in printing management or printing technology as well as two-year certificates in printing technology.

"Needless to say," ventured Matthews, "this facility was a major factor in our plant location choice, especially when combined with excellent interstate highway connections, rail location and distribution facilities."

On November 2, 1971, the company expanded again. It bought all the outstanding shares of the common stock of Wolf Composition Co. of Boston and Reading, Mass., as well as Book Graphics, Inc., a subsidiary, for "a consideration" of $680,491, with a proviso for additional payments of a possible 37,000 Krueger shares if net earnings warrant by December 31, 1976. The Wolf organization was purchased because it was a leading book composition house and had a facility in Watford, England, as well as in America. Before long, the Watford plant's advantages were to be fully appreciated.

The year 1972 began well. First quarter sales were up 22 percent and earnings up 169 percent! Business was improving at the New Berlin bindery. Monotype facilities at Watford were expanded and a new linotype department started. The Jonesboro plant was progressing on schedule. Contracts were signed with labor unions in Wisconsin and Watford—for three years in the former, 26 months in the latter. Negotiations with the Wolf unions in Boston, however, were still in progress.

In May 1972, 150,000 common shares were sold to help foot the bill for Krueger's share in the Jonesboro financing. In the prospectus for the shares, the company could boast it was one of America's ten largest lithographic printing concerns, producing magazines, books and commercial work. At the time, Jonesboro's total cost was being estimated at $6,250,000, with $5 million going into equipment, the rest into the buildings.

By mid-1972, Jonesboro had been started up and producing "live work" on the first of its two presses, a Cottrell M-1000. The plant was formally dedicated July 24. The Wolf plant in Watford, which had become operative in May, quickly sold its lino and mono time well into the fall. The New Berlin plant was busy too, reflecting a return of partial stability in the book business and, with the finalization of a new labor contract at Reading, Krueger had settled all such negotiations for the succeeding several years. By third-quarter 1972, Jonesboro was operating so well that the AMA authorized production of all four of its journals there starting in September. "This startup has been amazingly good and Jonesboro is more efficient at this point than we had anticipated," Matthews reported. Also by mid-1972, Phoenix operations were at record highs, producing 32 million magazines and catalogs a year and with *Arizona Highways* still leading the list of prize accounts.

By the end of 1972, as Matthews and his administration revealed in their annual report to stockholders, a sweeping reorganization of Krueger's basic operating procedures had been accomplished. Basic to that reorganization, but—as in the case of the Jonesboro announcement—almost wholly buried in it, was another, similar news blockbuster: the revelation that Krueger was embarking on another major new production expansion.

Clue to the big news was the announcement, in Matthews' annual message, of the establishment of a Short Run Magazine Group as one of three operating Groups (the others being the Books and Related Products Group and the Magazine and Commercial Products Group). In the "Notes to Consolidated Financial Statements," on the last page of the 1972 annual report, was notice that, to build a manufacturing facility in Senatobia, Miss., "the company is presently negotiating contracts for equipment purchases totaling $1,420,000 . . . Total expenditures for land, building and equipment are expected to approximate $3,041,000. Startup costs have been estimated at $645,000 for 1973, and will be amortized over three years. (In mid-1974 that plan was changed and decision announced to charge off all Senatobia costs after January 1, 1974 to current operations.) The company plans to finance the cost of the facility through a lease agreement with the City of Senatobia whereby the City will offer industrial revenue bonds in the principal amount of not more than $3 million."

While the actual contracts were not formally let until March of 1973, on the 9th of which month the board of directors gave the program its final approval, the planning had been a major management project of 1972. Concurrently, management had approved extensive production improvements during the year. It had added a unit to one of the Phoenix plant's two webs, updated and overhauled both, and installed there a new direct screening system. Brookfield ("cornerstone of the Magazine and Commercial Products Group") made substantial investments in direct screening and automatic plate processing equipment and ordered another perfect binder.

Thus, by the end of 1972, Krueger's operating organization had, according to president Matthews, been "re-structured along direct, profit-centered lines," giving all three new Groups "total responsibility for pricing, sales and manufacturing in their fields, and entrusting each to management by a Group Vice President." Here's how they lined up:

The Magazine and Commercial Products Group was composed of the Brookfield, Jonesboro and Phoenix plants;

The Book and Related Products Group was composed of the New Berlin plant and the Wolf Composition facilities in Reading, Mass. and Watford, England;

The Short Run Magazine Group was being built around the still-shrouded facility planned for Senatobia, Miss.

Also before the year was out, the company had set up a transportation division to "provide a nationwide, controlled distribution service," because of the "widening geographical spread" of its plants. The division consisted of a fleet of longterm leased trucks supplemented by trip-lease trucks.

As Krueger went into 1973, it appeared to have one main reservation about its production set-up. That reservation concerned the viability of the domestic composition operations of Wolf, its book manufacturing Group's typesetting facility. As Matthews reported in his year-end review of operations: "Practically all domestic book composition has been, or is being, shifted to foreign sources from England to Spain or Hong Kong or even Korea. The timing of our expansion (of the Wolf plant) in England proved fortuitous due to the lack of competitiveness of domestic costs for book composition." He warned: "The same lack of competitiveness will force us in 1973 to re-evaluate the Wolf plant in Reading, Mass., as to whether it can produce at profitable levels . . ."

In terms of production planning, then, Krueger entered 1973 with a mixture of energetic confidence and some reservations—confidence in its expansion and reorganization moves (especially in the Senatobia project), reservations mainly about its domestic book composition activities, and some also about the darkening clouds on the paper front.

By the end of the first quarter, the Wolf Composition's Reading plant was already in trouble, and Matthews was planning to re-deploy expansion capital to England rather than to Massachusetts. ("The domestic facilities will, in turn, be condensed to serve only the small remaining percentages of domestic composition," he declared. By the middle of the year, the Reading facility was in even deeper trouble. The staff had been reduced and a sale-leaseback agreement had been signed "with the lease being a very short-term affair")

Jonesboro, by mid-1973, was beginning to flourish. Its first web offset press—the six-unit M-1000—had been the nucleus of a production effort considered "most exemplary." The talk of the company, however—and indeed of many competitors—mostly concerned testing of the second of the plant's two webs. This was its $2 million, six-unit Baker-Perkins common impression cylinder press, the Orion model, with a 52″ web and a folder arrangement affording hundreds of variations in color combinations and folder configurations. Such color capability was, of course, vitally important to the production of medical journals requiring many full-color illustrations throughout the layout of every run.

Jonesboro's production, at the time, was 75 percent medium-run, nationally distributed magazines, 20 percent catalogs and the rest advertising inserts. Some 70 employees worked in its 80,000 sq. ft. plant, of which 60,000 were occupied by pressroom and bindery. Printing was being done with low-emission inks produced in-plant in a department run by Kohl & Madden Ink Corp. Equipment also featured a Hell Combi CT-258 Chromagraph scanner with double scanning head, capable of combining two four-color illustrations into one set of color separations. The plant's bindery was equipped to handle both perfect and saddle stitching jobs (included was a Sheridan 24-pocket rotary gatherer feeding into a Sheridan perfect binder). A 16-pocket inserter fed a Sheridan saddle stitcher. Both bindery lines fed into Magnacraft mailing operations.

As to Senatobia, Miss.—ground was broken on March 20 at a 15-acre site in an industrial park. Announcement on that date was the first to dub the Group's manufacturing effort officially as "Modular Publications, Inc." and it declared that the 56,800 sq. ft. plant would be "designed to house special-purpose manufacturing equipment to serve a select market of short-run magazines with a circulation in the 5,000 to 25,000 range."

In the third quarter of 1973, the domestic hot metal operations of Wolf Composition Co. were doomed, and arrangements made to phase them out before the year ended. The Baker-Perkins press installation at Jonesboro was reported "producing saleable merchandise since mid-August," a performance which Matthews dubbed "exemplary." As to Senatobia, while construction had been delayed by shortages, the delay was not at the time expected to be sufficient to affect planning. The big worry was paper. "In reality, only one cloud hangs over your company," President Matthews told shareholders in his third-quarter report. "That is the cloud of extreme shortages of paper." Supply problems, plus the disappearance of basis weights less than 50 lbs., had then "resulted in an increased cost of paper to our customers in the area of 50 percent and, with paper representing approximately one-half of the total cost of a catalog or a magazine, a real cost increase (to customers) of approximately 25 percent." And to this, Matthews added, there had to be appended "the substantial increase in postal costs due in January." He warned: "There is no question that cost increases such as these will affect the printing business." Despite the fact that Krueger backlogs were substantial, the prospects at the time seemed almost totally unpredictable as far as the new year was concerned.

All the above developments re third-quarter 1973 were reported in the same month (October) in which Krueger dedicated a 23″ four-color web offset press (Big Herman) at its New Berlin book plant and announced that photocomposition and camera operations in Reading would be relocated. (The company also reported that it was being forced to turn down "extraordinary sales opportunities" because of the paper situation.)

When all the chips were in and counted for 1973, sales were found to have risen 8.3 percent (to $56.5 million from $52.2 million), and net income was up 15.2 percent (to $1.75 million from $1.52 million). "Our capacity did not increase until the large new press was brought on-stream in Jonesboro," Matthews reported. That occurred during the fourth quarter. The big plus for the year, however, as Matthews says it, was the turnaround in the New Berlin manufacturing plant, which he declared had achieved an "almost miraculous" performance.

By the end of the first quarter of 1974 it had become apparent that Senatobia was not going to enter the production mainstream as smoothly as had been expected. It had begun operations as of mid-December 1973, but the sad fact appeared to be that Krueger's planners were at the mercy of their suppliers as far as implementation was concerned, and the suppliers were not proving capable of performing as per promise. At the 1974 annual meeting, held in April, Matthews reported that "the five-color press due to be delivered last August still has not been shipped . . . The software for our typesetting system has given everybody problems. And our building was late, due to non-delivery of this, that and you-name-it." He continued:

"As a result of all this, our people-training program has been substantially slowed down, so we cannot assimilate work which we had available under contract as fast as we wanted to . . . We expect that this year will be extremely difficult and that consolidated earnings will be affected due to these ongoing things, all of which are not calculable today. We don't know when that press is going to reach us, for example . . ."

While that question still dangled as this report was being composed, the pattern clearly established by all the foregoing seems to render it a relatively minor consideration in the total Krueger pattern. Pressing as such details can be at any given moment, what counts in the long run is problem-solving experience and ingenuity and quite plainly Krueger at the moment has little shortage of either.

People,
People Policies

Between 1934 and 1970, three men built W. A. Krueger Co. from an ant hill to one of the ten tallest dunes on commercial printing's shores. They effected in those 36 years a four hundredfold increase in personnel, and almost a three thousandfold increase in sales.

The builders were William A. Krueger, Robert A. Klaus and Harry Quadracci. In terms of background, they were an assorted trio. Founder Krueger joined his father's letterpress printing business in 1916 at age 14. Eighteen years later he was spoiling to split and join the competition. Klaus, a German-born adventurer with a degree from the London School of

Economics, arrived in America at age 24 to work in the foreign exchange department of a Wall Street bank. He was 29 and working for an international accounting firm when he threw in his lot with Krueger. Harry Quadracci was all of 21 when he left his own firm, Standard Printing Co., to become plant superintendent for the newly-minted W. A. Krueger Co.

Within five years the trio was operating a $100,000-a-year venture with 50 employees; within ten, a $230,000-a-year venture with 58 employees (a remarkable productivity gain), and within 15 years it was employing 110 and its sales were over $1 million a year. In their 23rd year, when they took their quantum leap into public finance, the trio's staff of 250 sold $4.5 million worth of lithography.

When the public ownership era began, William A. Krueger ended his 23-year tenure as president and became chairman, while Klaus took over the presidency and Quadracci continued to reign over production as executive vice president. That basic setup persisted for the next 13 years. In the first five of those years, company sales almost tripled; in the next five, they more than doubled again; in the last three years of the 13 they went from $29 million to $42 million.

In that final year, 1970, the forward momentum that had become somewhat of a hallmark of the triumvirate slowed as three economic factors combined to strip its gears. In the same fiscal period that suffered the first strike in Krueger history, the bottom dropped out of the el-hi textbook market (then half company sales) due to drastic cutbacks in federal education subsidies, and then the whole economy slipped into a worse slump phase. In a very immediate sense the founders' world had turned upside down. The corporate structure they now directed was complex and mammoth in comparison to that which they had nurtured through the years they were in their prime. It seemed time to offer the helm to successors. They took Robert C. Matthews out of sales and put him in the presidency. President Klaus became Chairman Klaus; chairman Krueger became chairman emeritus; only Harry Quadracci remained in place. Within a year, however, he was entering semi-retirement as a consultant.*

In the three and a half decades of their management, the K-K-Q trio had kept an exceptionally clean labor record. When they wrote their first stock prospectus, they could claim "the company has sustained no work stoppage or labor difficulty since its inception," some 23 years before. While they then claimed to operate a closed shop, "most" of their 120 litho production personnel in 1957 belonged to Local 7 of the then Amalgamated Lithographers of America (now Graphic Arts International Union). The company offered employees a pension and a profit sharing plan, plus other benefits such as Blue Cross, Blue Shield, health and welfare

---

*As of March 8, 1974, William A. Krueger, still a director and still chairman emeritus, was retired on $18,000 a year; Chairman Klaus was receiving an annual $25,000 as a consultant and director; Harry Quadracci, fully retired since October 1971, had two years to go as a $25,000-a-year consultant, after which he was to go on a $15,000 pension.

insurance and life insurance. It had its own personnel training program, and it sponsored a Loyalty League to reward employees with five years or more seniority. The Krueger pension plan was three years old in 1957, funded by an aggregate of 25 percent of net profit before taxes "after deducting an amount equal to 12 percent of net worth." Payments were made into the fund via issuance of $100 par value preferred stock. Stock options were also conferred on key employees.

By late 1965 the majority of Krueger's 650 production employees were union members. There were 800 employed in all. During fiscal 1964, which extended into mid-1965, some 20 percent of the company's work-force was attending either in-plant or college courses on a tuition-free program designed to refine their work-related skills and knowledge.

In addition to their concern for labor relations amenities, the veteran managers of Krueger proved their continuing alertness to societal trends, conforming thereto well before problems could develop. President Klaus, in his fiscal 1970 report to stockholders, pointed out that "we have long been an equal opportunity employer and have lived our conviction in our own training and hiring policies and through our participation in local organizations working to lift the economic level of minority groups." Under Klaus' leadership, W. A. Krueger Co, kept well ahead of the industry in its environmental protection policies, too. By the later Sixties the company was treating and recirculating its water and filtering its stacks.

When, in 1970, the "changing of the guard" inaugurated the management era of president Robert C. Matthews, environmental concern continued to rate almost as high as basic personnel relations. As a mater of fact, it linked the two. The first report Matthews made to stockholders (issued for the year ended June 30, 1971) was on recycled paper from Bergstrom Paper Co. The cover story emphasized the company's air pollution controls and reported that "for the past four months *Business Week* has been printed throughout with special experimental inks that are totally smoke-free and completely odorless." That announcement was followed by the environmental/people connective:

"At Krueger, environmental control also relates to people ... Our administrative services division has launched a broad educational program directed at alcoholism and drugs. While these two illnesses are not serious problems at our plants, we believe it is our responsibility and the responsibility of industry as a whole to discuss these matters fully with our people and, hopefully, with their entire families and to educate them to the dangers and ramifications of these problems. These programs shall continue on a consistent basis."

President Matthews wound up his special message by announcing that, in the interest of "vital incentives" and basic personnel relations, he was revising company profit-sharing and stock option plans in order to improve the Krueger employee pension plan. The pension plan reform was one of the first high-priority assignments he gave the long-range planning committee he appointed upon taking over the presidency. (Composed of Krueger's four principal executives, it also developed a Five-Year Plan covering expansion goals for "markets, sales volume, manufacturing capabilities and personnel development.")

Matthews told shareholders at the 1971 annual meeting that his board had concluded that the then-prevailing pension plan was "inadequate to fulfill the purpose of providing sufficient retirement benefits for the future security of employees and their families." He called revision "essential to attract and retain sufficient qualified employees vital to attainment of the company's long-range goals." The plan he espoused split company investment in the employee trust into a two-part formula providing (1) that company contributions to a pension plan *not* be dependent on profitability and (2) that a profit-sharing plan be adopted that limits company contributions to "exceptionally high profit years."

The new formula for calculating company contributions under the profit sharing plan was to provide for an annual contribution equal to 15 percent of net earnings before taxes after first deducting from such earnings an amount equal to 10 percent of net worth, which resulting amount was then to be reduced by 50 percent of the amount contributed to the pension plan for that year. Pension plan payments were to be based on past and current services of eligible employees, which were to be the same class of employees eligible for the former plant (870 out of a total of 1,400 employees). Contributions to the pension plan were to be calculated on an actuarial basis and were not to be allocated among individual employees.

Eligibles for the pension plan are all full-time employees except those covered by plans to which the company contributes via collective bargaining, providing the eligible employee retires on his "normal, early or deferred retirement date, with at least five years of credited service," or he terminates employment with "at least ten years of credited service." Normal monthly benefits are "the sum of (a) 0.75 percent of final average pay for each year of service and fraction thereof before January 1, 1972, and (b) 1.25 percent of final average pay for each year of service and fraction thereof after December 31, 1971, less 1.666 percent of the pensioner's primary Social Security benefit for each year of total credited service not in excess of 30 years." Definition of "final average pay" is "average monthly pay during the 60 consecutive months in which pensioner's pay from the company is highest in the 120 months immediately preceding his normal or early retirement date, or his termination of employment, whichever occurs first . . ."

Profit sharing under the Matthews reform plan is available to all employees eligible for pension benefits, payments beginning after the first year of service. Payments are figured following the close of each fiscal year. In outline, the amount credited each participant is the company's contribution multiplied by a fraction, the numerator of which is the participant's adjusted base compensation for the fiscal year and the denominator being the total adjusted base compensation received by all participants in the plan during the fiscal year. "Adjusted base compensation" for the pruposes of the plan is the participant's total base compensation for the year increased by 1 percent for each full year with the company (as of December 31 of that fiscal year) less a percentage based on the number of days absent from work (none for less than 25 days, 10 percent for less than 50 days, etc.).

As mentioned above, the compensation reform embodied in the new plans was a top priority Matthews project. His personal interest in it was so great that the afternoon he proposed them to the shareholdeds and they aproved them he went directly to his typewriter, scant hours later, and personally thanked them in the introduction to his next communication: his 1972 first-quarter report. "Morale," he wrote, "is now at an all-time high in all plants. We feel that the company is strongly en route to reaching its long-awaited goals and expectations."

The then-new president's elation was understandable. One of the first executive actions he had been obliged to take upon assuming office was to effect a sweeping workforce reduction, much of it at middle-administrative levels. At the company's New Berlin, Wis., operation, personnel was cut 13 percent; over-all personnel was reduced by 4 percent. On top of the unsettling necessity to pare the workforce, Matthews had been obliged to ask the company's production personnel to fill in, on a very heavy work-load basis, for extra production needed to hold the new American Medical Association account while the Jonesboro plant was being built to accommodate the AMA's needs. ("Our employees . . . have worked most Saturdays and Sundays since last spring, and when these long hours were combined with pinch-hitting for summer vacations, it presented an intolerable situation," he wrote.)

In the same general time-span, Matthews had been forced to sever the corporate cord to the Chicago Brock & Rankin bookbinding operation and to trim the size of the Wolf Composition facility at Reading, Mass. Yet, while he had implemented a number of basic administrative reorganizations in a tenure that was barely two years old, there had been notably little attrition in the ranks of the top executives he had inherited when he assumed control. That, and the labor peace which has prevailed to date seem clear auguries of sound progress. As Matthews observed at the close of the first quarter of 1973: "The fears that existed a year ago after we made a substantial reduction in administrative personnel have disappeared. Certainly the exempt employees are pulling together as a unit."

Nothing notably untoward, labor-wise, had happened well into 1974. Matthews' reforms seemed to have worked well and, if the K-K-Q trio which preceded him deserves to be called the builders of Krueger, he seemed well on the way to becoming a canny consolidator of all their gains. That, of course, is in addition to considerable building of his own.

Financial Management

On September 9, 1957, the W. A. Krueger Co. completed the most fateful step in its then 23-year corporate history: it went public: It had posted sales of $4,454,423 for the fiscal year ended June 30, 1957. Earned by a workforce of 250, they contrasted with 1935 sales of $16,320 earned by a workforce of eight.

While a fine growth rate had been established over the 23 years by the company, it was not a particularly unique one in terms of intensity. Nor was the company notably different from its peers in any other respects in those days. What was unique for the time however was the fact that a company of its size had the temerity to venture into the bigtime world of public finance.

The immediate aim of the Krueger foray into the open capital market was to realize $680,000 worth of capital by selling 100,000 shares of common (par value $5) at $8 per share. With all costs deducted, the monies raised were to be applied as follows: $130,000 to expand inventories, $400,000 for new plant construction and $150,000 for equipment expansion.

While their "bold venture" proved highly successful, it exacted its price. It meant for founder, William A. Krueger and his two chief sidekicks—Robert A Klaus and Harry Quadracci—a 37 percent reduction in the ratios of company stock each owned. It also meant a 20 percent reduction in their aggregate annual paycheck. Similarly affected was a fourth principal—Arthur M. Wood, vice president for sales, who had joined the firm in 1939.

Prior to the public offering, the four men controlled 87.6 percent of the company's stock: Chairman Krueger voted 92,672 shares, or 54.2 percent of common shares outstanding; President Klaus voted 38,920 shares, or 23 percent; Quadracci voted 10,920 shares, or 6.5 percent, and Wood 6,664 shares, or 3.9 percent. After the public sale, the four principals and their wives, etc., altogether controlled only 55.2 percent of the company's common: Krueger's control dropped to 34.1 percent; Klaus' to 14.5 percent, Quadracci's to 4.1 percent and Wood's to 2.5. For Chairman Krueger, that 20.1 percent drop represented the most significant change of all, for while it still left him with an imperious grip on his corporate offspring, it was no longer an unbreakable one.

In prior years the four principals had been earning an aggregate of $230,000. On June 28, 1957, just two days before the end of their last independent fiscal year, they anticipated their "income problem" and reduced its aggregate sum to just over $199,000—$60,000 for Krueger, $75,000 for Klaus, $34,000 for Quadracci and $30,000 for Wood. That aggregate was shortly to be reduced another $15,000 in accordance with terms of the underwriting agreement that they signed—an agreement which required that for the three-year period ending October 1, 1960 the income of the quartet could total no more than $184,000.

At the time its chiefs were publicly recapitalizing their corporate gamecock, a lot was going on at W. A. Krueger Co. The firm was on the verge of selling the 65,000 sq. ft. plant it owned in downtown Milwaukee and moving to a 135,000 sq. ft. plant it was building in Brookfield, on the outskirts. It was committed to an expenditure of $167,335 for a new press being installed there—which expenditure was due within 30 days of the public offering. It was paying off a 6 percent first mortgage of $163,600, which it had promised to retire out of proceeds of the sale of the downtown plant. It was seeking to negotiate a 6 percent first mortgage of $700,000 as a first lien on the Brookfield plant. It was committed to paying off $127,200 within two years—and the rest of $233,400 worth of 6 percent subordinated debentures within seven years.

All things considered, the decision to go public obviously reflected another—that it was time to break out of the common mold and "make it or bust," and soon. Krueger's managers lost little time. One of their first moves was to add web offset and buy Tyler Printing Co., Phoenix, the other major contractor on the *Arizona Highways* magazine account.

The next major, crossroads-type financial management decision to be implemented came on July 2, 1962, when the company acquired all of the outstanding common stock of Brock & Rankin, Chicago, a corporation engaged in the bookbinding business since 1892. The purchase cost was 157,000 shares of Krueger common, but it put the Wisconsin wunderkind solidly into a new field it had been probing since late 1958—book manufacturing, specifically the el-hi textbook field.

By 1965, with sales of $17.8 million, Krueger was rating itself among America's 12 to 15 largest enterprises engaged in color lithography and the printing and binding of books and magazines. (Eight years earlier, when it went public, it rated itself among the first 25 "producers of lithography.") In 1965 it offered for public sale 125,000 shares of common at $11.50 (up $3.50 per from the 1957 price)—a sale from which it planned to realize $1,318,750. Since going public, it had become a multi-plant organization seated in Brookfield and with large operations in Chicago (Brock & Rankin) and Phoenix (via the Tyler operation—which it had expanded appreciably by 1965).

The funds raised by the '65 offering were targeted for an addition to the Brookfield plant and the installation there of printing and binding equipment to cost $1.9 million. Another $750,000, from a loan arranged through an insurance company, was to make up the remainder of the needed financing. (Bank borrowings at the time—mainly taken to support costs of inventories and accounts receivable—were $1.3 million.) As adjusted to reflect the issuance of the new stock, stockholders' equity in 1965 was vested in 608,784 common shares ($5 par value) outstanding or an authorized million shares, and 7,139 shares of an authorized 8000 shares of 6 percent cumulative preferred stock of par value $100 (later to be called first preferred).

Despite the company's quadrupling of its sales since 1957, net earnings per share in 1965 were down slightly—from $1.41 a share in the earlier year to $1.38 a share in the later one. And while the Krueger-Klaus-Quadracci triumvirate remained at the top of the management pyramid as chairman, president and executive vice president, respectively, the pyramid's base had widened considerably. Among others, it now included as a vice president Donald C. Brock, who was also president of the Brock & Rankin subsidiary, and Robert C. Matthews, senior vice president for sales and marketing. By the time the stock sale was complete, the total common stock owned or controlled by founder Krueger amounted to 16 percent of the outstanding shares while those controlled by the Brock family amounted to 28.1 percent. No other common stock interests totaled more than ten percent.

In terms of voting control, however, the K-K-Q three still held sway, for at the time of the purchase of Brock & Rankin they had entered into an agreement with the Brocks whereby for five years they were granted an irrevocable proxy to vote all shares owned by all parties to the agreement. As salaries reflect management influence, here's the way the "sway" went in 1965: President Klaus, $71,000; Chairman Krueger, $52,000; Executive Vice President Quadracci, $50,000; Vice President Matthews, $47,500; Vice President Brock, $36,500.

In April of 1967, W. A. Krueger Co. sold its first 100,000 shares of a new Series A convertible second preferred stock at $25 per share, raising $2.35 million on the transaction. Each of the shares entitled the owner to one vote, and to annual dividends of $1.44 before common stock dividend payments could be paid. The new shares changed again the voting power-structure of the company. (By September 1, 1967, owners of more than 10 percent of either common stock or the new preferred were: Donald C. and Mrs. Marjorie Brock, 11.1 percent of common; William A. Krueger and allied interests, 11.9 percent of common; New York Mutual Life Insurance, 13.4 percent of preferred, and Northwestern National Insurance of Milwaukee, 10.1 percent of preferred. "Various nominees" represented by the First National City Bank of New York owned 20.8 percent of the new preferred.)

To the sum raised by the April sale of preferred the company planned to add $3 million from institutional financing. Actually, the offering was the first step in a program "to provide about $7 million additional outside capital funds for a projected three-to-four-year expansion and modernization program," president Klaus announced in his 1967 annual report message. "About $5 million of the expected total cost of approximately $12 million will be generated internally. When this program is completed in 1970, manufacturing capacity of the W. A. Krueger Co. will have been increased by at least 65 percent." By June 30, 1967, contractual commitments for plant construction and equipment purchases totaled $6.4 million, of which $1.23 million had been paid or accured. The balance of previous conditional sales contracts for machinery and equipment on that date was $505,632—which was left out of an original commitment total of $1.15 million.

At the end of August 1968, with its sales at $29.8 million, the company went again to the money market—this time to sell 130,000 shares of its $5 par value common, then priced at $23.875. Proceeds to the company—$2,889,250—were meant primarily to expand facilities at the Brookfield plant to accommodate the production requirements of what was then the biggest plum in Krueger's corporate history—the contract to print *Business Week* magazine. It was estimated that the total cost of the expansion would be about $4.8 million. Another $500,000 was needed for working capital and the company wanted also to buy back 5000 shares of its first preferred stock—the $100 par value stock base of the employee pension fund.

With that latest stock market offering allowed for, capitalization of W. A. Krueger Co. in latter-half 1968 stood at $24,415,438, of which $10,172,500 was debt in terms of notes and loans (the latest then being $3 million worth of 7-3/4 percent senior notes due 1984); $3,376,050 was equity in preferred and $10,866,933 was equity in common stock.

In the 11 years since it had gone public, then, the company's sales had been increased nearly 700 percent and the selling price of its common stock 300 percent. Its total indebtedness in September 1957 had been $2,562,295; by August 1968, that figure had increased by over 900 percent.

At the time of the company's 1969 annual meeting, other contrasts were almost as great. While he still served as chairman, William A. Krueger's salary had dropped to $35,000, mostly reflecting his semi-retirement, and his common stock ownership had dropped from 34.1 percent of 1957 common to under 10 percent of 1969 common (72,496 shares out of a total of 748,713 shares then outstanding). Robert A. Klaus was still president and chief executive officer, and his salary was substantially what it had been, but although he had added almost 11,000 common shares to his company portfolio, his equity had dropped to less than half what it had been in 1957. Harry Quadracci was still executive vice president and his "direct aggregate remuneration" had leaped from the $34,000 he was earning in 1957 to almost $60,000 in '69—yet he too had had his equity in the company halved despite having bought another 5152 common shares.

One of the soon-to-be-significant developments of 1969 was the latter-year appearance in top management ranks of the most powerful new star in the company's uppermost firmament—Robert C. Matthews. Matthews had joined the company in 1958 as director of sales for the Brock & Rankin subsidiary, then in 1962 became the subsidiary's vice president of sales. Two years later the parent company took him in as senior vice president, sales and marketing—adding a directorship in 1968 and in 1969 the portentous additional title of assistant to the president.

By October 30, 1969, no individual held even 10 percent of the company's common stock. The age of the bankers had arrived. The 1969 proxy statement showed that National City Bank of New York held 19.82 percent of Series A Convertible preferred stock in trust for "various nominees;" Mutual Life Insurance Co. of New York held 13.94 percent of that stock and another 10.51 percent of it was held by Northwestern National Insurance Co. of Milwaukee. Further, one of the main objectives of the annual meeting scheduled for that fall day would continue the dilution of individual ownership influence by increasing the number of authorized shares of common from one to two million. ("At present," read the annual meeting notice, "of one million authorized shares of common stock approximately 958,000 shares are outstanding or committed. It is believed that the existing condition is too restrictive and that an increase . . . is necessary to give the company flexibility in its long-range planning.")

[Following the offering of another 150,000 common shares—May 3, 1972, when the sale price had readjusted to $18.25 per—the total common stock interests of all officers and directors as a group amounted to 173,492 shares, or 23.4 percent of that stock class. Northern Trust Co. of Chicago alone held in trust 149,456 shares, or 19.91 percent of all common.]

To resume fiscal-year chronology: 1970 began (July 1, 1969) gingerly, then quickly delivered a haymaker. By the time the first quarter had expired, the company had undergone a 14-week strike that hobbled production at its Brookfield and New Berlin plants and ended a proud, quarter-century history of uninterrupted labor peace. The $301,000

Krueger collected in strike insurance was a pittance compared to the effect of the strike during a period when the national economic index had begun to slide alarmingly.

By the time the final tally for fiscal 1970 was in (June 30, 1970), the company had recovered nicely in terms of sales ($37 million as against 1969's $32.7 million), but it had taken a bath in more important fiscal areas: as compared to the respective 1969 figures, 1970 gross profit had dropped from $6.15 million to $4.75 million; operating profit from $2.77 million to $1.26 million; earnings before taxes from $2.3 million to $580,182 and—worst of all—net earnings had plummeted from $1.11 million to $307,182. Per share earnings for fiscal 1970 were 14¢ as against the 1969 figure of $1.23.

That the $301,000 strike insurance equated to band-aid medication for an amputation was evident in the company's 1970 statement of consolidated operations. It shows that the cost of sales for that year was $32,234,449 as compared to the previous period's $26,559,597. Other effects of the fiscal year's problems could be seen in such figures as "expenditures for plant and equipment, net." In fiscal 1970 they froze at $2 million, compared to the 1969 figure of $4.7 million, and 1968's $7.3 million.

Presumably in consequence of a battery of such factors—the strike, the rising importance of the sales cadre, the decision to hold the line in terms of production expansion, and the finally-dominant influence of outside, bank-controlled interests—the closing months of calendar 1970 witnessed a "changing of the guard" at W. A. Krueger Co. William A. Krueger relinquished his post as chairman for that of chairman emeritus; Robert A. Klaus relinquished the presidency for the chairmanship, and Robert C. Matthews assumed the post of president. Harry Quadracci kept his former post. All retained directorships.

The Advent of Matthews

Stockholders got their first clues to the potentials of the Matthews stewardship via the new president's 1971 fiscal first-half report, issued January 25, 1971. While he told of the disappointment at non-achievement of budgeted goals, he announced thereafter that the company's earnings for the period were 32¢ a common share, as against a *loss* for the preceding half-year of 83¢ a share.

"The significant factor affecting performance was extreme deficiencies at our new book plant in New Berlin," Matthews observed, adding: "measurable results (of drastic retrenchment as to systems and manning schedules) show that performance of this plant has been turned around." The July 1, 1970 to December 31, 1970 period recorded net sales of $20,640,000 as opposed to $15,356,000 for the comparable previous fiscal period, and net earnings of $341,000 as against a loss of $525,000. Largely responsible for that bottom-line improvement were a 13 percent workforce cut at New Berlin and a 4 percent workforce reduction for the company over-all. Another Matthews measure in that half-year interval was to bear down hard and fast on costs. The company's cost system was revamped and a new, standardized program instituted. Said Matthews: "Our billing cycle and the number of days invested in receivables have been reduced, which contrasts with contrary trends in business generally."

In his fiscal 1971 third-quarter report, President Matthews reported some good news and some bad news. The good news: with all markets softer than they had ever been in the corporation's public history, the magazine printing sales staff had turned in an excellent showing. His bad news: "Our Chicago book manufacturing plant (Brock & Rankin) is producing at a much lower level than it has in the past decade ... should this continue, we shall have to consider alternative courses of manufacturing to preserve profitability." By the end of fiscal 1971, despite worsening market conditions and continuing production problems, Matthews had a happy note to strike re sales and earnings. He delivered it sotto voce: "Sales for the year ended June 30, 1971 were slightly in excess of $42 million, representing an increase of 14 percent ... Earnings approximately $1.16 per share for fiscal 1971 compare favorably with earnings of 14¢ per share reported for the previous year ...."

With that bland phrasing, the new president characterized remarkable company performance during a year when the economy in general was depressed, and when his organization was not only recovering from a trauma of its own but was also adjusting to his new leadership. His accomplishment gave him ample sanction for his next moves, big ones, which came fast:

On August 30, 1971, Brock & Rankin entered into a contract for sale of "certain of its assets," including its name, and for sublease of its premises to John E. Hilton, a sales vice president of the W. A. Krueger Co. Total sale price for equipment was $301,526, payable in quarterly installments over two and three-quarter years. The inventory was sold for another $131,840. A month later, the operation passed into Hilton's full control and he resigned his Krueger post. All the Krueger bookbinding operations were subsequently consolidated at the plant in New Berlin. To stockholders, the cost of the liquidation amounted to 7¢ per common share out of the 11¢ those shares had earned in the previous two quarters.

The best news of the year came next. It was broken to stockholders in Matthews' report for the quarter ended September 30, 1971. For an announcement of such consequence, it was couched in curiously convoluted terms: "This afternoon (October 25) I announced that, based on the company establishing a new printing facility in Jonesboro, Ark., we have been awarded four new magazine contracts from the American Medical Association ..."

No mention of any Jonesboro plant plans had been made in previous annual, quarterly or mid-year reports. As a matter of fact, the pronouncement dated October 25 had been composed immediately following the 1971 annual shareholders meeting, held that day. No word of Jonesboro had appeared in the notice of that meeting, whose primary announced purpose—beside the election of directors—was to seek stockholder approval for reform of Krueger's pension plan and its incentive arrangements, notably as to stock options. (Matthews even began his report on that meeting by stating: "This afternoon we had a most wonderful reception at the annual meeting. Your management was extremely gratified as shareowners approved the Employees' Pension Plan, the Modified Profit-Sharing Plan, etc . . .")

Yet here was a newsbreak of profound importance to W. A. Krueger Co.'s future and its standing in the pecking order of the nation's primary printing paragons!

Next news about a major move came on November 2, 1971. On that date Krueger announced its purchase of Wolf Composition Co. of Boston, a leading producer of book composition, with plants in Reading, Mass., and Watford, England. Included in the purchase was the Wolf subsidiary, Book Graphics, Inc., of Reading. Initial consideration was $680,491, consisting of $199,000 in cash and $481,491 in the form of 28,383 shares of common at $17 per share (down from the $19.50 quoted stockholders a month before as the August 30 price). Agreement also stipulated that Krueger would issue a maximum of 37,000 more common shares to the sellers if "defined net earnings" of the organizations "exceeded a stated minimum" in the four years ended December 31, 1976.

Thus, by the end of calendar '71—which, incidentally marked the changeover of the company's fiscal year from one ended June 30 to a calendar year—Krueger had not only recovered from its 1970 slump but was strongly embarked on an expansionist offensive. Around it, the printing scene generally was in disarray, the economy almost in stasis, Washington was implementing controls to brake inflation and most business optimists were being measured for strait jackets.

How, against that background, could a Wisconsin printing management team field a plan for a 20 percent capacity expansion like a "Jonesboro"? Whence the venture capital for a multimillion dollar project entailing, just initially, commitments to building 85,000 sq. ft. of plant space in the middle of Arkansas, and hiring and training 400 new people?

As befits any good solution to a complex problem, the answer was simple:

In the first place, all the business needed to float the project was already signed on when Jonesboro's news was promulgated. Meanwhile, Brookfield was breaking its back to keep the basic contracts intact while the plant on which they depended was moving toward completion.

In the second place, the cost to Krueger in immediate, out-of-pocket terms was remarkably minimal. Here's why: Under an agreement between Krueger and the City of Jonesboro, the city financed part of the construction of the plant and the purchase of "certain equipment" with an estimated aggregate cost of $4.4 million by issuing 6-3/4 percent to 7-3/8 percent industrial revenue bonds in the amount of $3 million. Krueger provided the $1.4 million balance and in addition committed itself to acquiring approximately $1.85 million worth of equipment under a ten-year lease financed by an industrial lender.

Krueger's current occupancy of the plant is under the terms of an irrevocable lease lasting until 1987 and providing for rental payments averaging $323,000 a year, equal to the bond amortization, interest and carrying charges. Renewal and purchase options were also written into the lease. Prior to April 1, 1977, the company has the right to purchase land (31 acres), building and equipment only if: (1) there is major damage to the building, (2) it is condemned, (3) there are legal changes affecting the lease or bonds, or (4) there is curtailment of use or a premature lease termination. *After the bonds are retired, the purchase price of the building and equipment to Krueger will be $100, or the rental will be $100 per annum.* (Provision was even made to neutralize effect of the plant's startup costs, for such costs were being capitalized over a period of three years. "This procedure," noted president Matthews, "will minimize any detrimental effect on 1972 earnings while bringing on-stream this much needed and long overdue additional magazine facility.")

It was to raise the capital needed for its investment in Jonesboro that W. A. Krueger Co. floated an offering of 150,000 common shares (par value $5) on May 3, 1972, as mentioned above. That offering was sold out the first day. At the time, the estimated cost of the Jonesboro project had been "re-structured" to $6.25 million: $1.25 million for the building and $5 million for equipment. Proceeds of the stock sale amounted to $2.52 million. (Re the May '72 offering, a comment by Matthews seems significantly pointed: "Of great importance was our decision to broaden our shareowner base to a real national distribution by having the offering co-managed by Dean Witter and Robert W. Baird. None of these shares was sold to institutions and the number of round lot owners substantially increased." Apparently the weight of bank-oriented ownership was then becoming either onerous or impolitic.)

The year 1972 had begun very well for the company. First quarter results recorded a 22 percent sales increase ($12.4 million vs. $10.1 for the comparable 1971 quarter); a 140 percent earnings-before-taxes increase ($1,164,000 vs. $484,000) and a 144 percent increase in net earnings ($567,000 vs. $232,000). Per share earnings had gone from 24¢ to 67¢. At the time Matthews had cautioned, however, that those figures for 1972 included operations of the new composition subsidiaries, not included in the 1971 figures, and that "earnings for the quarter are not necessarily indicative of results for the entire year." By the half-year accounting, although Matthews could boast that "operating earnings for the period were the highest ever reported" the comparative sales/earnings ratios had tamed considerably. By that reckoning (June 30, 1972 vs. June 30, 1971), net sales were up 9 percent ($23.7 million vs. $21.8 million); net earnings 21 percent ($915,000 vs. $758,000) and net per share 16 percent ($1 vs 86¢).

By third-quarter '72, Matthews was unhappy. His first quarter precautionary admonition had been realized. "This quarter and its disappointing results did not live up to our expectations," he stated. Blaming results more on production mismanagement than on market weakness, he added: "Significant changes are already in the making to avoid a repetition of this performance." His rue traced to the fact that although sales had jumped 20 percent over those for the comparable '71 quarter ($14.2 million vs. $11.8 million), net after taxes had fallen to $426,000 vs. $430, 000 and per share earnings to 41¢ vs. 50¢

Reporting on the full fiscal performance of 1972 in the annual report for that year, Matthews had to tell stockholders that "although your company generated the second highest earnings in its history, we do not consider 1972 a satisfactory year." While sales had hit a record $52.2 million vs. $45.8 for '71, after tax net earnings were $1,518,000 as opposed to $1,575,000 in '71 and per share earnings $1.50 vs. $1.80. (Earnings in terms of percent of sales were 2.9 in 1972 as against 3.4 in 1971.) Blame for the disappointment was placed primarily on intense competition and poor pricing which traced to over-capacity in the printing industry. "Unfortunately," Matthews observed, with uncharacteristically simplistic logic, "our industry has not had the fortitude to follow the example of the paper industry and reduce capacity by silencing obsolete machines . . ." (What had actually silenced those obsolete paper machines was not economic statesmanship as much as the economic imperatives of potentially heavy losses from them the machines to be modified to conform to anti-pollution laws!)

Thus, after slightly over 15 years of public ownership, and 20 months of Matthews stewardship, W. A. Kruger Co.'s basic statistics included these:

W. A. Krueger Co. After 15 Years of Public Ownership

	1972	1957
Sales	$52,173,628	$4,454,432
Total Current Assets	$15,603,628	$1,417,602
Common Shares Authorized	2,000,000	500,000
Common Shares Outstanding	929,000	169,000
Common Share Selling Price	$18.25[1]	$8.00[2]
First Preferred ($100) Shares Authorized	25,000	8,000
First Preferred ($100) Shares Outstanding	9,953	1,632
Convertible Second Pref. Shares Outstanding	80,107	0
Book Value Property, Plant and Equipment	$20,745,593	$1,095,095
Plant Floor Space in Square Feet	750,000	135,000
Number of Plant Units	6	1
Inventories (raw materials, work in progress)	$ 4,177,124	$ 395,246

[1] As of May, 1972.
[2] As of September, 1957.

As of December 31, 1972, the largest single-ownership voting factor in the company's records was the Northern Trust Co., whose total voting power (one vote per second preferred and one per common share) was 15.59 percent. Its 12,000 shares of second preferred comprised 15.10 percent of that class and its 145,206 shares of common (including 50,000 held in trust for Donald C. Brock) comprised 15.38 percent of total outstanding common shares. Mutual Life Insurance Co. of New York held 13,400 shares of second preferred or 16.73 percent of the class and was at the time record owner of $2,774,000 of the company's unsecured notes due 1983-84. It had no common share ownership and its total voting power was only 1.33 percent. Wisconsin Securities Co. of Delaware, with 12.48 percent of second preferred (10,000 shares) and .53 percent of common (5000 shares) voted 1.49 percent of the company's total stock.

Northwestern National Insurance Co.'s 10,100 shares of second preferred (12.61 percent) gave it 1 percent of total voting power.

No individuals wielded ownership authority of any consequence. The above-mentioned trust and insurance companies held 56.92 percent of all second preferred (80,100 shares) outstanding. Founder William A. Krueger, fully retired, owned or controlled 53,207 common shares of 943,905 then outstanding. Director Donald C. Brock, also retired, controlled 63,277 shares, and Chairman Robert A. Klaus owned 49,980 shares. Klaus also owned beneficially 377 shares of $100 par value first preferred stock. President Matthews owned 2,243 shares of common. Harry Quadracci, as of October 31, 1971, had terminated active service, was no longer a director, and was on a five-year $25,000 consultancy period, following which his $15,000/year retirement agreement was to take effect.

As of December 31, 1973 Chairman Emeritus Krueger's share of common—out of 870,547 shares outstanding—remained at 53,207; Donald Brock's had jumped 500 shares to 63,777; Chairman Klaus' had been rounded off to 51,000. The Brock shares listed under that remained exlcusive of the other 50,000 held in trust by Northern Trust Co. and the Klaus fund of 377 shares of first preferred also remained unchanged. Far and away, they represented the major blocks of shares listed under individual ownership. Matthews' 2,243 shares also remaining unchanged, the precise identity of the holder who in second-quarter 1973 "elected to change his portfolio" by selling 58,400 shares back to the Krueger treasury eludes a search of public records.

During that year ended December 31, 1973, however, the bankers had relinquished substantial amounts of ownership. Northern Trust had sold 11,000 shares of second preferred and 52,700 shares of common, reducing its total voting power percentage from 15.59 to 9.85. Wisconsin Securities and Mutual Life of New York maintained its holdings during the year, but Northwestern's 1972 lot of 10,100 second preferred, which had given it 12.61 percent of all stock, disappeared from the rolls for 1973. The Dean Witter/Robert Baird stock offering of May '72 had considerably loosened the bankers' grip, as had been hoped. Whereas at the end of 1972 they had held 19.41 percent of total voting power (as recorded in the March 9, 1973 proxy statement), by the end of 1973 that percentage had fallen to 12.84.

To resume this chronology, the big fiscal commitment of 1973 was first announced to shareholders in the annual report for 1972.

In his introduction to that report, President Matthews described a managerial reorganization into three operating Groups, each with a group vice president: (1) Magazines and Commercial Products, (2) Books and Related Products, and (3) The Short Run Magazine Group. Back in the Notes to Consolidated Financial Statements, on page 24, the meaning of the Matthews reference to the new Group took shape. It was a most significant announcement despite its obscurity in the report's makeup: "In March, 1973, the board of directors authorized the construction of a manufacturing facility in Senatobia, Miss. The company is presently negotiating contracts for construction and equipment purchases and has made contractual commitments for equipment purchases totaling $1,420,000 as of March 9, 1973.

"Total expenditures for land, building and equipment are expected to approximate $3,041,000. Startup costs have been estimated at $645,000 for 1973 and will be amortized over three years.

"The company plans to finance the cost of the facility through a lease agreement with the City of Senatobia whereby the City will offer industrial revenue bonds in the principal amount of more than $3 million."

Financing was arranged by the Mississippi Agriculture and Industry Board, as well as the City of Senatobia. In addition, the state agreed to contribute "significant training assistance, both in time and material." Name of the new subsidiary is Modular Publications, Inc.

While negotiations such as that concerning Senatobia were being pursued, so were plans for internal financial management reorganization. A pioneer among printers in computerizing its financial record-keeping and related activities, Krueger was still dissatisfied with its efficiency. It hired Arthur Andersen & Co. to study its operation and in his April 27, 1973 report president Matthews declared that "corrective measures" recommended by Andersen to improve "our internal financial and information system are being taken . . . A strong system of financial controls is a prime goal for 1973."

By the end of 1973 the effect of the Anderson plan, the over-all reorganization of management was being credited by Matthews as largely responsible for the fact that 1973 "was a good year." As he put it: "Of considerable significance was the strengthening of the financial department, which provided better management tools in the form of more timely reports and more depth in reporting as a whole. Difficult items must include the added burden of governmental reporting, of wage and price control restraints, of expenditures to comply with OSHA requirements in all plants, and the continuing effort to upgrade our processes to fully comply with the Environmental Control Act."

While the year's sales were up an unspectacular 8.3 percent ($56.5 million as opposed to 1972's $52.2 million), earnings were up a comforting 15.2 percent ($1.7 million vs. $1.5 million).

First quarter results for 1974 were reported just as this study was being finalized. The quarter's sales were $13.9 million compared to the 1973 quarter's $11.5 million; primary earnings were 52¢ a share vs. 29¢. Initial operating losses on the Senatobia venture amounted to 18¢ a share, which brought 52¢ down to 34¢.

Senatobia, however, was being viewed as fiscal '74's Achilles heel. Planning on the project called for its breaking even by the year's end, but a series of delays in construction and equipment installations had already made clear by March 1974 that the hoped-for goal would not be reached. "As of this date," stated Matthews, "the total impact of these happenings on the consolidated earnings of the company for the year 1974 cannot be estimated, but management believes that the effect of the startup and related costs will be such that we will be fortunate if we are able to maintain the earnings level of 1973."

Ranking:	Among the top ten producers of periodicals and books as well as advertising printing. Prints magaiznes such as *Business Week, Arizona Highways, Journal of the American Medical Association, Jack & Jill, Dun's Review.* Manufactures books for Time-Life, Meredith Publishing, American Heritage, Rockville House, many of them encyclopedia sets. Total sales, 1974: $69,024,000.

Product Mix:

1971 (Sales: $42,418,000)
Periodicals . . . 42.7% ($18,114,000)
Books 34.7% ($14,726,000)
Commercial . . 22.6% ($ 9,578,000)

1972 (Sales: $52,174,000)
Periodicals . . . 41.4% ($21,594,000)
Books 31.2% ($16,258,000)
Commercial . . 27.4% ($14,322,000)

1973 (Sales: $56,499,000)
Periodicals . . . 40.9% ($23,119,000)
Books 35.4% ($19,993,000)
Commercial . . 23.7% ($13,387,000)

1974 (Sales: $69,024,000)
Periodicals . . . 42.1% ($29,045,000)
Books 33.1% ($22,857,000)
Commercial . . 24.8% ($17,122,000)

Plants:

Total, 800,000 sq. ft. (approx.)
Brookfield, Wis. (periodical, comml) - owned - 300,000 sq. ft. - built 1958
New Berlin, Wis. (book mfg.)   - owned - 250,000 sq. ft. - built 1968
Pasadena, Calif. (periodical, comml) - leased - 50,000 sq. ft. - built recently
Phoenix, Ariz.   (periodical, comml) - owned - 80,000 sq. ft. - built 1962
Jonesboro, Ark. (periodical, comml) - leased - 85,000 sq. ft. - built 1972
Senatobia, Miss. (short run period.) - leased - 56,800 sq. ft. - built 1973
Woburn, Mass.   (book composition) - leased - 19,000 sq. ft. - built 1965
Watford, England (book composition) - leased - 16,000 sq. ft. - built 1937

Notes: Plants operated under 15-year lease agreements with City of Jonesboro (1972) and City of Senatobia (1973). Both agreements require Krueger to provide rental payments equal to the bond principal amortization and interest. Company has option to purchase assets for nominal amounts on expiration of leases. Krueger has capitalized both leased assets and included aggregate rentals of $6 million in its accounts.

Employees:

as of 12/31/74, total 1,800, of whom 1,300 are in production
as of 12/31/73, total 1,622, of whom 1,328 were in production
as of 12/31/72, total 1,502, of whom 1,093 were in production

Sympathy for President Matthews' travail comes hard, since it is conveyed in a first-quarter report sporting a four-color cover showing Krueger's four largest, modern plants, two of which had come on-stream during the still-short span of his presidential tenure. That span had also seen the growth of sales from $42 million to $56.5 million; a growth of total assets from $31.5 million to $44.8 million, a growth in equity per common share from $15.83 to $19.63.

As of its 39th annual meeting, held April 24, 1974, here are salient fiscal facts about W. A. Krueger Co. as depicted to shareowners by Matthews:

"We are at the upper limits of our line of credit now, but we foresee that this is the peak and we shall be coming down later in the year." In 1973 Krueger's short-term banknotes had increased by $2,150,000, with an effective interest rate of 9.8 percent; long-term debt increased by approximately $2.2 million. Bank lines of credit approved by the board of directors totaled $4.5 million (carried by the Marshall and Ilsley Bank of Milwaukee and the First National Bank in Arizona). As of the date of the annual meeting, Krueger's borrowing position was "in the area of $4.2 million." These other yardsticks prevailed: The company's earnings were in the area of 3 percent on sales; its price-earnings multiple was "a little better than 5 percent"; its stock was selling at less than half book value; with 1973 assets of $18 million and sales of $56.5 million, book value per common share was $19.63.

"The Krueger company and the printing industry as a whole do not earn a reasonable return on investment," declares Matthews. "Return on stockholders' equity—that's what we're after."

W. A. Krueger Co.—Financial and Operating Data, 1964-1974

(Years since 1972 calendar years, audited; 1970 and 1971 are unaudited calendar years; years 1964 through 1969 are fiscal years ending June 30)

	Net Sales ($000)	Net Income ($000)	Share Earns ($)	Div./ Share ($)	Equity/ Share ($)	L/Term Debt ($000)	Work'g Capital ($000)	Current Assets ($000)	Current Liab's ($000)	Current Ratio
1974	$69,024	$1,692	$1.77	$0.50	$20.74	$11,409	$9,939	$19,887	$ 9,948	2.00
1973	56,499	1,749	1.76	.44	19.63	11,288	8,062	18,475	10,413	1.78
1972	52,174	1,518	1.50	.40	17.91	9,079	8,048	15,465	7,417	2.08
1971	45,752	1,575	1.80	.40	17.05	7,486	5,865	11,881	6,016	1.97
1970	42,099	1,198	1.31	.40	15.83	8,091	5,882	11,864	5,982	1.98
1969	32,712	1,109	1.23	.40	15.93	7,973	5,668	10,593	4,925	2.15
1968	29,776	888	1.09	.40	14.13	5,873	3,307	8,457	5,150	1.64
1967	28,783	1,145	1.73	.40	13.55	2,875	5,645	11,480	5,835	1.96
1966	21,528	834	1.39	.40	11.34	2,850	4,237	8,042	4,165	1.92
1965	17,788	690	1.39	.25	10.44	2,189	3,369	6,374	3,005	2.11
1964	16,183	573	1.16	.15	9.26	1,816	2,397	5,431	3,033	1.79

W. A. Krueger Co. Stock Record (OTC)

	Bid Hi	Lo	P/E Ratio
1974	8¾	5	7
1973	11¼	7	5
1972	20¼	11	7
1971	23½	15½	15
1970	27¼	16½	15
1969	34½	20	21
1968	29-7/8	21¼	28
1967	29	11¼	20
1966	11-5/8	11-3/8	9
1965	11-7/8	9¼	8
1964	11-7/8	6¾	11

W. A. Krueger Co.

	Prop'ty/ Plant/Eq. ($000)	Total Assets ($000)	Ratio PPE/TA (1:X)
1974	$24,280	$45,341	1.87
1973	23,580	44,865	1.90
1972	20,093	38,518	1.92
1971	19,492	32,469	1.67
1970	18,687	31,511	1.70
1969	18,174	29,823	1.64
1968	14,995	24,202	1.61
1967	8,830	20,850	2.36
1966	6,574	15,445	2.35
1965	4,548	11,244	2.47
1964	4,406	10,095	2.29

Krueger's per share earning have for the past few years "exceeded those of such leaders of our industry as R. R. Donnelley & Sons Co., Arcata National and Cuneo Press, and such fine competitors as the Goerge

Banta Co., the Maple Press, and others," Matthews reported. "Yet the Krueger company, like most of our competitors, still suffers with its common stock being valued at very low earnings and multiples . . ."

Incidentally, to study and possibly improve that situation as concerns W. A. Krueger Co., its board of directors has an audit committee composed of three outside directors which meets four times a year. It plans to increase the frequency of those meetings.

Milestones

1934 Organized on July 2 by William A. Krueger (4 employees; 4,000 sq. ft.).

1940 Micro-Color concept developed by Krueger craftsmen working with Eastman Kodak technicians at Krueger plant.

1943 New building in Milwaukee acquired (50,000 sq. ft.) and 60 employees added as sales market expands from local to national.

1949 Sales break $ million mark—$1,143,000.

1950 Krueger wins bid to do color sections of *Arizona Highways* magazine.

1957 Company goes public; begins experimenting with web offset.

1958 Brookfield, Wis., plant built (135,000 sq. ft. then) and occupied. First web offset press installed.

1961 Tyler Printing Co., Phoenix, co-contractor on *Arizona Highways*, is acquired; expansion begun via new plant construction.

1962 Brock & Rankin Co., Chicago bookbinding concern founded in 1892, is purchased. Tyler division occupies new plant (50,000 sq. ft.).

1965 Bright-Craft, Inc., Chicago, acquired.

1968 New book manufacturing plant in New Berlin, Wis., goes onstream in April. In August, Krueger enters weekly newsmagazine field with 11-year contract to print *Business Week*'s western, midwestern editions.

1970 First strike in company history, 14 weeks long, hits Wisconsin plants. Krueger, Klaus, Quadracci management era ends and Matthews elected president.

1971 Brock & Rankin subsidiary sold to John C. Hilton, Krueger sales vice president; all Krueger book manufacturing moved to New Berlin plant. Two new subsidiaries acquired: Wolf Composition Co., Boston and Reading, Mass., and the affiliated Book Graphics, Inc.

1972 Plans to build multi-million publication printing plant at Jonesboro, Ark., announced in January. By the third quarter, four AMA medical journals were being produced in the plant.

1973 Ground broken March 20 at 15-acre site in Senatobia, Miss., for plant of Modular Publications, Inc., especially-designed to produce periodicals for Krueger's new Short Run Magazine Group.

1974 Headquarters moved from Brookfield, Wis., to Scottsdale, Ariz.

Corporate Officers

Robert A. Klaus, chairman of the board. Born: 1905. Career: 1928-34, emigrated from Germany to become employee in foreign exchange dept., Wall Street bank, then employee of international accounting firm; 1934, joined W. A. Krueger Co.; 1935-50, vice president, sales and marketing; 1950-55, executive vice president; 1956-70, president.

Robert C. Matthews, president and chief executive officer. Born: 1920. Career: 1946-56, R. R. Donnelley & Sons Co.; 1956-58, president, Geographic Publishing Co.; 1958-62, director of sales, book manufacturing, W. A. Krueger Co.; 1962-64, vice president of sales, Brock & Rankin subsidiary; 1964-70, senior vice president, sales and marketing, W. A. Krueger Co.

Jack W. Fowler, group vice president—magazines and commercial products. Born: 1931. Career: Kingsport (Tenn.) Press, 12 years; Plimpton Press, 2 years; Arcata Graphics, 5 years. (Formerly group vice president, books and related products, W. A. Krueger Co.)

Jack B. Sandler, group vice president—books and related products. Born: 1932. Career: 1950-60, Concordia Publishing House; 1960-67, Color Associates, Inc. 1968-present, W. A. Krueger Co. 1972, vice president and general sales manager, books and related products.

Ross O. Nelson, senior vice president—national sales and Western region sales manager. Born: 1914. Career: 1945-48, founder and president, Los Angeles Publishing Co.; 1948-63, Pacific Press, Inc.; 1963, formed independent oil wildcatting operation; 1966-present, W. A. Krueger Co. 1970, senior vice president, sales and marketing.

Richard L. Seal, vice president—administration. Born: 1930. Career: 1953-58, USN; 1958-63, General Electric Co.; 1963-67, Clark Equipment Co.; 1968-present, W. A. Krueger Co.

Joseph A. Riggs, Jr. vice president—corporate planning and marketing. Born: 1933. Career: 1959-70, joined MGD Graphic Systems in sales management becoming vice president of marketing in 1970 and vice president and general manager of Commercial Web Division in 1972; joined Krueger in 1974 as director of corporate planning and marketing and was elected vice president in 1975.

Robert L. Knetzger, treasurer and assistant secretary. Born: 1924. Career: 1951-65, Square D. Co.; 1965-present, W. A. Krueger Co.

William V. Campbell, corporate controller. Born: 1930. Career: 1954-57, General Electric Co.; 1957-present, W. A. Krueger Co.

Robert J. Tiemeyer, assistant corporate controller for operations. Born: 1936. Career: 1958-present, W. A. Krueger Co.

Margaret A. Willoughby, secretary and legal counsel. Born: 1940. Career: 1966-69, private law practice; 1969-present, W. A. Krueger Co.

W. A. Krueger Co.
7301 East Helm Drive
Scottsdale, Arizona 85260

Krueger's Jonesboro, Arkansas plant.

Brookfield, Wisconsin plant.

120

Courier Corporation

Courier Celebrates
150 Years in the
Graphic Arts Field

The Murray Printing Company's
soft binding capabilities are
in part provided by this
Sheridan one- and two-up
18 pocket perfect binder.

This high-speed Hantscho
web press and custom book folder
helps the Murray Printing Company
to maintain a healthy mix
of general trade, school, college
and reference book production
at its Forge Village, Mass. facilities.

Synopsis Courier Corporation of Lowell, Mass.—a leading producer of telephone directories, forms and books—marked its 150th Anniversary in 1974. It was a year characterized by sharply escalating paper costs, an 18-day strike, and the spiraling cost of money. In spite of the impact of these forces on the business, Courier retained its position as one of the top ten producers of commercial printing in the United States with a sales volume of $66,102,000 in 1974.

Net income for the year amounted to $1,543,000, or $1.04 a share after a year-end adjustment for an accounting change in the method of valuing inventories from FIFO to LIFO. This step decreased earnings by $534,000 or $.36 per share.

Descended from *The Chelmsford Courier*, a newspaper established near Lowell in 1824, Courier Corp. sold its last interest in newspapering in 1939 and shortly thereafter significantly expanded in the forms business. Now forms generate 40 percent of sales, directories 33 percent and books the remainder. The company employs approximately 2500 people in 22 plants and offices all over the United States.

Capsule History Courier Corporation's ancestor, *The Chelmsford Courier*, first appeared May 25, 1824. It was purchased in 1867 by George A. Marden and Edward T. Rowell, 12 years after its rival, *Lowell Daily Citizen*, debuted. In 1882, the *Citizen* was bought by the Citizens Newspaper Co., composed of local influentials, among them Peter W. Reilly, who had been utilizing the Citizen's press idle time by printing telephone directories. The rivalry between the Courier and Citizen factions ended in 1894, when they merged to form the Courier-Citizen Co. By that time, the Citizen had been producing telephone directories for 16 years, and it was sufficiently immersed in the business to buy, in 1898, its first specially-designed directory press. The trend to non-newspaper business continued until, by 1906, Courier-Citizen was doing much commercial printing for the Boston market and had gotten rather heavily into production of forms and service printing for telephone companies and other major customers. In 1906, Phillip Marden succeeded his father as president of C-C and Peter W. Reilly was named vice president. Marden was to remain president until his death in 1963, while Peter W. Reilly's son, Peter W. Reilly, Jr., who joined the company in 1920 was to succeed Marden as president until 1966 and then to serve as board chairman until retiring in 1973.

By 1939 forms printing was challenging directory printing for first place in Courier-Citizen Co.'s product hierarchy. In May of that year, C-C sold its newspaper interests off entirely to the *Lowell Sun*, and two years later it bought Uniform Printing & Supply Co. of Chicago, a top producer of forms for the fire and casualty insurance business. From then on, commercial printing was Courier-Citizen's whole "bag."

In 1966, Courier-Citizen bought the Murray Printing Co. of Forge Village, Mass. and entered the book field. That same year James F. Conway, Jr., who had been with the firm since 1951, was named president and chief executive officer. Under Conway's guidance, the company went public in 1972 and changed its name to Courier Corp.

The Divisions   *Synopsis:* Courier Corp. has three divisions: a directory division, a forms division, and a book division comprising Murray Printing Co. and Courier Color. The form's division's sales in fiscal 1974 were $26,920,000 as against $24,527,000 in 1973. Directory sales declined slightly in 1974 to $21,531,000 from a total of $21,610,000 in 1973. The book division, however, increased sales substantially, from $13,926,000 in 1973 to $17,651,000 in 1974.

Directory   In 1878, the Citizen's Newspaper Co., forebear of Courier-Corp., printed its
Division   first directory—barely two years after the telephone was patented. Title of the directory was "Telephone Dispatch Co.," and it carried the first subscriber list of 68 Boston merchants. Its preface was prophetic: "Every bank, office, business house, and profession in this city are expected to connect with this central office system." Before long, the telephone directory account became the Citizen's largest one.

The division operates a major production plant in Lowell, and strategically placed composition and traffic record plants in Latham, N.Y., East Rutherford, N.J., and Hamden, Conn. Also located in East Rutherford is Ruthco, Inc., a wholly-owned subsidiary operating a service order editing bureau for the New Jersey Bell Telephone Co. This operation receives, edits and microfilms directory updating information obtained through 30 high-speed teletype machines which link the Ruthco office with the telephone company service order network.

In addition to manufacturing over 350 of the familiar white and Yellow Page telephone directories, the division also provides daily updated listings to a network of Directory Assistance Bureaus which are located in the northeast.

Courier's present work is handled through contracts with Western Electric for the New England Telephone Co., Southern New England Telephone Co., New York (Upstate) Telephone Co., and New Jersey Bell Telephone Co.

In spite of an increase in the number of directory pages, sales for the telephone directory business remained stationary for fiscal year 1974 due to the reduction in the number of books ordered by the telephone companies.

During the year, a new plant was opened in North Billerica, Mass. to perform the typesetting of yellow page display advertisements using computerized photocomposition. Company personnel are being retrained to operate the new typesetting equipment. Approximately $250,000 was expended in 1974 to initiate this operation.

As cold type gradually replaces the use of hot metal composition in the telephone directories it produces, the company is completing the development of a relief printing plate which can be made from film. This new plate, which by-passes the traditional stereo plates, will become the standard directory press plate.

The company expects that the number of phone books ordered by the telephone companies will resume their growth trend and that the number of pages per book will continue to grow in the years ahead. The demand for telephone directories and their use will rise sharply, when the phone companies receive permission to charge for directory assistance calls. A new Wood Hoe press, with a capacity of printing 144 pages at a time, is scheduled to be installed early in 1976 at a cost of $1.75 million to meet the increased demands.

The division operates under the supervision of Alden French, Jr. who is vice president and general manager of the company.

Forms Division

Begun before 1900 but not formalized by division status until 1941 (when Courier-Citizen bought Uniform Printing & Supply Co. of Chicago), forms production is now the company's biggest breadwinner. The division has sales offices in Lowell, Atlanta, Columbus, Dallas, Des Moines, Hartford, New York, Philadelphia, Chicago and Albany. It has 21 rotary offset presses operating in four manufacturing plants (Lowell, Chicago, South San Francisco and Pleasanton, Calif.), whose floor space exceeds 280,000 sq. ft.

A nationwide network of nine imprinting/warehousing centers occupy over 380,000 sq. ft.

More space was added in 1974 to the Stafford Springs, Allentown and Gainesville plants, and a new warehouse was opened in Jacksonville, Texas to meet the company's expanding needs in the Southwest.

During the first six months of fiscal year 1974, the Forms Division showed no improvement in sales compared to 1973, and profit margins fell significantly. Phase IV and work stoppage in Lowell were principally responsible for the poor results of this period. However, starting April 1, 1974, the division recorded sharp sales increases and increasingly higher profit margins. For the full year, sales volume amounted to $26,920,000, a gain of $2,393,000 or 10 percent over fiscal year 1973.

Major customers include Aetna Life & Casulty, C.I.T. Financial Corp., Dun & Bradstreet, The Home Insurance, The Transamerica Group, Howard Johnson, American Express, Blue Cross, Ingersoll Rand, and Insurance Services Offices. A number of new customers were added during the year, including the California Dental Service, Metropolitan Property and Liability Insurance, and Zayre Corp. Additional work is being performed for the United States Government.

Services offered include complete forms surveys, the engineering and designing of forms, printing, imprinting, warehousing, distribution, EDP controls and reports. The division produces flat, snap-apart, and continuous forms, rate charts, checks, drafts, brochures, letterheads and envelopes.

"Authentic" policies and endorsements of coverage for the buyers of home, property and auto insurance account for a major proportion of the division's business. The "authentic" service includes updating of insurance forms to reflect changes resulting from new industry practices or state regulations. Customers are advised of changes and offered new or revised forms. The division's computer provides inventory, fulfillment, cost and tax information on forms production and handling to the headquarters of many major financial, health, insurance and industrial manufacturing companies.

Vice president Robert M. Markus, who was executive vice president of Arkwright Interlaken, Inc., before joining Courier in 1972, is general manager of the division.

Book Printing

The book printing segment of Courier Corp. is made up of two entities: The Murray Printing Co., Forge Village, Mass., a wholly-owned subsidiary, and Courier Color, of Lowell, Mass.

The Murray Printing Co. was founded in 1897 by Albert N. Murray, grandfather of Albert C. Murray, who headed it as president until 1972 and who currently serves as its chairman. The Murray Co. was acquired by Courier in 1966. John Walantis is the president and treasurer of Murray.

A major supplier of quality educational, scientific and technical books, Murray specializes in one- and two-color medium and long-run jobs. It also produces short-run one-color and two-color books (sheet and web-fed) in a wide variety of sizes. Facilities include 11 sheetfed presses, one- or two-color, and six webs which also offer one- or two-color capabilities. Last year, the company bound nearly 70 percent of its book production in soft covers, and it claims that it processes more plates than any other book manufacturer in the United States.

Courier Color Division, established five years ago, is now a leading supplier of educational materials, specialty magazines, catalogs, brochures and direct mailing pieces, as well as perfect bound and saddle-stitched books. It also does printing for other corporate divisions, one of its major jobs being the multicolor covers of all the directory division's telephone books.

The division's services include everything from project conception and design to warehousing and distribution—with artwork, composition, and color separations all done in-house—as well as printing and binding. Facilities include two four-color offset web presses, a 25 x 38″ perfecting five-color sheetfed offset press, and two 35 x 45″ offset sheetfeds, one a one-color and the other a two-color. Newest equipment includes an automated 32″ process color camera and light system. Color proofing is done via 3M Transfer-Key system and DuPont Dylux prints.

During fiscal year 1974, book manufacturing sales increased to $17,651,000, up from $13,926,000 during 1973. The sales increases were recorded by both Courier Color and Murray Printing Co. and reflect the fact that throughout the paper shortage they were able to maintain adequate inventories of paper for publishers.

The Book Division's mix of trade, school, college and reference books has kept a healthy balance of reprints and new titles flowing through the plants. General trade books included several best-sellers, such as Simon & Schuster's *All the President's Men, A Bridge Too Far, Our Bodies Ourselves* and *Cashelmara.* Several new accounts were developed in the school and college textbook areas.

Murray Printing Co. is currently installing a new high speed web press with a newly designed book folder. A third shift was added to the soft cover binding line during May 1974, and has been effective in decreasing manufacturing cost by increasing productivity. A new hard-binding line was delivered late in the first quarter of fiscal 1975 and was productive during the second quarter. The new hard-binding line together with the expanded soft cover binding will increase bookbinding capacity 19 percent and provide the capability of binding 60 percent of the division's total printed products.

During 1974, F. Russell McDonnell joined Courier as vice president and general manager of the Courier Color Division. He has had extensive experience in the book publishing and educational services industry, an area in which Courier has a growing business interest.

Going Public

A major milestone in company growth was the decision on May 19, 1972 by the Courier-Citizen Co. board of directors to change the company name and proceed with a public offering. On August 7 of that year, the Courier-Citizen Co. merged with the newly-organized Courier Corp., and on November 16, Courier Corp. stock was successfully offered to the public by an underwriting syndicate headed by Paine, Webber, Jackson & Curtis, Inc.

A total of 383,637 shares were offered; of that total, 208,637 shares were sold by then-current shareholders and 175,000 were sold by the company. The stock was offered at $15 per share over the counter. The transaction raised $2,625,000 for the company. That money is being used to finance plant and equipment expansion.

"The progress Courier has made over the past five years—which have been less than an economic bonanza—indicates that we know the printing business and how to control costs," declares President James F. Conway, Jr. He added: "We'll continue to grow. We plan to broaden the application of our know-how and resources by acquiring companies in the printing industries or allied fields.

"However," he added, "growth will take place in the direction of larger printing groups—not in unrelated conglomerates as in the past decade. Businessmen will have to study their businesses for themselves and not rely on forecasts and projections furnished by so-called experts. People who know their business and their specialties—and stick to them—will not only survive the current recession but will continue to thrive in the future."

Corporate Officers

James F. Conway, Jr., president and chief executive officer.

Jefferson R. Mansfield, Jr., vice president and treasurer.

Kennon D. Heusinkveld, vice president—finance.

Leonard W. Doolan, III, vice president—engineering.

Alden French, Jr., vice president and general manager, Directory Division.

Arnold Greenfield, vice president, Forms Division.

Edward J. Kelly, vice president, Marketing and Administration, Forms Division.

James Kelso, vice president and general manager of West Coast Operations, Forms Division.

Robert M. Markus, vice president and general manager, Forms Division.

F. Russell McDonnell, vice president and general manager, Courier Color.

George J. O'Brien, vice president and New York sales manager, Forms Division.

Walter B. Reilly, Jr., vice president, corporate staff.

J. Williams Seekins, vice president, Product Development.

Charles R. Wilson, vice president and New England sales manager, Forms Division.

Michael A. Carpinella, Jr., controller.

Five Year Summary

Fiscal Years Ending September:

For the Year	1974	1973	1972	1971	1970
Sales	$66,102,000	$60,063,000	$53,871,000	$47,172,000	$45,913,000
Net income	1,543,000*	2,464,000	1,956,000	1,268,000	945,000
Net income as % of sales	2.3%*	4.1%	3.6%	2.7%	2.1%
Depreciation and amortization	1,560,000	1,509,000	1,536,000	1,472,000	1,426,000
Cash flow	3,103,000*	3,973,000	3,492,000	2,740,000	2,371,000
At Year End					
Current assets	$20,973,000*	$19,690,000	$18,396,000	$18,058,000	$14,990,000
Current liabilities	8,595,000	6,429,000	6,895,000	7,747,000	5,917,000
Working capital	12,377,000*	13,261,000	11,501,000	10,311,000	9,073,000
Long-term debt	3,254,000	3,998,000	4,789,000	5,982,000	6,773,000
Debt as a % of total capitalization	12.0%	15.0%	21.1%	29.2%	31.1%
Stockholders' equity	23,711,000*	22,554,000	17,942,000	16,008,000	15,020,000
Shares outstanding	1,486,520	1,486,520	1,268,320	1,227,640	1,243,400
Per Share					
Net income—fully diluted	$ 1.04*	$ 1.70	$ 1.51	$ .99	$ .77
Depreciation and amortization*	1.05	1.04	1.22	1.20	1.19
Cash flow*	2.09*	2.74	2.78	2.23	1.98
Dividends**	.26	.22	.19	.12	.11
Book value***	15.95*	15.17	14.15	13.04	12.08

*1974 results reflect a change to the LIFO method of accounting for certain inventories. The change had the effect of reducing inventories by $1,113,000 and net income and working capital by $534,000 (equal to $.36 per share).
**1974 dividends per share were $.06, $.06, $.07 and $.07 in the first, second, third, and fourth quarters respectively.
***Based on shares outstanding at year-end.

Net Sales by Divisions

Revenues (000 Omitted)
Fiscal Year Ended

	September 28, 1974	September 29, 1973	September 30, 1972	September 25, 1971	September 26, 1970
Forms	$26,920	$24,527	$20,393	$17,690	$16,737
Telephone Directories	21,531	21,610	19,505	16,986	16,112
Books	17,651	13,926	13,973	12,496	13,064
	$66,102	$60,063	$53,871	$47,172	$45,913

Plants, Warehouses, Sales Offices

Corporate Offices
165 Jackson Street
Lowell, Mass. 01852
(617) 458-6351

Forms Division Manufacturing
Courier-Citizen Company
Wellman Industrial Park
North Chelmsford, Mass. 01863
(617) 458-6351

Courier-Citizen Company
339 Harbor Way
South San Francisco, Cal. 94080
(415) 761-0950

Courier-Citizen Company
7069 Commerce Circle
Pleasanton, Cal. 94566
(415) 761-0950

Uniform Printing & Supply Co.
Div. of Courier-Citizen Company
7460 N. Lehigh Avenue
Chicago, Ill. 60648
(312) 774-3600

Forms Division
Warehouse/Distribution
Uniform Printing & Supply Co.
div. of Courier-Citizen Company
2401 W. Emaus Avenue
Allentwon, Pa. 18103
(215) 797-5731

Uniform Pringint & Supply Co.
Div. of Courier-Citizen Company
979 Riverside Drive, N.E.
P.O. Box 1378
Gainesville, Ga. 30501
(404) 534-4488

Uniform Printing & Supply Co.
Div. of Courier-Citizen Company
Highway 6 West
P.O. Box 253
Kendallville, Ind. 46755
(219) 347-3000

Uniform Printing & Supply Co.
Div. of Courier-Citizen Company
132 Flatbush Avenue
P.O. Box 820
Kingston, N.Y. 12401
(914) 339-3703

Courier-Citizen Company
1540 Church Road
Montebello, Cal. 90640
(213) 724-0896

Uniform Printing & Supply Co.
Div. of Courier-Citizen Company
Scitico Road
P.O. Box C
Somersville Industrial Park,
   Conn. 06072
(203) 684-4273

Courier-Citizen Company
East Grantline Road
P.O. Box 120
Tracy, Cal. 95376
(209) 835-6761

Courier-Citizen Company
Center Street
P.O. Box 343
Raymond, N.H. 03077
(603) 895-3373 or 895-3375

Uniform Printing & Supply Co.
Div. of Courier-Citizen Company
Hihway 204
Jacksonville, Texas 75766
(214) 586-3775

Forms Division Sales Offices
Uniform Printing & Supply Co.
Div. of Courier-Citizen Company
688 New Loudon Road
Latham, N.Y. 12110
(518) 783-6600

Uniform Printing & Supply Co.
Div. of Courier-Citizen Company
92 Luckie Street, N.W., Suite 704
Atlanta, Ga. 30303
(404) 524-1595

Uniform Printing & Supply Co.
Div. of Courier-Citizen Company
High Long Building
5 E. Long Street
Columbus, Ohio 43215
(614) 221-6591

Uniform Printing & Supply Co.
Div. of Courier-Citizen Company
271 Garden Mall—Exchange Park
Dallas, Tex. 75235
(214) 358-1561 or 1562

Uniform Printing & Supply Co.
Div. of Courier-Citizen Company
401 N. Seventh Street
Indianola, Iowa 50125
(515) 961-3217

Uniform Printing & Supply Co.
Div. of Courier-Citizen Company
1107 New Britain Avenue
Elmwood, Conn. 06110
(203) 236-0896

Courier-Citizen Company
2411 W. 8th Street
P.O. Box 17128
Los Angeles, Cal. 90017
(213) 385-6197

Courier-Citizen Company
165 Jackson Street
Lowell, Mass. 01852
(617) 458-6351

Uniform Printing & Supply Co.
Div. of Courier-Citizen Company
501 E. St. Clair
Sheridan, Mich. 48884
(571) 291-3659

Uniform Printing & SupOly Co.
Div. of Courier-Citizen Company
156 William Street
New York, N.Y. 10038
(212) 227-1555

Uniform Printing & Supply Co.
Div. of Courier-Citizen Company
P.O. Box 27067
Philadelphia, Pa. 19118
(215) 247-2865

Courier-Citizen Company
World Trade Center
Suire 292
San Francisco, Cal. 94111
(415) 421-6070

Uniform Printing & SupOly Co.
Div. of Courier-Citizen Company
4350 Oakton Street
Skokie, Ill. 60078
(312) 647-8500

Uniform Printing & Supply Co.
Div. of Courier-Citizen Company
P.O. Box 6094
South Bend, Ind. 46615
(219) 288-9322

Directory Division
Facilities and Manufacturing
Courier-Citizen Company
688 New Loudon Road
Latham, N.Y. 12110
(518) 785-3244

Courier-Citizen Company
1685 Dixwell Avenue
Hamden, Conn. 06514
(203) 288-8231 or 8232

Courier-Citizen Company
230 Boiling Springs Avenue
East Rutherford, N.J. 07073
(201) 935-2555

Courier-Citizen Company
17 Hall Street
Lowell, Mass. 01854
(617) 458-6351

Courier-Citizen Company
8 Executive Park Dirve
North Billerica, Mass. 01862
(617) 667-3846

The Murray Printing Company
Sales and Manufacturing
The Murray Printing Company
Pleasant Street
Forge Village, Mass. 01828
(617) 692-6321

The Murray Printing Company
60 E. 42nd Street
New York, N.Y. 10017
(212) Mu 2-0641

Courier Color
Sales and Manufacturing
Courier Color
Div. of Courier-Citizen Company
790 Chelmsford Street
Lowell, Mass. 01851
(617) 458-6351

Vice President Leonard W. Doolan III,
who is responsible for manufacturing operations
in Courier's directory division,
observes the operation of a new
Harris Model 2200 terminal
at the firm's Billerica, Mass. plant
where Yellow Page displays ads are
produced by computerized photocomposition.

Together with expanded
soft binding facilities,
this newly acquired Smyth
hard-binding line at
the Murray Printing Company
plants in Forge Village, Mass.
has increased book binding capacity
by 19 percent and given the firm
the capability of binding
60 percent of its total printed product.

Starline Corporation

Shrewd Planning,
Steady Growth for
Southwest Printer

Starline's modern headquarters
in Albuquerque, New Mexico.

Small pressroom where limited
orders for regular clients
are produced and finished.

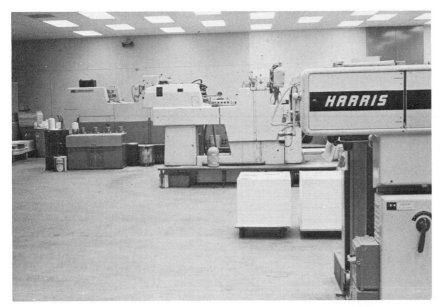

Battery of Harris offset presses.
There is ample space in pressroom for traffic.

Headquartered in a new $500,000 lithographic printing plant and office building in Albuquerque, New Mexico, Starline Corp. topped the million-dollar sales mark in 1973, thereby breaking, so to speak, the "sound barrier" in printing volume for this state. The 18-year-old company is the first printing establishment in New Mexico to expand its market into adjacent states and initiate an aggressive program of competition with larger firms in the Southwest.

Sales leaped again in 1974 to $3,664,109 from 1973's $1,126,868 (an impressive 225 percent), although earnings declined 33 percent to $92,368 from $137,479 the previous year. The decrease was attributed to inflation, recession, and troublesome internal conditions (e.g., operating losses in the Starline Creative Printing of California subsidiary, which has since been restructured into a graphic services facility under the name of Starline-California Graphics).

Growth/
Acquisitions

Robert L. Walker, chairman and president, launched Starline operations in 1957 with a Multilith press as his sole equipment. As both sales force and production department, he sold printing by day, turned it out in the evening, and delivered it the next day. The firm was incorporated with his brother, Harley E. Walker, as secretary/treasurer, and several other shareholders. Vice president William J. Houston joined the company in 1961.

Gradually, over the years, Bob Walker and Bill Houston have divided their duties. The former is the outside contact man, and Houston is in charge of plant operations.

In his annual report to shareholders on May 5, 1973, President Walker said: "We believe there will be sweeping changes in the printing industry. We see many smaller firms going the way of the corner grocery. We intend to acquire some of these and join them to us in a comprehensive, efficient organization. There may be possibilities in printing specialties. We are set up for growth—on the threshold of an exciting future."

Since the time of this statement, Starline Corp. has made several external expansion moves. In the process, the thrust of the corporation's operations has changed to directing services and products toward clients outside the printing field. This approach is, however, fully consistent with marketing goals of broadening Starline's reach in graphic arts and meeting as many needs of their customers as possible.

Starline Corp. now has three wholly-owned subsidiaries and five divisions. The former are Fine Papers, Inc. and Starline Management Group, Ltd., both in Albuquerque, and Starline-California Graphics (Starline Creative Printing of California) in San Diego. Two of the divisions—Starline Creative Printing and Starline Color Laboratories—are located in Albuquerque. The West Texas divisions, headquartered in Midland, Texas, include: West Texas Business Machines, Odessa; West Texas Office Supply, Lubbock, Midland, and Odessa, and West Texas Creative Printing, Midland.

The auxiliary service of Fine Papers, Inc. sells paper and graphic supplies to both its parent firm, Starline Creative Printing, and outside clients. Starline Color Laboratories supports the corporation's lithographic printing facilities and also markets its separation work. Starline Management, Inc. offers expertise in the management consultant field to businesses and institutions.

Starline-California Graphics (Starline Creative Printing of California, Inc.), formerly KB Graphics before its August, 1973 takeover by Starline in a cash-for-assets transaction, became the corporation's first out-of-state acquisition. This subsidiary is headquartered in a new plant in a fast developing area of San Diego where it serves the southern California market.

Starline Corp. purchased the $230,000 net assets of its three newest divisions in Texas in exchange for 103,500 shares of Starline common stock. The proceedings were closed in April, 1974 and became effective retroactive to January 1 of that year.

Going Public   Starline established another first in the New Mexico printing industry with its initial public offering of shares for over-the-counter trading at the close of 1972. Authorized capital stock has already been increased from 250,000 to two million shares at $1.00 par value. This stock was all in the hands of officers and directors of the corporation.

The December, 1972 public offering resulted in 125,000 shares being underwritten locally at $4.00 per share. The total number of shares held by the public in 1973 amounted to 419,768 and 523,268 in 1974. Net earnings per average share increased from 25¢ in 1972 to 33¢ in 1973, but declined to 18¢ in 1974.

President Walker firmly believes that the decision to take the company "public" has been one of the soundest moves made by management, as "the benefits derived have allowed Starline to grow rapidly and soundly."

Marketing Policy   Starline's marketing policy is to be all things to the buyer of lithographic printing. That is, not only to print specific orders, but to get involved in the customer's problems, learn all aspects of his business, then design the type of graphic communications that are needed to further his aims. In other words, enter into his total circumstances, and look at his printing needs from an inside point of view.

"We are essentially persuaders," says Walker. "The majority of our sales volume is based on the use of persuasion literature to help clients sell ideas or get people to think favorably of their operations. To do that we have to look at things from their side."

Being all things to the buyer of printing means, in Starline terms, to help establish plans, produce ideas, design the appropriate printed matter, do the art work, and print the job. The close relations thus established with clients have been responsible for Starline's garnering of 400-500 active accounts, mostly in the local community.

"Naturally, we couldn't have built a client relationship like this without the help of a dedicated nucleus of workers in our plants. All of them are sales-minded. We encourage clients to go into the plant and talk with these key people. They stay with us and work as a team. We know they will make a favorable impression," Walker declares.

Another reason why Starline has so many regular clients is the rather diversified nature of New Mexico's economy. Aside from producers of raw materials such as oil and gas, potash, copper and uranium, there are no really large industries. Most of these facilities belong to major corporations with headquarters in other states. The same holds true of the relatively few manufacturing operations. Cattle raising, farming, tourism and winter sports are actually the principal bulwarks of the state's economy.

But in a city of more than 300,000 population such as Albuquerque, there are a number of comparatively large service companies—utilities, holding companies, investment firms, banks, land developers, and builders. In serving these, Starline has developed a strong position in corporate and advertising printing.

For years it has been Bob Walker's custom to have breakfast and lunch practically every day with one or another of the firm's clients. In his first year in Albuquerque he single-handedly sold and produced $40,000 worth of printing.

Starline now maintains a sales staff of four persons in Albuquerque, two in southern California, and four in the West Texas printing division. The expansion into the office machine and business supply areas has enabled the company to offer more diverse goods and services to its clients.

Self Advertising

Direct mail advertising has been an important element of Starline's sales promotion. From the very first, Starline has practiced what it preached. It has used direct mail printed matter to introduce and represent itself as an up-and-coming graphic arts organization.

The first mailings consisted of humorous mottoes printed on cards that could be hung up or slipped under a glass-topped desk. These proved to be an immediate hit and even attracted inquiries from firms not on the mailing list. The little printed reminders and name sellers are still sent out once a month.

In recent years, direct mail advertising has been stepped up. An especially distinctive program is the mailing of 8″x10″ full-color lithographic reprints of original paintings by southwestern artists. The originals themselves are displayed in the long corridor connecting the office building with the production department in Starline Creative Printing's new home.

The reproductions are printed and mounted on heavy cover paper, 12″x 23″ with two folds down to a 9″x12″. They are sent out in specially made white envelopes and cost $2.00 each to mail. These mailings initially went out quarterly to a select list of large printing buyers. They made quite an impression on prospects and customers who had never seen a small printing company, or any other company in Albuquerque, attempt anything so elaborate. After each mailing, dozens of requests came in for additional copies. Over-runs were made to meet the demand.

The king-size mailing pieces, each on a different color stock, are numbered, and contain two paragraphs of copy, one about the artist and one about the painting. The series is entitled "Southwestern Art." Starline's copy is merely a signature with the line "Creative Printers and Lithographers." The series has been especially well received because, in the colorful Southwest, people are highly art conscious. Two mailings are now made each year to 5,800 concerns in New Mexico, Texas and California.

Promotion outlays in the New Mexico division and subsidiaries have average $20,000 each year, with corresponding sales figures indicating how handsome the program's rewards have been. While the costs of producing high quality reproductions of paintings is substantial, Starline's management credits the series with helping to open doors at top level corporations.

Operations   Although its volume is considerable, Starline Creative Printing, flagship of the corporation, is a rather small organization. There's plenty of room to expand in the 20,000 sq. ft. plant which opened in August, 1972 and is located on four acres adjacent to Interstate Highway 25. The sales force has doubled in recent years to cover a larger marketing area.

The production department is equipped with about $500,000 worth of machinery and equipment, including a Harris 25"x38" four-color sheet-fed lithographic press, the first in New Mexico, and three other Harris offset presses: a 25"x38" two-color; a 23"x29" one-color, and a 14"x20" one-color.

Supplemental equipment includes a Macey nine-station Multi-Binder with a capacity of 32 pages and cover; a Pako high-speed automatic film processor; a 3M automated plate developer; a Western camera, and a nuArc line-up table.

In a segregated section of the pressroom, a small press department is equipped with a Miehle vertical, a Heidelberg 14"x22" platen hand press, two small ATF Chief offset presses, and a Multilith. These presses are used for producing and finished small orders from regular clients. Other than these, small commercial orders are not solicited.

Starline has never had any typesetting equipment. All repros are bought from Typographic Service, Inc., of Albuquerque, which offers over 1,500 type faces. The two plants are about eight miles apart, so to speed up communications, they are interconnected by a Xerox Telecopier.

Captions and other small segments of copy, with layouts, are sent facsimile to the typographer the first thing each morning. At that time his linotype machines are ready to go. Repros of this material are usually delivered by noon, permitting tight scheduling in the Starline plant. Longer texts are picked up by the typographer and delivered later. This operation has proved to be highly satisfactory at both ends of the line.

Paper is stored in a corner of the 100x300-ft. pressroom. Air conditioning and humidifying equipment keeps the paper from drying out in Albuquerque's arid climate.

All film used on jobs is retained in a separate storage room. A filing systems keeps it available for future use.

The new plant is a rather startling innovation for a printing company in New Mexico. It consists of two buildings, a 16,000 sq. ft. concrete and steel production building and a frame stucco office facility. The reception area, offices and board room are finished in walnut, rosewood and cork. Furniture is carefully keyed to the decor. Dividers are custom-carved paneling, with decorative corner pieces to enhance the graphics. It's a tasteful corporate and operating headquarters—worthy of a bank.

Starline's Origins

Robert L. Walker, Starline's chairman, president and chief executive officer, began his printing experience at 16. He lived in a small town in Oklahoma, where he got a job with a local weekly newspaper. Later he moved to Norman, Okla., where he worked up to plant superintendent with the Hooper Printing Co.

He settled in Albuquerque in 1957 at age 26 with nine years of printing experience behind him. He was looking for a place to grow up with the economy and he found it. As he recalls:

"Albuquerque was a newly arrived metropolitan center. It was expanding in population and economic stature. But I felt that local printers had not kept up with the possibilities, and there was an opening for an aggressive full-service printer.

"Some of the choicest printing jobs were being sent out to distant cities, and the local printers hadn't had a chance to show what they could do. Top bracket buyers of printing were hiring advertising agents who had little confidence in home town production. Rather than take a chance on it they advised their clients to have their color printing done in a larger city.

"I concluded that to break the deadlock would take a crash program of educational promotion and all-round service to back it up—art, layout, copy and finished job."

From the first, when Walker was the entire company working in rented quarters, he attracted attention with the excellence of his work on a little Multilith 1250. By 1961 he had a small staff and was able to build a new brick and steel plant. One of his helpers then was William J. Houston, now vice president.

In ensuing years, as Starline's workforce grew, a number of regular accounts were won by surprise demonstrations of speed in production. For example, an out-of-town businessman came in for some letterheads. Walker quietly put through the order and kept the man talking for a while then presented him with the completed job. The man was so impressed that he kept on sending in orders by mail. Starline salesmen all carry electronic pocket buzzer instruments so they can get to a phone and receive word to call on a client before coming in.

After seven years in business, Starline was spending $20,000 a year on advertising—8 percent of its gross volume of $250,000. Always the emphasis was on good results for its clients. Two years after it was built, the plant was doubled both in size and new equipment added.

On a wall in the new plant there are 31 plaques attesting to the company's craftsmanship. Walker is an organization man. He is past president of Creative Printers of America, a former board member of Master Printers of America, past president of the Printing Industry of New Mexico and of the Executive Association of Greater Albuquerque. He is a graduate of PIA-Case Western Reserve University's Executive Development program.

Active in local affairs, Walker is a trustee of the University of Albuquerque and he played a key role in the Albuquerque Chamber of Commerce's fund-raising campaign to set up an industrial foundation to attract new business.

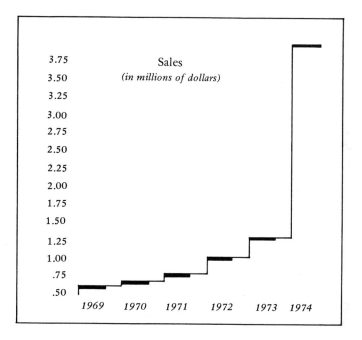

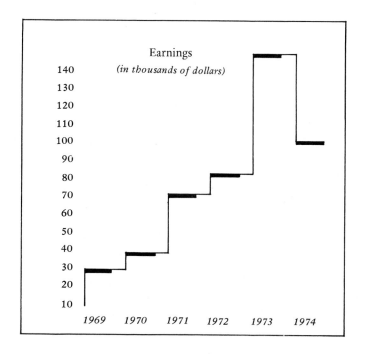

	1967	1972	1973
Financial Printing	$ 22,000	$ 91,000	$ 54,000
Corporate Printing	84,000	218,000	397,000
Advertising Printing	77,000	192,000	281,000
General Commercial Printing	297,000	385,000	395,000

	Sales	Net Income	Income Per Share	Average Shares Outstanding	Long-Term Debt	Working Capital	Current Assets	Current Liabilities	Current Ratio
1969	$ 527,403	$ 29,164	$.20	147,032	$ 78,201	$ 82,142	$ 128,435	$ 46,293	2.8
1970	591,986	37,925	.24	157,263	70,915	135,397	171,773	36,376	4.7
1971	685,173	65,644	.33	201,821	456,260	323,245	521,601	198,356	2.6
1972	886,131	74,368	.25	295,453	417,967	541,661	676,756	135,095	5.0
1973	1,126,868	137,479	.33	419,768	395,338		585,704	163,910	
1974	3,664,019	92,368	.18	523,268	981,721	421,794	1,294,465	349,317	3.6

Starline's pressroom in its new plant.
View from rear with Harris
four-color offset press in foreground.

Starline Corporation
7111 Pan American Highway, N.E.
Albuquerque, New Mexico 87110

140

George Banta Company, Inc.

"All in the Family" Approach
a Key Factor in Banta Success Saga

Banta Company, Menasha, Wisconsin.

Synopsis　At the April 1974 annual meeting for shareholders, William H. Fieweger, president of the George Banta Co., closed his talk with the statement: "...It is our expectation that consolidated sales will approximate $96 million; our obvious aspiration will be to become a $100 million company in 1974."

In the autumn of 1974, with telltale signs of recession covering the business landscape with the profusion of falling leaves, Fieweger told shareholders in the report for the quarter ending September 1974: "Our evaluations of the fourth quarter indicate we will exceed our 1974 sales projections of $96 million." By year's end, when the nation's economy had slipped to a worrisome level, Fieweger rang down the curtain on Banta's history for 1974 with the good news that: "At the close of 1974, George Banta Co. reached a significant milestone . . . sales for the first time in our 73-year history exceeded $100 million."

The final sales figure of $103,004,000 represented a 23-percent increase over that for 1973 and double that for five years ago. Net earnings of $3,499,000 were 18 percent greater than the prior year and nearly twice those of five years before.

In a period when annual reports, however emblazoned with four-color process photos and eye-catching charts and graphs, either showed pallid gains or none at all, Banta's shareholders continued to find their annual reports some of the best reading available.

The Banta Company and its subsidiaries continue to build a graphic arts family maintaining its upward mobility by never moving far from the technical and marketing base it understands best. Acquisitions are planned to augment the company's position and to establish new bastions in a business terrain well known for its potential.

On November 18, 1974, George Banta III, chairman of the board of George Banta Co., and Richard E. Bogt, chairman of the board of KCS Industries of Milwaukee, Wis., jointly disclosed an agreement to sell KCS to Banta. KCS Industries, founded in 1909, is a creator and producer of point-of-purchase advertising materials, industrial and consumer product labels and brand identification signs. The firm employs more than 170 people in two Milwaukee plants. One of the plants is a 78,000-sq.-ft. facility completed in 1973.

KCS Industries' customer list includes nationally prominent industrial and consumer companies. The firm's sales for 1974 exceeded $4 million. In greeting KCS as a member of the Banta family in early 1975, Fieweger stressed the prospects for extending the parent firm's services to the graphic arts. He commented: "Many mutual opportunities will exist for interfacing the strengths of KCS and our other nine autonomous Banta companies."

Production expansion keeps pace on another level matching the acquisition of new companies by Banta management. Donald S. Koskinen, president of the Banta Division (the corporation's largest operating unit), announced on December 26, 1974, purchase of a new web offset press, the eighteenth press of its kind now operated by the Banta Division. Confident of sustained growth during 1975, Koskinen asserts the press will be needed to help the book manufacturing branch of the corporation keep pace with the needs of its present customers and increased business.

Several months before the purchase of the web offset press, the division announced the purchase of a second $1.1 million Cameron Belt Press, which, when filled to capacity, is expected to generate an additional $5 million in annual business. Installation of this fully automated book production press enrolls Banta among the few companies operating two or more Camerons either in the United States or abroad. The press is said to turn out a completely finished book from printing through all intermediate operations to packing ready for distribution in a matter of minutes. Banta Division also slated for installation in 1975 a fourth $500,000 binder for paperback books, a five-color sheet-fed offset press, an additional casebinding line and a saddle-wire binder.

Purchase of equipment costing several millions of dollars to acquire and install is evidence of the certainty of Banta's management that sales trends are inexorably upward. Says George Banta: "There fortunately is a strong industry consolidation trend underway. As an example, mergers in printing and publishing were substantially up in the fourth quarter of 1974 at a time when the all-industry trend was down. Nowhere is this more evident than in book manufacturing. In the last two years, close to 30 competitors of the Banta Division have gone out of business or merged with others. Instead of overcapacity, this Banta unit now exists in a climate of close to fully utilized capacity."

Commenting on general market trends within the specialized elementary-high school educational materials field, Thomas Hicks, vice president of marketing, says: "Educational publishers' sales for 1973 were up 10.3 percent over 1972, one of the largest gains in their history of marketing. Forecasts are for an even larger 1974 increase—two record years back to back."

Aside from the company's continued climb toward higher sales and production levels in educational publishing in general, Hicks points to what he describes as "unparalleled growth from multi-media (materials for educational instruction)." He adds: "Publishers' media sales have grown an average of 34 percent annually over the past five years. Banta sales are expected (at the time of his address to the annual meeting, April 19, 1974) to increase over 200 percent in 1974 compared to 1973 to over $2 million."

In the September, 1974 quarterly report to shareholders, President Fieweger singled out three divisions of the company as notable for performance during the first nine months of 1974. He commented that Daniels Packaging, the Banta Division, and The Hart Press showed exceptional strength with sales up 34 percent to $10 million in Daniels Packaging alone. The Banta Division and The Hart Press, in spite of strikes lasting about two weeks each, showed gains of 13 percent and 12 percent respectively.

Daniels Packaging is viewed as offering special promise within the next several years, principally because of its novel cold seal packaging technology. This technology has attractive earning potential when applied to candy and medical packaging requirements especially. Daniels recently installed a new $300,000 flexographic press.

Fieweger envisions further growth through the acquisition route, probably by an exchange of stock. "We have a five-year plan of acquisitions," he advises, "and it's such a good plan that we envision we'll do better in the next five years than in the past five in spite of what appears to be a sustained downturn in the economy."

In the next five years, says Fieweger, the character of the George Banta Co. and its divisions will retain a consistent shape as producers of general graphic arts materials. "We don't want to develop any of the characteristics of the conglomerate. We expect to stay close to the graphic arts emphasizing book publishing manufacturing.'"

In October, 1974, John G. Strange, retired president and current vice chairman of the board of trustees of the Institute of Paper Chemistry, was elected to the Banta board of directors. Commenting on Strange's addition, board chairman George Banta said: "At a time when there is some scarcity of paper and when standards of quality may be variable, we are glad to have a man of John Strange's connections and special knowledge. We feel his background will help Banta maintain the quality standards that have won the company a position of eminence in the educational publishing field."

Banta, unlike most book publishers, furnishes nearly all of the paper on which it prints and maintains inventories of all grades commonly used by the company in its various specialties. The majority of other book printers rely on the publishers they serve to provide them with paper stocks.

Chairman Banta views the company's moves into gravure as having a significant potential for a sustained technical and financial advance within the next several years. The last 15 years, he says, have seen the rise of offset printing, particularly web offset, in the publishing field. He feels that gravure will show the greatest technical virtuosity in the next 15 to 20 years in the publishing field.

Contemplating a changing complexion in the printing industry in the next decade, Banta sees a reduction in the number of small commercial printers. He envisions a trend toward fewer, better equipped and staffed plants with ample financing to enable management to take advantage of new technological advances. Larger economic units are requisite to the health of the industry in his view. Gains will be derived from deeper and broader management, marketing and technological skills; from the availability of funds for new plants and equipment and for acquisitions; from market synergism, and from more effective procurement of materials and supplies.

Background

The Banta organization was founded in 1901 in Menasha, Wis., by George Banta Sr. (b. 1859; d. 1935). He had begun his career as an insurance agent whose hobby was printing. By the turn of the century his hobby had overturned his interest in insurance, and he decided to become a printer of business and insurance forms. Later he began to specialize in the production of fraternity and sorority magazines. That specialty came naturally since his father was at the time dean of the University of Indiana's Law School, and George Banta himself was a leading light in Phi Delta Theta, a national fraternity.

He first got the contract to print Phi Delta Theta national magazine, then won contracts for a number of similar fraternity and sorority magazines.

By 1910 the job shop which had opened in 1901 was hopelessly outgrown. Banta that year built its first plant on the site of what is now its Menasha headquarters building. (The two-story 7,200 sq. ft. edifice has been thoroughly "overgrown" by additions which make it the core of the present 156,000 sq. ft. facility there.)

In the pre-World War I era, Banta's interest in printing for the educational community had become deep-seated. By the early teens, it was printing 184 scholarly, technical and academic journals. The war years and their immediate aftermath were hard ones, but then an "explosion in education" began to develop in the second half of the 1920s.

While Banta was well situated already to ride the swell of that development, the key to its most energetic participation was forged by an inordinately fortunate bit of happenstance. In the late '20s elementary school workbooks appeared and one of the first was written by Russell Sharp, a brother-in-law of George Banta Jr., son of the founder. Banta went into production immediately and by 1929 it had become the first of the major producers of such workbooks. (It now produces millions of them annually for use in schools from elementary through graduate levels.)

Its educational interests having seen it safely through the depression years, Banta kept close tabs on developments both technical and marketing which would sustain its growth. In 1941 it installed the first of its 29 corporate web presses and by 1950—when the web offset process was still widely considered a primitive one—was doing quality four-color work on it.

By 1946 Banta was well on the way to becoming a major factor in the American printing community. That year it built its Midway plant (halfway between Menasha and Appleton), a 41,800-sq.-ft. facility that has since grown to 480,000 sq. ft.

Banta Milestones

1901 Establishment of George Banta Printing Co. by George Banta, Sr., in rented quarters in downtown Menasha, Wis.

1903 Name changed to George Banta Publishing Co.

1910 Builds first plant on present site—7,200 sq. ft. devoted primarily to printing books and periodicals for educational world.

1929 Begins printing of elementary school workbooks. (Then a new tool, but Banta now prints 108 million annually.)

1940 Installs first web offset press. (Now operates 19 such presses.)

1946 Build second plant midway between Menasha and Appleton; 41,805 sq. ft. (Now grown to 480,000 sq. ft. Midway plant is believed to be America's largest single book printing facility.)

1954 Company name changed to George Banta Co. Inc.

1969 Acquires Daniels Mfg. Co. of Rhinelander, Wis. (1974 annual sales in food packaging converting: $13,939,000). Now Daniels Packaging Co. Inc., a subsidiary.

1970 Acquires (April) all outstanding stock of The Hart Press, Long Prairie, Minn., lithographic printer of trade and religious periodicals and journals. (Net 1974 sales $8,350,000.)

1970 Acquires (May) Northwestern Engraving Co., Menasha (now Northwestern Colorgaphics, Inc.), producer of photoengravings, offset color separations and offset films. (Net sales 1974: $1,989,000.)

1971 Banta goes public March 9, with offering of 454,900 common shares at $12.50 per.

1972 Acquires (Jan.) Demco Educational Corp., Madison, Wis. Manufacturer and supplier of instructional products for schools, libraries. (1974 annual sales: $13,003,000.)

1972 Buys (March) $1 million Cameron belt press book mfg. system (fourth in United States). Announces $1 million expansion for Daniels Packaging Co.

1972 Acquires (March) Columbus Bank Note Co., Dublin, Ohio, general commercial printer, check and imprint manufacturer. (1974 annual sales: $4,600,000.)

1972 Restructures (Sept.) GBCo printing activities as the Banta Division, to do typesetting, printing, binding, mailing for two Menasha plants; and establishes a Publications Group; Media Group (for multi-media instructional materials) to serve specific markets.

1972 Introduces (Oct.) Banta Viv·id·Tone—"the answer to economical and speedy color separations."

1973 Acquires (March) Levison McNally Co., Reno, Nev., and Ling Packaging Co., Neenah, Wis. Former, a book manufacturer, renamed Banta Levison. Its name was changed again to Banta West in 1974 (1974 annual sales: $2,200,000). Ling, paper and plastic packaging manufacturer, is renamed Ling Products Inc. (1974 annual sales: $1,400,000).

1973 Acquires (May) Springfield (Ohio) Gravure Corp. (1974 annual sales: $3,100,000.)

1974 Corporate revenues exceed $100,000,000 for the first time.

1975 KCS Industries Inc., a Milwaukee creator-producer of point-of-purchase advertising materials, industrial and consumer product labels, and brand identification signs, joins the Banta family.

Management Methods/ Philosophy

In the late sixties there was a decisive changing of the guard at Banta. The old order, having done its work superbly in its time (overseeing a sales growth from the hundreds of thousands to $30 million) retired and/or became less active. Its formula had been to build from within, recruiting ever larger numbers of larger and larger publishers of educational printing. As they grew, Banta grew, and the company's compounding expansion at 8.4 percent per year was eloquent evidence of how well they were attuned to their time.

But the Sixties wrote their own rhythm, and they wrenched the orderly processes of times past right out of their sockets. From every direction came the blandishments of the new order—in the terms of offers from high-riding conglomerates and the acceleration of competitive hazards and opportunities based on the increasing battering the old technology was taking from new technology rooted in electronics and computerization.

Banta met the challenge first by seating a new generation of managers. Reins were firmly in their hands when they made their big move in 1969. That year they drew up the company's first long-range expansion plan. It had three main tenets:

1. Emphasis on corporate independence and on growth from within (notably from educational sources) would continue;

2. A prime source of expansion in the future would be through acquisitions of selected, small, midwestern firms;

3. Banta would not only adopt new technology but would innovate and pioneer new methods and directions.

Basic to the plan was the recognition that the printing industry is "becoming increasingly capital intensive and that the real long-term profit opportunities lie in larger economic units."

To remain independent and yet effect the growth that would keep it in a leadership position in an industry in which ever-larger units were being forged by mergers, Banta went public.

In March 1971, at a price of $12.50, a total of 454,900 shares were offered by the selling shareholders as 29 percent of the 1,555,604 shares then outstanding. The stock is traded over the counter and a market is made in the company's shares by three regional and one national brokerage house. Coupled with the decision to go public were two primary complementary decisions.

The first was to accelerate the company philosophy of investing heavily in advanced technology to hold or improve productivity levels. Evidence of this was the funding of a $1.2 million Cameron belt press system, installation of a computerized phototypesetting unit dominated by a Harris cathode-ray tube (CRT)*, new presses for the Banta and Hart Press web offset batteries, and new flexographic press equipment for Daniels Packaging.

The second primary, complementary decision was to continue an active and aggressive acquisition program for printing and/or market related companies.

Acquisitions which took the company into commercial printing and periodical printing on a new scale—and which introduced it to package manufacturing as well as production of equipment and supplies for libraries—tested Banta management's muscle as much as its theorizing.

"We are trying to avoid the image of a conglomerate," declared president Fieweger in 1972. Banta's way of avoiding that image was to acquire enterprises that were relatively small, sound, related in primary

*Ed note: This operation has since been terminated because Banta "could not achieve adequate profitability for the foreseeable future."

nature to printing and compatible with Banta's loyalty to the educational base on which it is built.

In pursuit of that aim, Banta purchased The Hart Press and Demco; reorganized at Menasha and Midway in 1972 to form the Banta Division, then organized its Media Group to serve the growing nonprint area of its educational accounts.

Thus reorganized, with George Banta Co. as parent and the Banta Division and the eight subsidiaries as operating units, Banta formulated a policy for financial accountability of subsidiary operations while at the same time insisting on autonomy for each in the setting of objectives and their achievement.

"All of our subsidiaries operate under rigid budgetary controls," said George Banta III. "At the close of each three-month period we critically but constructively examine past performance and update operations for the next quarter."

In each case, after each acquisition, "Banta was able to make a substantial contribution to improved performance," George Banta reported. In 1970, the first full year under the expansion program, overall sales increased 27 percent and per share earnings 11 percent. In 1971, consolidated sales rose 9 percent to a new high of $56 million while earnings jumped 17 percent. In 1972, sales shot up 19 percent and net income 24 percent. In 1973, sales rose 25 percent and net earnings increased 15 percent. For 1974, the comparable gains were 23 percent and 18 percent, respectively.

As sales grow and production demand accelerates, the search for the men to man expanded operations has posed a problem for many a printing firm. Banta is finding its acquisition policies synergistic in this respect:

"As a company like Banta grows through acquisitions, it is important to be ever-mindful of the need to ensure continued effective management," President Fieweger told the company's 1973 annual stockholders' meeting. He boasted:

"The depth and adequacy of our young management team was recently confirmed when two important vacancies were filled by promotions from within the company."

It might logically be supposed that a track record such as Banta's would have investors lining up for a crack as its shares. Lamentably, reported Fieweger at the company's March 1973 meeting, that is not the case:

"Our corporate achievements have not yet impressed the American investor," he sighed. "Our record deserves a price/earnings ratio greater than nine times last year's fully diluted earnings. . . . We are, therefore, conscientiously pursuing an investor relations program in keeping with the solid character of our company. . . .

"Presentations have been made to analyst groups in Columbus, Detroit, and New York. All this, of course, in addition to our regular releases to shareholders, analysts and the media."

In composing those presentations, the Banta spokesmen have some comforting data to cull:

Since World War II the company has grown about 15 percent per year in sales and earnings (actually, since 1969, despite two recessions per share earnings have increased at an average annual rate of 20 percent.)

After-tax return on shareholders' equity has increased each year, beginning in 1969 to the current 11.9 percent level.

All those considerations, plus the company record of progress since the dawn of the Sixties and through the depths of the recession just experienced, indicate that Banta's prospects are among the best in the industry. A not inconsiderable factor in those prospects is the way the company has equipped itself to weather droughts in printing activity:

In 1967-68, when printing for education was in a slump, packaging and commercial printing were booming. During the recession of 1969-71, educational printing recovered while the commercial printing and packaging fields were down. As presently constituted, indications are that Banta will be able to rely on one or the other field to see it through any recurrence of such selective traumas with the minimum of damage to the over-all organizations.

With the company so constituted—and still searching for selective, "well managed companies in related areas of the graphic arts field where mutual gains will result"—growth seems assured. So does relative security in times of stress.

Withal, the present Banta management seems well on the way to realizing the main conditions of the basic principles of its expansion planning tenets:

"In order to prosper, a firm will have to be big enough to:

"1. Afford the expensive modern equipment necessary to offset rapidly rising labor costs;

"2. Purchase materials and supplies at favorable rates;

"3. Support specialists in all important segments of the business;

"4. Support a technical effort of a scope sufficient to contribute to, or at least keep abreast of, rapidly changing technology."

Growth/ Growth Planning

One conspicuous result of Banta's participation in the educational information market has been consistent growth, independent of the fortunes of the general printing and publishing market. For instance, between 1960 and 1970 the company's sales increased at a compound annual rate of 8.4 percent, acquisitions excluded. (In only one year, 1967, did sales fail to increase and that was a year in which textbook publishers universally suffered because of cutbacks in federal appropriations for education). The real thrust of that 8.4 percent growth in sales came from the expanded demand of Banta's educational clientele.

In the 30 years between 1926 and 1956 Banta's sales more than doubled each decade, rising from $601,677 in 1926 to $1,393,652 in 1936 and then to $3,594,545 in 1946. In the following decade, they tripled— rising to a 1956 total of $10,929,669—reflecting the mass return of World War II veterans to the educational scene, the influx of a secondary wave of Korean War veterans, and a general population increase of elementary and high school age children. By 1966, the sales curve had again taken a sharp upturn, leaping from the $11 million vicinity to close to $30 million ($29,650,744). Through fiscal 1969, they registered another $10 million gain—to $40,119,396—all, as in the preceding decades, without external stimulus other than growth of demand in its specialty field, education.

The Sixties, of course, were the years in which the conglomerates began their explosive growth. Many large, independent printing companies bought their pitch and hopped the easy-money bandwagon. Banta did not.

"We had many beautiful offers to sell out to conglomerates," chairman George Banta III recalls, "but we decided to remain independent. To do that, it was best to go public."

In 1969 Banta formulated the strategy for its first long-range expansion drive. A ten-year campaign was mapped, the first half of which was to concentrate on three growth aspects: internal expansion; acquisitions; development of special projects. In 1970, the first full year under the plan, over-all sales increased by $11 million, about 27 percent, and earnings per share went up 11 percent. By the end of that year, the Banta fold included Daniels Packaging Co., The Hart Press and Northwestern Engraving Co. (now Northwestern Colorgraphics, Inc.)

In the recession year 1971, sales climbed another $5 million (from $51 to about $56 million) while the company went public. In 1972 it plunged back into the acquisition race, adding Demco Educational Corp. in January, and Columbus Bank Note Co. in March. Meanwhile, it committed $1 million to an expansion of Daniels Packaging facilities, and set up two new marketing segments—the Media Group and the Publications Group—while reorganizing Menasha-plant operations into the Banta Division.

While its five acquisitions between 1969 and 1972 thrust the Banta banner into a number of new competitive fields—packaging, check and advertising printing, trade services and even library furnishing manufacture—the company's educational printing operations continued to be dominant. (About 47 percent of the organization's 1974 sales were the product of its educational operations, which remain of sufficient magnitude to rank it as a leading printer in that field.

In short, in the three-year interval ended 1972, sales climbed about 55 percent as new acquisitions began to pay off and educational subsidies recovered their old steam.

During 1973, Banta acquired three more firms. In March, Levison McNally Co. of Reno, Nev. (first renamed Banta Levison and now Banta West), a book manufacturer, and Ling Packaging Co. of Neenah, Wis., renamed Ling Products, Inc.), a paper and plastic packaging manufacturer, joined the fold. Then, in May of that year, Springfield (Ohio) Gravure Corp. teamed up with Banta.

Acquisition Planning/ Rationale

Banta's acquisition policy is designed, according to president W. H. Fieweger, "to achieve the advantages conglomerates sought without incurring the severe penalties they suffered."

Acquisition strategy has been "to expand laterally across the various kinds of printing—not to move into the ranks of suppliers (such as paper firms) or publishers." By purchasing primarily printing-related firms, Banta has found it is able to share customers—"each one of our new companies has opened doors for the others."

According to Fieweger, Banta limits its acquisition targets "to well-managed, small companies, preferably not in metropolitan communities." He adds: "It has not been a coincidence" that a high proportion of early acquisitions have been "in the Wisconsin area . . . a very desirable area because of (a) availability of raw materials, (b) ease of distribution of materials to customers throughout the country, and (c) locations in smaller communities as aid community and employee relations."

While its earlier acquisitions had been mostly for cash, in late 1971 Banta announced that the company would also use common stock and preferred stock in the future—which it promptly did in acquisitions following that pronouncement.

Banta
Marketing

The Banta Division, seat of the company's enormous educational printing output, is responsible for over half of its sales (in 1974, for $56 million of a total of $103 million).

The 12 largest customers of the company account for approximately 33 percent of total sales and have been customers for over ten years. The company's largest customer accounts for approximately 5 percent of total sales. Most of the Division's sales are to customers of long standing, many over 30 years.

In late 1972, when the two Banta Menasha plants were put under the direction of Donald S. Koskinen, and declared an operating division, two additional marketing arms were created at the same time: the Publications Group and the Media Group. They are decisive heralds of a new era for Banta's marketing thrust.

Purpose of the Publications Group is to generate suitable additional magazine customers for The Banta Division and Banta West—and also The Hart Press, Columbus Bank Note Co., Northwestern Colorgraphics, and Springfield Gravure. The last four named concentrate, respectively, on serving the periodical, promotional-and-banking, and trade service needs of the company's commercial printing customers. The Banta Division and the Banta West operation remained oriented as before—serving, respectively, the educational textbook, workbook and testing materials fields and the book publisher.

Banta Division, however, is now increasing its emphasis on commercial printing as well as on production of trade books. The Division's purchase in 1972 and 1974 of two Cameron belt presses signalled its decision to increase its capabilities to handle short run books, trade as well as educational. Evidence of the Division's heightened interest in commercial printing activity lies in the 100 new accounts it acquired in 1974.

The Media Group's purpose is to specialize in the manufacture of multi-media instructional materials, considered one of the fastest-growing segments of the educational communications industry. Formed also in late 1972, it uses mainly, the facilities of the Banta Division, which has the capability to produce many parts of the MG's output. That output "involves the total interchange of student informational sources, using electronics, television, tape and computer programs to supplement printed books and materials."

While the Media Group and Publications Group represent fresh and specific marketing thrusts for Banta, they complement and broaden service to the company's two oldest customer segments—periodical and educational publishers. In the area of magazines, the corporation is able to consider a wider variety of publications, ranging from medium to long run print quantities, as Banta subsidiary companies (gravure, sheetfed, and web off-set) expand in this field through the Publications Group.

The Media Group assists educational publishers in developing instructional kits and coordinates the manufacturing functions, as the company has done traditionally for textbooks and workbooks. No media-kits are produced or sold by the Banta Division in competition to a publisher, just as books are not published by Banta.

Prior to the post-1970 acquisition drive, Banta's product lines, as percentages of total sales, were:

Paperbound textbooks, workbooks and testing materials: 53 percent
Periodicals (educational, trade, religious, fraternal): 21 percent*
Conversion of flexible packaging materials: 15 percent
Commercial printing, color separations, engraving, composition and plating: 11 percent

As currently constituted, over-all Banta 1974 sales stack up—again in terms of approximate percentages by type of output—as follows:

Paperbound textbooks, workbooks and testing materials: 45 percent
Periodicals: 13 percent
Packaging materials: 15 percent
Commercial printing, color separations, engraving, composition and plating: 14 percent
Educational and library materials manufacture and distribution: 13 percent

The Banta Division

Banta Division, Menasha, Wisconsin. Formed September 13, 1972 to perform typesetting, printing, binding and related functions of Banta's two Menasha plants. Operations of the Division in 1974 were responsible for approximately $56 million of the organization's total annual sales of $103,004,000.

Operations: Specializes in production of educational materials including workbooks, testing materials and other paperbound books, periodicals and journals as well as clothbound books. Also, commercial printing, including sales brochures, catalogs and magazines. Consumes over 60,000 tons of paper annually, or some five carloads per workday.

Banta specializes in this type of magazine rather than the larger-circulation consumer magazines "because they are less subject to cyclical variations in number of ad pages and because regular, planned growth is easier to achieve, since each new periodical adds only modestly to sales."—ED. NOTE.

Facilities: Menasha plant, on site of an original 1910 plant, contains 156,000 square feet. The second plant (Midway) contains about 480,000 sq. ft.

During 1974, a new preparatory studio of 22,500 sq. ft., attached to the Midway plant, was constructed at a cost of nearly $1 million.

Capital Equipment Latest major equipment installation was the 1974 emplacement of a second $1.1 million Cameron belt press primarily to print short-run, lower-cost paperbacks—college and trade. When filled to capacity, it is expected to generate $5 million of additional business. Total 1974 plant and capital equipment expenditures were $3,090,000 for the Banta Division with $3,791,000 planned for 1975.

Press facilities: The Division operates 19 web offset presses, two of them single-color, nine two-color, and eight four-color. Nine sheet-fed offset presses include four single-color, three five-color, one two-color, and one three-color. In addition, the Division operates a number of letter presses, but these are gradually being phased out.

Bindery facilities include Smyth, McCain, Singer and Sheridan equipment for sewing, stitching, and perfect binding. Also Spiral, Wire-O, Lino-lok and plastic. A fourth $500,000 perfect binder, an additional casebinding line, and a new saddlewire binder were schedule for installation in 1975.

Typesetting facilities include monotype and linotype equipment, especially for scientific and professional books and journals where tabular matter and technical formulae are involved. Hot metal typesetting, although steadily being reduced, makes use of the company's IBM 3640 computer.

Employees of the Division: 1,400, all unionized except office employees. "Substantially all" covered by non-contributor pension plans.

Sales The Division's sales volume grew 13% to $56 million. Earnings gains topped growth in sales for the second consecutive year, in spite of a costly 10-day strike in April, 1974.

Banta Division facilities are heavily targeted as the production source for sales generated by the Publications Group (which plans greater penetration into the magazine field) and Media Group (which specializes in assisting educational accounts in the creation of informational materials such as audio-visuals and computer programs integrating with printed materials).

Sales offices: Boston, Chicago, New York, Washington, Los Altos, Calif., Menasha, Wis.

Acquired Companies September 1969 *Daniels Packaging Co., Rhinelander, Wis.* Founded 1915, its 1968 calendar year sales were $6,700,000, earnings $2,200.00. Banta's purchase price: $2.4 million.

Operations: Prints, coats and laminates films, foils, polyethylenes and glassines. Names like General Foods, General Mills, Procter and Gamble, Hershey and Nabisco dominate Daniels' account list.

Facilities: Include 110,000 sq. ft. of manufacturing space; 50,000 sq. ft. of warehousing space; nearly 5,000 sq. ft. of storage space were added in 1974 for inks, solvents and coatings. Capital equipment includes nine multi-color flexographic presses (a tenth was ordered in 1974), seven slitter-rewinders, a 54″-wide, four-section printer-coater-laminator and a new adhesive laminator. A capital investment of about $500,000 is planned for each of the next five years.

Employees: 210

Sales: $13,939,000 in 1974, up 36 percent over 1973; earnings also showed a solid increase.

April 1970 *The Hart Press Inc., Long Prairie, Minn.* Founded 1920; its sales for last full fiscal year before purchase were $4,138,559, earnings $196,545. Banta's purchase price: $1.9 million, $480,000 down and rest is seven equal annual installments.

Operations: Produces over 50 million of nearly 100 publications, including catalogs.

Facilities: 95,000 sq. ft. manufacturing space, 15,000 sq. ft. warehousing space. Owns city block in Long Praire, served by rail siding; 18.5 acre plot for expansion.

Capital Equipment: Four web offset presses (one a six-unit machine), four sheet-fed offset presses, perfect binding equipment, two saddle-wire stitchers and one side wire stitcher; also, automated mailing and distribution equipment.

Employees: 260

Sales: 1974 sales of $8,350,000 were up 13% from the previous year. Earnings declined slightly primarily due to a two-week work stoppage.

May 1970 *Northwestern Colorgraphics, Inc. (formerly Northwestern Engraving Co.), Menasha, Wis.* Founded in 1934; its sales for year acquired were $1,156,651 and net earnings $107,991. Acquired through stock exchange.

Operations: Produces over half America's Sunday four-color comic strips via fluorography. Another specialty is Viv-vi-tone, a proprietary method of producing color separations for lithography used primarily by staff of 30 in Northwestern's Appleton plant in preparation of school textbooks and other school aids. Largest photoengraver in Wisconsin, Northwestern offers full range of offset color separation services, black-and-white film processing and photoengravings.

Facilities: 20,000 sq. ft. in Menasha leased month-to-month from a corporation it owns 50 percent.

Employees: 75

Sales: Increased nearly $100,000 in 1974 to $1,989,000. Earnings improved as investments in new equipment, such as a computer-controlled scanner and four-color production press, began to impact on productivity. Note: Sales to other Banta organizations were close to $600,000.

January 1972   *Demco Educational Corp., Madison Wis.* Founded in 1906 as a division of Democrat Printing Co., it was incorporated in 1931. Sales for fiscal year preceding purchase by Banta were $6,431,000. Banta's purchase price: $2,940,870, representing fair value of 37,000 shares of $.10 par value Banta common stock and 30,000 shares of $10 par value preferred.

Operations: The company is a major manufacturer and distributor of supplies and instructional materials for libraries and schools. Demco makes library furniture, book jacket covers, catalog cards, and other supplies. It stocks supplementary audio-visual learning materials for elementary and secondary schools, represents nearly 100 publishers with over 25,000 titles. Included in lines are filmstrips, slides, overhead transparencies, records, cassettes, audio tapes, etc. In October 1973, Demco acquired American Library and Educational Services (ALESCO) of Paramus, NJ. The merger added hard-cover library book distribution and subscription services to Demco's existing product lines. ALESCO is now operating as a division of Demco.

Facilities: Include an 83,000 sq. ft. plant and warehouse in DeForest, Wis. on 20 acres; an 8,000 sq. ft. distribution center in Fresno, Calif., and the ALESCO plant in Paramus, NJ.

Employees: 200 plus

Sales: Increased 56% in 1974 over 1973 to $13,003,000. Earnings also improved, although modestly.

March 1972   *Columbus Bank Note Co., Dublin, Ohio.* Founded 1894, its fiscal 1971 sales were $3,871,000, earnings $41,665. Banta's purchase price: 100,000 shares of Banta $.10 par value common stock.

Operations: Basic volume (about 50 percent) is commercial printing, 25 percent check preparation, 25 percent promotional equipment. Artists and copywriters on staff help produce annual reports, displays, banners, company publications. Clients include Scott Seed, Coca-Cola, Sears, Roebuck & Co., Stouffers, Calgon, Nestle, Rubbermaid, Borden's, Tappan. (Over 80 percent of work is four-color.)

Facilities: A model, 53,000-sq.-ft. showplace plant on 22-acre wildlife refuge 15 miles from downtown Columbus.

Capital Equipment: two 52x76 and two 25x38 four-color presses, plus bindery and mailing facilities, a complete check printing department, and a new color separation department.

Employees: 145

Sales: 1974 sales were $4,600,000, up from $4,451,000 in 1973; earnings kept a proportionate pace.

February 1973   *Banta West, Inc. (originally Levison McNally Co., then Banta Levison Co.), Sparks, Nev.* Founded 1971, its 1972 sales were $1.3 million, earnings $568,000 (loss). Banta's purchase price: $100,000 in cash and 7,040 shares of Banta common stock.

Operations: A medium-sized book manufacturing company, it now functions as a Banta affiliate specializing in trade and educational titles. Many Banta Division accounts add volume to Banta West. The latter's expanded sales force—and a new customer service organizatin—were also instrumental in adding another 32 new customers in 1974.

Facilities: 100,000 sq. ft. in modern building.

Capital Equipment: One- and two-color 77″ presses include a Miehle perfector capable of producing 128 book pages in a single pass; bindery facilities for cloth and paper back books of all types, including stitched, sewn, adhesive bindings. The preparatory department was upgraded significantly, equipment was added to print and coat book covers, and fulfillment service capability was increased during 1974.

Employees: 100

Sales: 1974 sales rose to $2,200,000—29% over 1973. Earnings also showed a gratifying gain.

March 1973   *Ling Products Inc. (formerly Ling Packaging Co., Inc.), Neenah, Wis.* Founded 1969, its 1972 sales were $750,000. Banta's purchase price: $46,000 and 4,015 shares of Banta $.10 common stock.

Operations: Specialty polyethylene and spunbound film conversion. A major marketing move in 1974 was preparation for the introduction of "Sorb-Oil"®—a patented product created to absorb and remove oil from water.

Facilities: 40,000 sq. ft. of manufacturing and warehousing space.

Capital Equipment: Includes Ling-Seals, Ling-Cut, and die-cutting equipment. During 1974, a high-speed rewinder to facilitate initial converging techniques and a poly-film line for glove fabrication were added. Capacity to print, convert and package disposable tablecloths was also increased.

Employees: 60

Sales: 1974 sales of $1,400,000 were double those of $708,000 in 1973. In spite of higher prices for petrochemical plastics, net earnings increased to $77,000. A major step in improving earnings was the elimination of contract manufacturing.

May 1973   *Springfield Gravure Corp., Springfield, Ohio.* Founded 1957, its 1971 sales were $3.3 million. (Plant was idled by strike from March 1972 until purchase.) Banta's purchase price: $1,500,000.

Operations: In 1974, Springfield made the transition from a trade service house, whose main function was to provide other printers with gravure separations, to a printing-oriented company, serving advertising agencies, retail stores and consumer manufacturers, such as Winston Cigarettes. A new line of package inserts was developed with Clairol as the first account.

Facilities: 50,000 sq. ft. manufacturing space, 5,000 sq. ft. warehousing space.

Capital Equipment: Includes an 11-unit Albert Press, four-unit Motter press, proof press, and extensive photographic and preparatory equipment. Among the new equipment put into operation in 1974 were a solvent recovery system, a Goss folder, a Butler splicer, and press register controls. Bindery equipment is being installed also.

Employees: 80

Sales: In 1974, sales were over $3,100,000. Capital equipment outlays, coupled with reorganization costs, resulted in an earnings loss. However, continued increased sales and internal improvements are expected to reverse the situation.

January 1975   *KCS Industries Inc., Milwaukee, Wis.* Founded in 1909, the company has had a history of steady growth. Banta's purchase Price: $350,000 and issuance of a note for $950,000 payable with interest at 8 percent over four years.

Operations: Point-of-purchase merchandising, industrial and product package labels and brand identification signage. Customers include a wide range of consumer and industrial markets.

Facilities: 68,000 sq. ft. building located on an 11-acre City of Milwaukee site. A second plant is leased in the city.

Capital Equipment: Injection molding, vacuum forming, tool making, hot stamping, metal forming, color finishing, and other processes. Graphic arts processes include letterpress, flexographic and silk screen printing.

Sales: 1974 net sales were $4,612,000, and net earnings were $173,000. Sales offices are maintained in Chicago, New York, Detroit and Atlanta with expansion to the West Coast now underway.

Banta's Presidents

George Banta, Sr., (founder)—1901-1935
Ellen Lee Banta (founder's wife)—1935-1951
Richard E. Thickens—1951-1954
George Banta, Jr. (son of founder)—1954-1960
John H. Wilterding—1961-1964
George Banta III—1965—1971*
William H. Fieweger—1971-

Top Executive Officers

George Banta III, chairman of the board, chief executive officer, George Banta Co., Inc. Born 1923. Education: Lawrence University. Prior work experience: sales office and various service and production departments, George Banta Co.

William H. Fieweger, president, George Banta Co. Inc. Born 1914. Education: University of Notre Dame. Prior work experience: vice president and director, Kimberly-Clark Corp.

John E. Wall, president, Demco Educational Corp. Born 1926. Education: Xavier University, Marquette University, Northwestern University, Illinois Institute of Technology, University of Wisconsin. Prior work experience: vice president and general manager, Cook Electric Co.; production manager, Reliable Electric Co.; manager of operations, Spic & Span.

Now chairman of the board, chief executive officer

Jack T. LaBlonde, president of Daniels Packaging Co., Inc. Born 1923. Education: General Motors Institute. Prior work experience: Cadillac and Chevrolet divisions, General Motors Corp.

Harris H. Hanson, president, The Hart Press Inc. Born 1918. Education: University of Minnesota; Harvard Business School. Prior work experience: office manager, corporate secretary, corporate treasurer, Hart Press.

Carlton E. Kuck, president, Northwestern Colorgraphics, Inc. Born 1915. Education: University of Wisconsin. Prior work experience: owner and president, Northwestern Engraving Co.

John P. Gould, president, The Columbus Bank Note Co.

Gordon A. Plum, chief executive officer, Springfield Gravure Corp. Born 1931. Education: North Dakota State School of Sciences; University of North Dakota; Rochester Institute of Technology. Prior work experience: vice president of manufacturing, The Hart Press Inc; production manager, The Dakota Farmer Co.

Donald S. Koskinen, president, Banta Division and Banta West Inc. Born 1928. Education: Lawrence University. Prior work experience: sales office, director sales service, vice president of sales, George Banta Co.

Charles J. Lingelbach, president, Ling Products Inc. Born 1917. Education: Michigan Tech University. Prior work experience: brew master, Pabst Brewing Co.; Research Associate, Institute of Paper Chemistry; head of product development (film and unsupported film), American Can Co.

Earl R. Vogt, president, KCS Industries Inc.

George Banta Company, Inc.
Curtis Reed Plaza
Menasha, Wisconsin 54952

Lee Enterprises, Inc.

*A Single Newspaper
Spawns Closely Knit
Multi-Media Family*

Lee Enterprises built this $6.5 million
plant for NAPP Systems (USA)
at San Marcos, California,
where some 3.6 million plates
a year are produced.

159

The LaCrosse, Wisconsin Tribune
Plant which prints by offset.

Lee Enterprises Inc. is primarily a multi-media corporation owning 14 medium-sized to large newspapers, four television stations, three FM radio stations and two AM stations. All but one of these are in the midwest and northwest, and largely in prime growth areas. The corporation is also involved in newspaper production equipment sales.

More than 80 percent of the $48.4 million revenue for Lee's 1974 fiscal year, which ended last September 30, came from the newspapers.

Every year for the last eleven the company has shown increased earnings and profits, and its after-tax earnings for 1974 exceeded $5.5 million.

What has become the Lee corporate enterprise of today had its beginnings 95 years ago with a single newspaper, the Ottumwa (Iowa) *Courier*. The *Courier* is still a part of Lee Enterprises, which now employs about 2,500 persons.

But while the company takes pleasure from its long history, its eye is riveted ahead to what it confidently sees as even greater opportunity for public service as well as profit. Here are some of the major items seen as contributing to Lee's prospects:

A marketing operation has begun for a new photopolymer printing plate, called NAPP, which Lee maintains is uniquely capable of performing cost-cutting and operational wonders for the printing business. A $6.5 million manufacturing complex at San Marcos, Calif., has been operating in the black. (As of the end of 1974, 157 newspapers in the United States and elsewhere had signed contracts for the NAPP plates.)

All the company's printing operations have now been converted to cold type.

As rapidly as can be managed, a conversion to automated "front end" systems is being carried out at all newspapers. These systems use video display terminals, a computer and advanced typesetting equipment to capture the original keystroke of the reporter, editor or classified ad taker and convert into type the impulse generated.

Lee is determined to reverse the traditional state of affairs in which more money was spent on production costs than in gathering and editing the news. Great strides toward this goal have been made through new technology. Lee says it is now investing much more money in news than composition, while still returning higher profits.

During the past ten years or so the company has spent $30 million on plant and equipment upgrading. The tab for fiscal 1974 alone was over $2.5 million.

The company avers that it now is probably the most technologically sophisticated newspaper group in America.

"Growth is no longer optional for Lee," says president Lloyd G. Schermer. "It's mandatory!"

"We're future oriented," adds the company's director of special projects, Jules S. Tewlow. "We don't necessarily want to be the biggest in the business, but we sure as hell want to be the best."

In addition to the Ottumwa Courier, Iowa papers in the Lee group are the Davenport Times-Democrat, Mason City Globe-Gazette and Muscatine Journal.

Montana likewise has four Lee papers: The Billings Gazette, the Montana Standard in Butte, the Missoulian in Missoula and the Independent Record in Helena.

The other publications are the Wisconsin State Journal in Madison, the Journal Times at Racine, Wis., La Crosse Tribune in La Crosse, Wis., the Star-Courier in Kewanee, Ill., the Corvallis Gazette-Times in Oregon and the Lincoln Star in Nebraska.

Lee's investment in associated nonconsolidated companies—in addition to NAPP Systems (USA)—includes a 49¾ percent ownership in the Journal-Star Printing Co., Lincoln, Neb. (at an investment cost of $1,118,445) and a 50-percent interest in Madison Newspapers Inc., Madison, Wis., (investment cost $237,480).

Broadcast facilities are WSAZ-TV at Huntington-Charleston, W. Va.; WTAD, AM and FM radio in Quincy, Ill.; KGLO-TV and KGLO AM radio, Mason City, Iowa; KEYC-TV and KEYC FM radio, Mankato, Minn.; WMDR FM radio, Moline, Ill., and KHQA-TV, in Hannibal, Mo., and Quincy, Ill.

Additionally, Lee has a 24.3 percent interest in KFAB AM and FM radio in Omaha.

Milestones   *1880* A. W. Lee, who had worked on the Journal at Muscatine, Iowa, acquires for $16,000 the Courier at Ottumwa with the idea of eventually establishing a newspaper group.

1889 Davenport (Iowa) Times is purchased.

1903 Muscatine (Iowa) Journal added to group.

1907 La Crosse (Wis.) Tribune acquired.

1915 Davenport (Iowa) Democrat bought.

1919 Wisconsin State Journal becomes part of group.

1925 Mason City (Iowa) Globe-Gazette purchased.

1926 Kewanee (Ill.) Star-Courier added.

1930 Lincoln (Neb.) Star bought.

1937 Entry into broadcasting with launching of Radio Station KGLO in Mason City, Iowa.

1944 WTAD in Quincy, Ill., is purchased.

1948 WTAD service expanded to FM transmission.

1953 Lee enters television with KHQA-TV, serving the area of Quincy, Ill., and Hannibal, Mo.

1954 KGLO-TV, Mason City, Iowa, goes on air.

1959 Company headquarters moved from Mason City to Davenport, and largest newspaper acquisition made. Eight Montana papers purchased from Anaconda Copper Co. The papers were located at Billings, Butte, Missoula, Livingston, Anaconda and Helena. Later, some were discontinued, sold or combined with others.

1960 KEYC-TV in Mankato, Minn., added to Lee group.

1968 KEYC-FM goes on air at Mankato, Racine Journal Times becomes part of newspaper operations as does Corvallis Gazette-Times.

1969 Lee becomes one of first newspaper groups to make public stock offering. Stock traded on American Exchange since March 17, 1970, under symbol LNT.

1970 WSAZ-TV purchased at Huntington-Charleston, W. Va.; WMDR-FM goes on air at Moline, Ill.

1972 Lee and Nippon Paint Co. of Osaka, Japan, form NAPP Systems (USA), Inc., to manufacture and merchandise new NAPP photopolymer printing plate.

1973 Plate production begins at new $6.5 million manufacturing complex at San Marcos, Calif.

1974 Revenues advanced to a new high of $48.4 million.

Lee's
Presidents

A. W. Lee (founder)—1880-1907
E. P. Adler—1907-1949
Lee P. Loomis—1949-1960
Philip D. Adler—1960-1970
David K. Gottlieb—1970-1973
Lloyd G. Schermer—Elected mid-1973

The NAPP
Plate

Not only are its own newspapers using the new Japanese-developed NAPP photopolymer printing plate but the company now is busy manufacturing and selling the plates to others.

A $6.5 million manufacturing complex went into operation at San Marcos, Calif., last year, and the new plates found such ready acceptance in the newspaper and commercial printing fields that the business was operating in the black within five months. Eighty workers currently are employed. The workforce will be expanded to about 120 men when full production of 3.6 million plates a year is reached.

"There is a vast market for the NAPP plate in both the newspaper industry and commercial printing, since the plate prints beautifully on any newsprint-like stock," according to the company.

"We set the machinery for the NAPP plate system in motion at Lee with cold type conversions for the use of photopolymer plates years before any photopolymer plates existed. If no plate would meet our standards when we needed it, we would make it happen—and that is exactly what happened. It is the reason we are selling NAPP plates today."

More specifically, what happened was that several years ago David K. Gottlieb, Lee president who died last year, started scouring the world trying to find the photopolymer plate which met his norms best. His search ended at the Nippon Paint Co. of Osaka, Japan, a century-old chemical company. Nippon Paint's scientists and engineers had put in five years working on a prototype plate. Once satisfied that they had the real thing, they offered it to Japanese newspapers in 1967. Nippon Paint also designed the equipment to manufacture and process the plate.

Lee gave it a tryout with extensive testing on the Davenport Times-Democrat and soon concluded that the process was a real winner. The company subsequently (in July 1972) formed a joint venture with Nippon Paint: NAPP Systems (USA) Inc. The two firms share NAPP 50-50.

Lee cites as advantages of the NAPP plates these claims: minimal capital investment in processing equipment; superior printing quality; ease of equipment installation; minimal training needed to process plates; excellent quality consistently; superior plate production per hour; capacity for use as pattern plates, from which conventional stereotype plates can be created, and superior color reproduction.

"When a publisher signs a NAPP contract," says Lee, "he gets the plate itself, competitively priced at $3.60, plus the equipment, the training and the technical service which go with the plate."

Lee says that what it calls the NAPP System I equipment enables a lone worker to process 24 plates an hour. This sells for a little less than $30,000 and includes two exposure units, two washout units and two ovens. The double units mean that the publisher has built-in backup in case of temporary equipment failure. Selling for slightly less than $55,000, NAPP's automatic plate processing equipment reportedly enables one man to handle 60 plates an hour.

The company requires that purchasers must send two employees to the NAPP training facility at San Marcos, Calif., or Davenport, Iowa for training. It claims a good man can master the essentials in less than an hour. ("The secret to superb printing reproduction lies not in the plate processing, but in the camera-work which precedes it. Thus trainees spend many hours learning to perfect their camera work. . . . If the negative is good, NAPP reproduction will be good.")

Customers don't have to worry about plates wearing out. Though nobody is yet sure just how long one will last, one national weekly publication using the plate prints up to one million copies each run with no plate wear.

The NAPP plate has a layer of polymer 28/1000ths of an inch thick, joined to a sheet of aluminum 12/1000ths of an inch thick. The tolerance is plus or minus 1/1000th of an inch.

Another prime virtue claimed for the plate system is the avoidance of safety and pollution headaches. The plate is washed by ordinary tap water heated to 105 degrees Fahrenheit, and the polymer which has not been hardened by exposure to the light source simply dissolves into the water without polluting it. The waste can be drained away without special treatment.

Moreover, there is a reclamation value to used plates. The hardened polymer is dissolved by soaking in water a day or two, leaving a clean sheet of aluminum the size of a newspaper page. The sheets can be sold for use again in many ways.

NAPP's technical service people are trained to help install and service the processing equipment, train workers at the customer's plant and make sure the best possible results are obtained.

After a customer gets into production, NAPP takes a three-month subscription to his paper and watches it carefully. If any reproduction problem is spotted, a technical representative will be dispatched to correct it—even if the customer hasn't complained.

Lee Enterprises suffered a severe shock last year when its president, David K. Gottlieb, died unexpectedly on July 4. Gottlieb, who had been with the company over 35 years, had served it on every level from back shop through editorial, advertising and finally front office. An outspoken herald and crusader for technological development in newspaper production, he was a prime mover in establishing the groundwork for the advanced technical systems now employed by newspapers in the Lee chain. He eloquently forwarded industry interests in such progress during his terms (1971-72) as president of the American Newspaper Publishers Association Research Institute.

Chosen to succeed Gottlieb was Lloyd G. Schermer, who had been vice president of the company and assistant to the president in the area of newspapers and executive staff. Of Gottlieb, Schermer said recently:

"As Dave insisted, Lee must be more than one man. He provided for the orderly transition of management by building an effective management team. That team has great depth and has responded magnificently."

Schermer earlier had been vice president of Lee's Montana divisions, and was publisher of The Missoulian at Missoula. It was at Missoula in 1967 that he led Lee's first successful conversion to photocomposition/offset. Subsequently, working closely with Gottlieb, Schermer helped develop many of the top managers and staff directors Lee has today.

Other top-level members of the Lee team now include:

James E. Burgess, vice president of newspaper operations and director.

Lloyd Loers, vice president of broadcasting. He is also general manager of KGLO and KGLO-TV, Mason City, Iowa.

John Stemlar, financial vice president and treasurer.

Tom Williams, operations manager of the Metro newspaper group which includes the papers at Davenport, La Crosse and Racine, and publisher of the Davenport *Times-Democrat*.

John Talbot, operations manager of the western group, embracing the Billings *Gazette*, the *Missoulian*, the *Montana Standard*, the Helena *Independent Record* and Corvallis *Gazette-Times*, and publisher of the *Missoulian*.

Steve Sturm, Iowa-Illinois newspaper operations manager and publisher, *Globe-Gazette*.

Jules Tewlow, director of special projects.

Ronald Semple, assistant to the president and staff director.

While the terminology may sound a bit unusual for a major corporation in this day and time, Lee has no hesitancy at all in saying frankly that it wants "Gee Whiz" people for its management. The kind it postively does not want is the "So What" type.

"When we discuss a topic such as the revolution in Newspaper Technology," says President Schermer, "the world divides itself into two groups: the 'Gee Whiz' people and the 'So What' people. The vast majority of our management team, more than 160 men and women, are 'Gee Whiz' people.

"Why is that important? Because it reflects human attitudes—the attitudes of people expected to translate the new 'shiz bangs' and 'widgets' into realities that are vital . . .''

Schermer asserts that the major goal of his leadership is to provide maximum opportunity for company people "to develop to their fullest potential and to gain a sense of self-accomplishment." He continues: "We have a management team—publishers, general managers, station managers and corporate staff directors—whose average age is 43.

"The foundation of our management philosophy is *decentralization.* We define this as *the delegation of authority and responsibility for every decision to the lowest possible level where the decision can be made effectively and with accountability.*

"As a corporation," Schermer continues, "we have succeeded in walking the line between local autonomy on the one hand, where the only connection between properties is a publicly listed stock, and centralized decision-making from corporate headquarters on the other."

The Business Picture

As Lee sees it, business looks great right now and even greater for the future. Technological changes are credited with making an important contribution to record progress in the 1974 fiscal year ended September 30.

Revenue was approximately $48.4 million, or about $3.4 million more than the previous year. Net earnings increased to $5.5 million. Net earnings per share increased 16.5 percent to $1.65, based on 3,352,429 average common shares outstanding in 1974, compared to 3,347,611 shares in 1973. Shareholders' equity increased to $13.94 per share, from $12.63 per share a year before. During the year the company distributed cash dividends of 35 cents per share, for a total of $1,157,000. The previous year the dividend was 30 cents.

During fiscal 1974, a total of $2.5 million was spent on new plants, equipment and other growth programs. At the same time long-term debt was reduced by $4,328,000.

Newspaper revenue was up 8.5 percent and broadcasting 5.2 percent.

The quarterly dividend was increased from 9 cents a share to 10 cents effective January 2, 1975. Altogether, dividends were raised by 33 percent in 12 months.

A sore situation for most newspaper publishers these days is the shortage and growing price of newsprint. Lee has long-term contacts adequate to cover basic newsprint needs, although it is seeking additional tonnage to cover the company's expected growth.

Progress in Technics

All the Lee newspapers have recently been shifted to the use of Photocomposition systems, coupled with either offset printing presses or letterpresses using the new NAPP photopolymer printing plates.

The *Times-Democrat* at Davenport has become a showcase as well as a training ground for personnel of other papers with the first installation and operation of the "front end" system. This is the use of Harris video display terminals, computer and advanced phototypesetting equipment in such a way that type is set by impulses from keystrokes of reporters, editors and classified ad takers. Many other Lee newspapers are being converted to this system.

The *Times-Democrat* also has automated its mail room. Additionally, it did extensive field testing and research on both Japanese and American manufactured NAPP printing plates, did research and development on a new press saddle to be used in conjunction with a NAPP plate, and remodeled its building.

At La Crosse, Wisc., the *Tribune* constructed and has moved into a new building which contains the latest photocomposition equipment as well as a new Goss Urbanite offset press. The Racine *Journal-Times* converted completely to photocomposition and put in the NAPP plate system.

At Madison, the *Wisconsin State Journal* has ordered a 12-unit Goss Metro offset press, expected to start rolling in 1975 and is constructing a new $9 million plant. The *Journal* has expanded its cold-type production capabilities and converted to NAPP printing also.

Other company conversions to the NAPP system have been completed by the *Globe-Gazette* at Mason City, Iowa; the *Star-Courier* at Kewanee, Ill.; the Lincoln *Journal-Star* in Nebraska and the *Independent Record* in Helena, Mont.

While converting to photocomposition, the Muscatine *Journal* in Iowa remodeled its existing building and constructed an addition to house a new Goss Community offset press and is using video display terminals.

At Lincoln, the *Journal-Star* extensively remodeled its building and implemented the first on-site computer applications system developed by Lee's corporate staff.

In Montana, the *Missoulian* has taken the first steps toward automating its mail room. The Helena *Independent Record* also modernized its building.

In a recent report to shareholders, President Schermer said that "our next move will be into the area of video display tubes, optical character readers and other computer-oriented devices yet un-named." He continued: "Improved production technology has done more for Lee than simply increase profits. It has allowed us to improve the quality of our newspapers.

"Newspapers usually are forced to spend more money to set type than to gather, write and edit news. That may not make sense, but it is impossible to spend more money on news when a great hunk of revenue is being gobbled up by a money-eating dinosaur of a composing room. Ten years ago, we at Lee created a plan to redress that imbalance; and we have. Today we have more people in our newsrooms than in our composing rooms. . . ."

From Jules Tewlow comes the confident prediction that "when we're through, our production probably will require the lowest number of man-hours per page in the world!"

Five Year Review

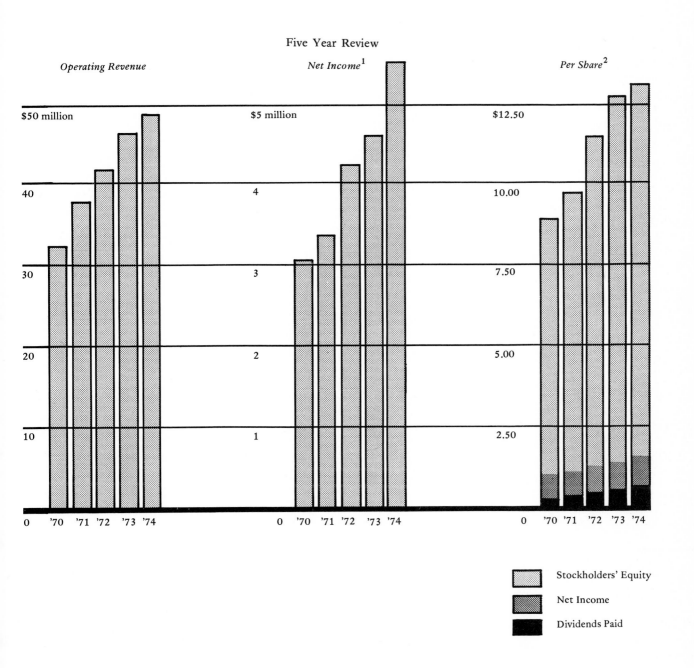

Operating Revenue   Net Income[1]   *Per Share*[2]

	1974	1973	1972	1971	1970
Dividends Paid	$ 1,157,000	$ 996,000	$ 910,000	$ 793,000	$ 783,000
Stockholders' Equity	$46,717,000	$42,347,000	$38,431,000	$28,609,000	$25,983,000
Property & Equipment Add'ns	$ 2,526,000	$ 3,881,000	$ 2,098,000	$ 4,744,000	$ 2,378,000

Shares are traded on the American Stock Exchange, symbol LNT.

[1] Before extraordinary items. Year 1970 excludes extraordinary net gain of $1,355,000, or $.69 per share, from sale of certain properties and interests. No extraordinary items in other years.

[2] Stockholders' equity per share is based on shares outstanding at end of year. Net income per share is based on average number of shares outstanding during year.

Ten-Year Financial Review

Year (9/30)	Revenues (000)	After Tax Earnings (000)	Equity in Affiliates (000)	Net Earnings (000)	Earnings per Share	Dividends	Price Range
1974	$48,409	$4,253	$1,274	$5,527	$1.65	$0.35	10¾ - 16¼
1973	44,980	3,766	978	4,744	1.42	0.30	10 - 25
1972	41,470	3,004	1,192	4,196	1.31	0.28	17½ - 30
1971	37,700	2,309	1,100	3,409	1.16	0.27	12½ - 20-1/8
1970	34,640	2,143	885	3,028	1.03*	0.27	8 - 16-7/8
1969	31,940	2,133	748	2,881	0.99	0.27	10-3/8 - 15-3/8
1968	26,870	1,768	648	2,416	0.84	0.25	Private†
1967	25,900	2,012	645	2,658	0.91	0.19	Private†
1966	24,780	1,862	574	2,436	0.80	0.18	Private†
1965	27,760	1,634	544	2,178	0.71	0.16	Private†
1964	21,640	1,397	325	1,722	0.56	0.12	Private†

Adjusted for 3-1 split in 1967, 4-1 split in 1968, and 50-percent stock dividend in 1971.
*Excludes credit of 30 cents per share from gain on sales of assets.
†Offered in March, 1969, at $13.67 (adjusted).
Source: February 5, 1974 analysis of Lee Enterprises by Lamson Bros., Chicago.

Newspaper Revenue

(000)

Year	Advertising	Circulation	Editorial Fees
1974	$27,548	$8,304	$2,409*
1973	25,600	8,988	1,920
1972	23,112	8,600	1,808
1971	21,491	8,070	1,657
1970	20,457	7,364	1,514
1969	18,530	6,739	1,423
1968	15,244	5,576	1,294
1967	14,774	5,259	1,201
1966	14,162	5,045	1,123
1965	12,709	4,831	1,063
1964	12,002	4,656	1,032

*1974 figure includes management fees from associated companies.

	1974	1973	1972	1971	1970
Dividends Paid	$ 1,157,000	$ 996,000	$ 910,000	$ 793,000	$ 783,000
Stockholders' Equity	$46,717,000	$42,347,000	$38,431,000	$28,609,000	$25,983,000
Property & Equipment Add'ns	$ 2,526,000	$ 3,881,000	$ 2,098,000	$ 4,744,000	$ 2,378,000

Shares are traded on the American Stock Exchange, symbol LNT.
[1] Before extraordinary items. Year 1970 excludes extraordinary net gain of $1,355,000, or $.69 per share, from sale of certain properties and interests. No extraordinary items in other years.
[2] Stockholders' equity per share is based on shares outstanding at end of year. Net income per share is based on average number of shares outstanding during year.

This is the Davenport
Times-Democrat NAPP plate department.

Lee Enterprises, Inc.
130 East Second Street
Davenport, Iowa 52801

Progressive Printing

As a final fillip, we tell the story of Progressive Printing, a current inhabitant of the Land of the Small Printer, where live over 85 percent of America's 30,000 commercial printers. In their tens of thousands, their total annual take is just over $3 billion, or approximately what the industry's "top 50" earn in a year. These are the printers who employ less than 20 people and are owned and operated by entrepreneurs who work (mom and pop) 60-hour weeks and worry mainly about two things: keeping going, and leaving the business to the kids. The Luebckes—Walt and Betty and son Jim—are cut from the molds from which the Donnelleys came, and the Bantas, Kruegers, etc. While still in the industry's lowlands, if they can hang on they will almost inevitably be moving up. The determination's there; now they need the "break." Time is on their side. But, when they do move up, another will quickly take their place, for despite technology and the prophets, for as long as hope "springs eternal" there will always be a Land of Small Printers.

An Idenity Crisis

Walt Luebcke, president, chief stockholder, and archetypal father of Progressive Printing in Salt Lake City, once described his entry into the printing business as "a hobby that got out of hand." Primarily a craftsman, he has been known to spend two hours running 500 postcards in order to lay down the ink "just right."

When Walt was discharged from the Army in 1945, he and his wife Betty settled in Salt Lake City, Utah. Since neither one had any particular skills to fall back on other than farming, Betty began an in-home typing service to meet the family's expenses.

As Betty began to get more long-run typing assignments, Walt decided they should expand into a duplicating service. Knowing little about printing but driven by a farm boy's fascination with machinery and the craft, Walt invested their savings in a small duplicating machine.

The next step was to buy out the old Hart Sisters' Letter Shop. The letter service operation has since faded with the front door paint, but at that point in 1947, Progressive Printing was on its way.

For Walt and Betty, Progressive has been their entire life. Rarely do they go home before 10:00 p.m. They would have been content to let Progressive go on as it had; a small duplicating shop which could provide comfortably for one family's needs.

But five years ago the Luebckes were faced with a crisis. They had always hoped their only child, Jim, would enter the family business and eventually take over the reins. Through hard work and reinvestment, Walt and Betty had managed to pay for the two Multilith 1250's and the land and building, although one had to be careful not to stack paper under certain areas of the roof when it rained.

Yet Jim Luebcke is a study in contrasts when compared to Walt. Where Walt is easy-going and quick to flash a patient smile, Jim is restless and aggressive. Inheriting the Luebcke affability but champing under the bit of Walt's lackadaisical attitude toward business, Jim left for San Francisco in order "to build an empire."

Walt and Betty were crestfallen. Knowing they wanted to pass the business along to Jim more than anything else, they realized they would have to grant him autonomy. To lure him back, Walt and Betty told Jim he could have full control of business expansion, and Walt would confine himself to his love—printing.

So after 26 years a business built with the caution of a family budget entered its present expansionist phase. The need was there. Over the past ten years, small printing companies have faced a mounting challenge. Traditionally serving individual customers wanting 100 copies of a letter, the growth of quick-print chains with national advertising, xerography and electrostatic printing has cut dramatically into their market.

Also, small printing companies have always competed against the man with a duplicator in his basement. Having no overhead and business taxes to pay, small offset printing will continue to attract the moonlighter. Further, small printing companies face cutthroat competition from each other. Rather than laying off trained personnel, an ebbing business is usually more than willing to take a job at cost or below.

In Salt Lake City the printing climate is one of non-union shops with a corresponding over-abundance of small printers. Not having to pay union wages, the small printer can run profitably a two-man business and have the satisfaction of calling it his own.

The over-all result is that Salt Lake City is a buyer's market. Shopping for printing is commonplace and usually will pay off. As a side effect, the low wage and profit margins spur Los Angeles and Las Vegas buyers to have their printing done in Salt Lake. It is cheaper to print in Salt Lake and ship than to produce the same product in Southern California.

Besides these particulars there are other overriding problems for small printing companies which are less tangible. To begin with, they are begun by craftsmen rather than businessmen, Walt Luebcke being a case in point. It seems that job printing is the last bastion of the rugged individualist. His hours are his own, and a small printer will work long days at cost to keep the business, his lifeblood, alive. As with most small businesses having frequent contacts with supplier and customer publics, personalities have large impact on success. For Progressive Printing the Luebcke smile has been the vital humor.

But when the quick-print phenomenon hit, Jim realized a smile was not enough. In the early 1970's business seemed to stagnate at the $40,000 gross sales per year level, and the market was slipping.

Progressive had been doing some business with a local savings and loan association. So when the purchasing agent asked Jim if he would buy a used Multilith from their former captive shop, Jim agreed, providing State Savings placed its specialty printing with Progressive.

The rush of new, more complicated work was heady, yet a second crisis developed. The workload was becoming too much. Without new equipment and personnel, Progressive would lose the account. Smoothing out a worried Walt's furrowed brow, Jim decided Progressive had to move dramatically then or not at all.

The aim in expansion was to make Progressive totally independent in production for better job control and efficiency. Before 1973 all typesetting and negative work had to be sent out. Progressive's schedule was dictated by the exigencies of the trade shop. Constant wrangling erupted, and Progressive was forced to pay rush order charges to make its delivery dates for the savings and loan.

The decision to purchase new equipment is an inexorable one for small printing companies as well as large. We are all under the lion's paw. Since the profit margin in the industry as a whole is low, each new piece of technology has a raison d'etre of its own. A vicious circle is drawn. You can't afford the new piece of machinery, but you can't successfully keep your business without it.

So the family business, just paid for, went into debt for a second time. Small beads of perspiration became noticeable on Walt's upper lip. Looking forward to retirement (which for him translates into an eight-hour day), Walt's plans were muddied. Although he subconsciously knew expansion was necessary, he still harbored a small businessman's fear of over-extension. For 26 years Progressive Printing consisted of two Multiliths and a Frankensteinian platemaker, which scratched as many hands as it did plates. Yet in one year the business saw an almost cancerous growth of machinery.

The first step was to construct a complete darkroom facility. The rush charges on negative work done outside were shaving profits. Jim secured a used Miller process camera with a few bugs. Slop in the worm gears meant inexact enlargements and reductions, and the vacuum back was not parallel at all points with the copy board. But Progresssive learned to live with the bugs or constructed Rube Goldberg apparatuses to lessen the errors.

Since specialty printing often calls for large blocks of solids or tints, the Multiliths soon proved to be inadequate for the State Savings account. The next move was to purchase an ATF Profiteer 25″ press. The large number of ink rollers, the ability to handle 133 line screens, and the suitable price made it a logical choice.

After the moving men unloaded the Profiteer, Walt stared at the monolith in quiet awe and vexation. Everyone felt what was running through his mind. "My God! Can we make it work?"

With the purchase of the 25″ press, Progressive had to come to grips with the signature. It soon became obvious Walt's manual paper cutter was a relic. Fatalistically, an automated paper cutter became the next acquisition.

But Progressive still faced the bugaboo of typesetting. It was useless to have a darkroom and a 25″ press languishing for lack of type for the trade shop. It could get by without a headliner, yet too much of its new work was not camera ready. After some investigation it was decided that a Compuwriter Jr. was best suited for Progressive's needs. So Walt picked a few bills and some lint from his proprietary wallet, and a photocomposer became the fourth purchase in 1973.

The next acquisition may seem to be an anachronism. With all this updating of equipment, why would Progressive need a letterpress? But the company still had no numbering, die-cutting, embossing or scoring capability. When Jim stumbled upon an old letterpress for sale from a small weekly newspaper going offset, he grabbed the beast for $200.

With a new stitcher in the bindery and a Baumfolder on order, Progressive now had complete control of production. Yet like the evolutionary tree, each new piece of production technology posed a problem in adaptation. New equipment alone wouldn't solve Progressive's dilemma. Somehow, the company had to make the new machinery work in tandem for utmost efficiency.

Along with the equipment, Progressive began to hire new personnel. For 25 years the business had been run by a three-member family. Since 1972 Progressive has hired five employees—a production manager, an offset pressman, a layout artist and photographer, and two bindery and delivery persons.

But a psychological block for Walt and Betty loomed in 1972 when the company was forced to hire its first outside employee. Walt no longer could handle the workload, and Jim had had it with ink on his hands when his children refused to let him touch them with his blackened fingers.

Two people applied for the job. One was a recent graduate from a technical college, and the other was a long-haired, bearded actor recently discharged from the Army, where he ran a press. Not really wanting to hire anyone, Walt and Betty nixed the long hair and hired the former. When he turned off his press after his first hour on the job and went for coffee, the Luebckes realized they had let culture shock distort their hiring. The actor was called back, and he has been with Progressive ever since. The older Luebckes refused to see it as merely business personnel expansion. Rather, they enlarged their family by one.

The new employee was a hard worker, but only had duplicator experience. Since Progressive was unable to pay the going wages for skilled personnel for the new equipment, it became necessary to retrain extant personnel. Correspondingly, a second problem arose. Besides making the machinery work in tandem, Progressive had to restructure its billing. How could the company charge for its production time and still remain competitive, while paying overtime to those same employees trying to find their way on the new equipment? There were still kinks in the production operation that had to be ironed out.

Mothballing Progressive's proprietorship in 1973 was one measure of self-help. Jim realized the company had to enter the 20th century of business. With incorporation Progressive got a tax break, and more important, better cost analysis. Looking toward the future, Jim incorporated the business under the name "Prog Inc." to allow for later corporate expansion.

Walt couldn't help gazing back over his shoulder. For the first time he had to take a salary. The old days were indeed gone. He too had become an employee of the "sprawling conglomerate."

Incorporation,
Systemization
Have Changed
The Ballgame

Ulcers were never a problem for Walt Luebcke. Of course, the primary years of Progressive Printing had been hectic, but Walt and Betty were younger then and they met the strain with vigor. The only impairment to their constitution was an occasional sore back from sleeping on the shop floor after meeting a wee-hour headline.

But after incorporation and equipment expansion, Walt's feet blossomed with a rosy fungus. The doctor said his condition was due to excess perspiration, more commonly translated as nerves.

The pressure on Walt's feet was understandable. Never before had the business undertaken such a quantum leap. Where would the money for the expanded equipment payments come from? How much could credit be extended?

Progressive and all small printing companies have always labored under a curse. Such businesses usually begin undercapitalized and, as in the case of Progressive, 27 years later the company is still undercapitalized. Business moves on a month-to-month basis. There is no corporate slush fund, and large, overdue accounts can be devastating.

Before incorporation, credit for Progressive Printing was tied to Walt's good name. When the business needed expanding, Walt's home was mortgaged or his personal, real property was pledged as an asset. Since incorporation in 1973, borrowing has been done with the Progressive Printing building and equipment as collateral.

The company purchased its new equipment through dealer financing. Progressive found the interest rates generally favorable, if indeed there is such an animal in today's tight money market.

The primary reason Progressive made use of dealer financing plans was the frequent hassle the company had experienced with the commercial loan system. Jim Luebcke, vice president in charge of ramrodding, became tired of the questioning eye he received every time he presented his case to a commercial loan officer. It seemed he had to continually resell the prospective piece of equipment to every person in the chain of command before he could obtain the loan.

Dealers, on the other hand, are only too aware of a printing company's equipment needs. Bringing the bad news "from Ghent to Aix," they had long been cryers of technological determinism. In their latter-day Darwinian creed, only the strong will survive, and they will be the first to point out that you just cannot make an honest go of it without their new piece of technology.

Besides favorable interest rates, dealers ask only 10 percent down in their financing plans. Progressive found commercial lenders a poor second with their 25-30 percent initial cash payment.

Progressive has sought capital borrowing only during tax time on 60-day notes for a few thousand dollars on signature. No assets have been pledged. The company was never borrowed for long-term financing capital. Although Jim is aware of the potential corporate advantages, the vagaries of an inflationary economy and a professed lack of borrowing acumen have made Progressive leery of long-term loans.

Investment credit has been another perplexing phenomenon since incorporation. Progressive can claim a $200 depreciation on its $814 per month machinery payments, but investment credit really does not allow for the planned obsolescence inherent in the printing industry's technology. The one-time investment credit granted by the federal government for the actual purchase of the piece of machinery is insufficient. To make matters even more aggravating, the state of Utah disallows any investment credit whatsoever in its corporate tax schedule.

Yet, on the whole, incorporation has been a positive factor for the company. It has forced a detailed itemizing of costs and the establishment of a break-even point in production. For the first time in 27 years, Progressive has a cost accounting system. Under the previous proprietorship, it did not seem necessary, as Walt would simply take home whatever was left over at the end of the month.

The over-all effect of cost accounting has been flexible planning, and as a corollary, better estimating in bids. Progressive now finds itself being awarded more bids than before incorporation.

The problem of slack time, a common malady in the printing industry, also has eased somewhat. Confident of its bidding procedures, Progressive has actively solicited municipal bids to buffer the production operation. Such work generally is not tied to strict delivery dates and lead schedules, and the profit margin is acceptable, provided that everything follows the initial plan.

Yet incorporation has not been a panacea for Progressive Printing. In spite of the new cost accounting system, the company desperately needs more enlightened accounting procedures. In this regard Walt's bookkeeper of 27 years can no longer help. To up the profit margin, the business could use the services of a specialized CPA firm aware of the printing industry's peculiarities.

In December of 1973, Progressive's net profit margin hovered at the 1-percent level, and had become a bone of contention between Walt and Jim. Jim maintained the figure was misleading. Although a 1 percent profit margin is not an auspicious beginning for an "empire," since 1972-73 the company coffers had provided for four new employees taking home $25,000 a year plus raises and over $50,000 worth of new equipment. Jim felt it was indeed laudable to put that much profit back into the business and still have a 1 percent profit margin, considering the tumultuousness of the year. He even could have reminded Walt that the federal government views equipment payments as taxable income, but what son would rub salt into his father's perspiration-saturated, reddened feet.

Walt took another tack. He admitted gross sales had burgeoned. In 1970 and '71, sales were stagnating at the $42,000-per-year mark. When

Progressive hired its first new employee in 1972, the figure jumped to $60,000. With incorporation and two more employees in 1973, sales were up 37 percent to $82,000. With the final returns still out, gross sales for 1974 should top $130,000.

Yet for all Progressive's apparent success, Walt asked if its owners were any happier or wealthier. Inflation accounted for some portion of the skyrocketing gross sales. Moreover, they still could not go home at 5:30. They still were paying overtime to employees finding their way on the new equipment. They still were not efficient enough to justify an increase in their billing rates. Somewhere the operation needed tightening.

Walt's observations struck a chord in Jim. Indeed, increased sales and new equipment were not enough. It is easy to compliment oneself on dramatically hiked volume, but unless productivity rises correspondingly, a company's new equipment is not being utilized to its fullest advantage. Wiping its brow while running in place, Progressive had a basic lack of production management expertise.

With this in mind, Jim began looking for help. In January of 1974 Progressive hired its fifth new employee, the disgruntled production manager of a printing company in Salt Lake City having sales of more than $500,000.

A pragmatic, dollars and cents man with more than 12 years experience building his own and other people's printing businesses, Al Lancaster quickly sensed Progressive's problem. The company lacked a systems approach to production. Tackling the situation with tactical zeal, Progressive's new production manager began turning the Mom-and-Pop shop into a printing company.

To begin with, Al revamped the billing method. Beforehand, billing had been tied to Walt's memory. For one excruciating week of penance at the end of each month, Walt had to sit down and try and recount the sins and omissions of the billing period. It was not uncommon to receive a late-hour call from a weary Walt asking, "Do you happen to remember how much time you spent in pasteup on this job?"

As sales shot upward, the old billing method proved woefully inadequate. In its place Al instituted unitized time keeping under departmentalized production. An hour was broken into twelve six-minute increments. For the first time in the company's 27-year history, Progressive Printing bought a clock.

Besides facilitating billing, Al's system of unitized time keeping also revealed a few glaring errors in previously unbilled time. In the past Walt had never charged to the minute for the time it took to cut paper, thinking it was inconsequential. Under the new system, Progressive found the company spent an average of ten hours a week at the cutter.

The departmentalization of production has worked, but only up to a point. In a small printing company, there still has to be some slop in operations. People become ill or go on vacation. A small shop operation is one where people must work in close harmony, not just departments. Inevitably in a printing company with relatively low volume, not all departments will have an equal workload. Some days a person has to cross departmental lines, and ideally, production should not suffer. the philosophy of "it's not my job, man" simply will not work.

A comprehensive job numbering system was the second addition in the systems approach. Al keyed the entire production process to one number. When an order is taken, the information is typed simultaneously on a job packet, production sheet and delivery receipt. In turn, the job jacket physically moves with the work through each of the departments, the production sheet goes to Jim for paper and ink ordering, and the delivery receipt is placed in the bindery for final clearance.

The job jacket and production sheet system has helped Progressive alleviate one of its major bugaboos, mistakes, by cutting down communication errors. Under the new system, the profit margin has inched to a solid 2 percent and continues to move upwards.

There is no longer any question on materials costs. Utilizing job numbers, Progressive has instituted an automatic charge-back system with its suppliers. If the company has not yet received an invoice, a call to the paper or chemical distributor results in a quick itemizing of materials costs for a particular job.

As a final benefit, job numbering has been a tremendous help in filing. Reruns no longer need to become lost in molding boxes in the basement. Old plates are found quickly and cranked onto the press without any loss in production time. Hide-and-seek is a necessary casualty in growing up.

Inevitably, the systems approach to production leads to a weekly time card synopsis. The results will often be disheartening, but without the feedback of hard facts and figures for use as tools, the systems approach is worthless. It would be like trying to tune a watch with a wrench.

Since the advent of unitized time keeping, Progressive found that 67 percent of its production time is billable. This amounts to an average cost per hour of doing business of $15.55, including both salaried and hourly personnel. More important, Progressive's weekly time card synopsis has revealed some previously hidden deficiencies in the production operation.

The 25″ press, potentially the company's biggest money-maker, is not being used to full capacity. At a billing rate of $20 per hour, the Chief must run for 15 hours a month just to cover its payments. Currently, the press operates an average of 11 hours per week. Correspondingly, Progressive has been forced to change its marketing techniques. The company must sell even more specialty printing, since that is meat and potatoes for the Chief.

The Compuwriter Jr. has been a monetary success. Billed at $16 per hour, the machine more than pays for itself. Its only drawback is its font library. Progressive has only three type styles and five point sizes. Any time a job needs a point size other than what the company can offer directly off the machine, the company must make PMT's in the darkroom and absorb the cost in time and materials.

Oddly enough, Progressive's anachronistic letterpress has been the star of the show. Since it was purchased for $200 in cash, any work done on the machine is cream. Moreover, the company no longer need run business cards and invitations on the Multiliths, a job for which they are woefully inefficient. The only problem with the letterpress is "how ya gonna keep 'em down on the farm" after they've worked on the Chief.

In the darkroom, Progressive has saved money by bottling chemicals. For uncomplicated exposures the company uses Kodaline film with Supermatic 55 developer because it can be stored and reused. For tricky camera work, the company uses conventional Gevaert chemistry. However, the chemicals are lost after a few hours in the open air.

For plates and negatives some developing systems are interchangeable, but often the results suffer. Progressive found it is best to find one system and stick with it, then take enough lead time in reordering to prevent having to switch to a new, temporary system while former chemicals are "momentarily unavailable."

Maddeningly, there is an eternal triangle in the systems approach to production. As one department becomes efficient and a profit-maker, another begins to ache. The process starts anew. More equipment has to be purchased, the system must be recoordinated, and new cost control procedures need to be instituted. So, like Progressive Printing, take some salt tablets, apply a fungicidal, and damn the perspiration, full speed ahead.

Image Building, Marketeering

Progressive Printing's location on Salt Lake City's west side was once labeled "across the tracks." All too often, Walt and Betty Luebcke had to relocate slumbering drunks sprawled at the foot of the door in order to open the shop.

Now, central Salt Lake City is going through a redevelopment boom. Increased convention traffic is spawning the construction of hotels in the Progressive Printing locale. New office-building/hotel hybrids dwarf the fading, circa-1900 building that houses the Luebcke business. The winos are moving further west, but as they emigrate, Progressive's property assessments reflect their departure. Rumors become rampant. There is talk of a liquor store or another hotel, and Progressive begins to fear the encroachment of urban redevelopment and eminent domain. Like most small printing companies, Progressive has little in excess funds to spruce up the building. So for the time being, the company's exterior will have to remain looking as though the occupants left with the last invasion of crickets.

The building's interior, on the other hand, has undergone substantial change. As part of the systems approach to production, Progressive analyzed the company's work-flow. Frederick Taylor's theories on the economy of motion underscore the fact that the shortest distance between two points is still a straight line. Under the tutelage of Progressive's new production manager, the company has been moving machinery and departments to facilitate logistics.

But Progressive is quickly facing a problem of space and structural limitations. The new folder on order cannot operate in a vacuum, yet one can tear down only so many walls in a turn-of-the-century building before the rest come crashing in. Walt is afraid Progressive may mistakenly institute a new dimension in the industry—the first open-air, drive-through printing company. To make matters worse, OSHA poses as still another drain on the already stretched capital improvement budget.

Yet house maintenance has never been a major capital outflow for Progressive Printing. During its period of growth pains, the company has utilized its own personnel. When a darkroom needs constructing, or the building cries for paint, or machinery falls into disrepair, resources have had to be found within the company. In a very real sense, the family business still relies on its "sons."

For instance, the wiring for the darkroom and process camera cost a mere $5.50. Flashing the Luebcke smile, Jim wheedled his father-in-law, an electrical engineer, into doing the job for a bottle of tequila, but not in advance. One must be business-like, you know. If the printing end ever falls, Progressive could always be successful in the salvage business. Outside of the new machinery, there are few office fixtures or secondary pieces of equipment remaining in their congenital state. Sometimes the physical deficiencies go beyond the laughable stage. The electrical wiring of the former tater-dog factory that is now Progressive Printing certainly does not complement a modern printing company. Too often, operations have to be staggered so certain machines will not have to run on the same circuit at the same time.

But the physical problems Progressive faces are minor compared to the rapidly changing market. The company found it could count on its old customers. They come to Progressive for the personal service and printing quality, and the fading paint, chipping mortar and other stresses and strains do not bother them. Yet the old market remains just that—old. The jobs have not changed in years. The notepads and 500 copies of a letter simply will not feed the jaws of five extra employees and $50,000 worth of equipment.

The essenial problem for Progressive, and any small printing company specializing for the market, is how to marshal its new, expanded forces to do battle with the printing Goliaths while still protecting its over-extended neck.

One measure of self-help Progressive found both inexpensive and fruitful was a forms facelift. Realizing it was a printing company without any printing of its own, Progressive decided there is no faster way to become a modern printing business with design in mind than to create that self image oneself.

In updating its letterhead, envelopes and invoices, the company tried to adopt a style in keeping with the connotations of "progressive." The task almost resulted in a company trauma. Not since 1953, when Walt and Betty paid an artist $50 to wipe some paint and letters on a piece of paper, had Progressive applied any external cosmetics. Everyone in the shop had to have his say. Any "I'm-not-sure's" resulted in another design. The entire weight of the newly expanded Progressive Printing seemed to rest on the letterhead. A good foundation was paramount, and because it was their signature, it had to be perfect.

Finally, everyone agreed on Blippo Bold for the type style, since the characters have a rolling, moving quality emblematic of a printing press.

Hoping to educate its public with the printing process, the company also designed a logotype graphically symbolizing copy preparation, photography, printing and binding.

Customer response was heady. Comments typically ran, "It's almost a pleasure to pay a bill so decoratively presented." Of immeasurable worth, the Progressive Printing correspondence design stays in customer minds and generates more sales subconsciously, even if it does not prompt faster payment.

But the real trick in market specialization is to generate sales consciously through a well researched, planned attack. For a small printing company, this can be a perplexing problem. Progressive's new production data indicated it had to find new job work in order to make its 25" press more profitable. Job quantities also had to be upped. Where once the company was pleased with an order for 1,000 copies, now it had to seek jobs calling for 10,000 or more.

Upon entering a new market, the ideal is to have an aggressive sales force with icy nerves who are not afraid of suffering numb knuckles from rapping on cold-call doors. In Progressive's case, it had Jim. Not being able to afford a full-time salesman, and unable to find one who would work on commission, Jim was forced to add still another hat to the top of his already teetering load.

The result was unsatisfactory. Jim, who did not have the time to blindly ferret out new business, merely wound up retrieving work from existing accounts. The 25" press still remained dormant two days a week. In turn, Progressive had to fall back on other less palpable resources in its attempt at market specialization.

Walt's watchwords and the cornerstone of his business for 27 years have been "quality and service." Because he has refused to compromise that slogan, Progressive has had an edge in CPA printing in Salt Lake City. Granting its limitations, the company felt it should use that same approach in its endeavor to broaden its market.

Borrowing on his experience with the savings and loan account, Jim pinpointed a few types of businesses using a good deal of specialty printing, especially direct-mail advertising. As it turned out, the hours spent waiting in the outer sanctums of bank and hotel purchasing agents and advertising agency production managers was time well spent.

Quality and service from a company in business since 1947 is still a salable commodity and functions independently of size. Leaving four-color work to the Goliaths, Progressive has managed to get its foot in the door of specialty printing to the point where the company now needs a man working full-time on the 25" press rather than commuting between it and the Multiliths.

But Progressive's move into specialty printing fostered a set of problems the company had never before experienced. Advertising agencies were a new breed of customer. Although pleased with Progressive's quality, they are insensitive to any schedules other than their own. Trying to satisfy its expanded market, Progressive began working weekends to meet Monday morning deadlines after 5:00 p.m. Friday dropoffs. Unfortunately, Progressive's entry into specialty printing also coincided with the paper shortage, and advertising agencies are becoming notorious for specifying paper stocks with the availability of papyrus and currency rag.

For the first time, Progressive faced problems in ordering and lead-time that were compounded by budget and space limitations disallowing inventory stockpiling. Jim began spending a major portion of his days on the phone ordering bits and pieces from one paper house and then another in order to have enough for the eventual run. To prevent further head-aches, Jim found it was to Progressive's and the advertising agencies' advantage for him to communicate constant feedback on paper availability.

Walt did not have much to say. Again, he could not help looking backward. The euphoric days of 20# bond had slipped away forever. Feeling like a displaced person, Walt also had to remain mute while he watched another old friend being laid to rest. Using the shield of general housecleaning and logistics for protection. Al committed what amounted to a venial sin in Walt's eyes when he said Walt's setups would have to go. But Walt Luebcke refused to take part in that mayhem and quietly retired to the front office while the company scavengers plundered his nest.

From the vantage point of hindsight, it is evident people are the crucial intangible in the success of any small printing company. Without that special mixture of talent and personality, the violent wrenching of a previously sheltered business to meet a new market would end in gross over-extension and inevitable failure.

Walt and Jim Luebcke have always maintained that business should be more than profit alone. There has been no time-clock syndrome at Progressive Printing. In its place is a mutual respect for the company and its employees. Consequently, personnel turnover during expansion has been nil, and Progressive has been able to attract new, skilled people to its climate despite lower initial wages. Because of this, the company has developed a good rapport with its suppliers to the point where it has had the same paper and chemical salesmen for the past ten to 20 years. These salesmen have not become wealthy with the Progressive account, yet they still come every week, always with doughnuts, largely for the sake of friendship and perhaps a little business.

During hard times, suppliers have carried Progressive for 120 days. They will tolerate the company's odd-lot orders, a service critical for small printing companies, and give pricing breaks when they possibly can. Progressive, in turn, reciprocates by concentrating its purchasing. Provided that the customer is not unduly cost-conscious, Progressive will not necessarily shop for the lowest price.

Usually, this "high finance" takes place in the lunch room, the point from which all life radiates at Progressive Printing. There the salesmen find peace in their schedule, and employees iron out the production operations for the day.

The Wrap-up;
The Vision

One national quick-print chain has borrowed the familiar profile of America's premier printer for instant tradition. Another tolls the public bell incessantly over the radiowaves with a voice that could shatter glass, exhorting it to have its printing done while it waits. Hampered by budgets unable to absorb the cost of similar advertising, many small printing companies have been easy prey in competition for the quick-print dollar. The Mom-and-Pop shop has been dealt a diktat—either change your market or suffer a dwindling business.

Progressive Printing sensed the trend and made its move into specialty printing. Walt and Jim Luebcke briefly pondered the idea of advertising, but a look into the company coffers halted that speculation. Still, the company had a problem. How could it get the new, expanded image of Progressive Printing before the public?

Instead of advertising, Progressive is developing a public relations approach. The anticipated returns probably will not pay off until the distant future, but a PR program falls within the realm and resources of any small printing company.

Progressive's first attempt at public relations could be better termed as an exercise in avoiding disgruntled customers. To its detriment, the printing industry has failed to educate the public. Because the only common knowledge of printing is the mimeograph, printers will continue to hear the everyday complaint, "Why does it cost so much?"

Since small printers tend to deal more with individuals on a limited budget than with large corporations, rising printing costs can have a drastic effect on their market by forcing more potential customers to scurry to the waiting arms of instant printing chains. Copy which is not camera-ready further compounds the problem. Since the initial art costs can be high, the estimated bid can needlessly frighten away the customer, and the more profitable rerun for the client and printer alike is lost.

Faced with this predicament, Progressive is designing a copy preparation booklet. In addition, this brochure will explain the modern offset printing process to the public, as well as the paper and petrochemical shortages and their maniacal brother-in-law, cost-push inflation.

To help customers, especially advertising agencies, plan their product better, they should be made aware of what they can expect from the paper industry in terms of prices, variety and availability. Because distributors will stockpile only high turnover varieties, Progressive's booklet will ask customers to plan for substantial lead time when specifying specialty papers.

Notepads and desk blotters, perennial favorites for printing companies, will be another complimentary come on in Progressive's public relations program. The company intends to screen the Progressive logo at the bottom of each note sheet. The advantage to this is that its name will be spread with the geometric progression of paper shuffling.

It is a cliche these days that business runs on paper. But the smart printing company can use this phenomenon to other advantages besides the obvious ones.

Because better management often demands standardization, Progressive is devising a query letter to its customers. In the questionnaire, Progressive's clients will be asked for their views on standardizing their job ordering. If they agree, this would help both Progressive and its customers by easing the problem of paper ordering and inventory control. The company would also like its clients to order longer runs as a hedge against future paper unavailability. Positive responses from the query letter to these two questions could someday lead to the use of a computer, but don't tell Walt. His feet are still sensitive.

Unless printing companies want to suffer the same wrath the public bestowed upon gas stations during the energy crisis, they will have to deal with the paper shortage more conscientiously. The shortage is a problem, yet the enterprising printing company could mold it into a public and corporate benefit. The public's desire to recycle is a fertile public relations target. Too often, communities want to recycle paper but do not know where to deposit their old magazines and newspapers. A recycling dumpster placed prominently in front of a printing company is bound to attract public good will. A coordinated effort by small printing companies would lessen the expense of pick up. Progressive does not have a recycling dumpster for the public yet. Because of its Skid Row neighbors, the company is afraid the only paper the bin would attract would be liquor bottle labels, although winos have never been accused of tidiness. But with the current price of glass, that also could be a profitable venture.

Basically, the problem presented by its building and its exterior confounds Progressive's management. The company's business demands a location in downtown Salt Lake City, yet Progressive will soon overflow its walls and spill out onto the street.

Rather than moving to an industrial park far from its clients, Progressive is considering buying the vacant lot next door. Although land in downtown Salt Lake City is at a premium, the cost would be worth it in the long run. Again with public relations in mind, Progressive hopes to adopt a green belt concept. By tearing down the old building and constructing a new one on two lots, Progressive could utilize the existing trees to its benefit by becoming a verdant focal point in a growing, concretized Salt Lake City. A company open house, in turn, would help advertise Progressive's concern for proper urban planning.

With the addition of a few key persons, a small printing company could move into the broader field of print advertising. Progressive is slowly developing an in-house design service. Because the company now has complete production facilities, it can offer a total print package, especially for direct mail advertisers. In turn, economy is passed along to the customer through job control and deletion of the advertising agency middleman.

The main problem for Progressive is the potential conflict with its primary customers, advertising agencies, who supply the butter work for the 25″ press. Yet a canvass of Progressive's agency clients revealed most would welcome such a service and even make referrals. Too often, advertising agencies do not have the manpower to represent adequately the small businessman who only needs a small print campaign. Their strength is their ability to handle a complete media approach.

The rise of "associationism" in America also merits consideration. With a design service and a facile copywriter, a small printing company could enter the publishing business. Small association executive secretaries often do not have the time or expertise to put out a monthly newsletter and could become a potential customer for the printer who can offer the complete service. Rather than wringing his hands, the small printer could be making his size work for him. The key terms in his rise from the ashes should be "management by objective."

Although the company was relatively unaware of what it was doing, Progressive's expansion program was an exercise in management by objective. First, the company realized it had to alter its market. To do so, it needed more equipment and personnel. But the new, bulging muscles on the former scarecrow contracted at different times and worked against one another. So Progressive was forced to pursue a second objective—a systemization of work flow and costs.

Coupled with incorporation, the systems approach to production allowed management better control over its costs and scheduling. By unitizing time under departments, Progressive was able to pinpoint its softspots, and a diagnosis of the problem is the essential first step in any recovery process.

Now the production operation was geared to push work through the back door economically, but the new efficiencies demanded even more food. The company relying upon a few, large accounts for its bill of fare is one step from the tar pits. Good business health allowing for steady growth calls for a diet of varied, uninterrupted work, and Progressive realized it had to peddle its product better. Correspondingly, the company assembled its strengths and devised an attack designed to meet its third objective— marketing.

If at all possible, a company should formulate its management objectives in a calm climate where deliberate, informed action can be taken before problems arise. Progressive Printing was forced into many of its decisions. Rather than considering the entire formula, Progressive kept adding and deleting fundamental parts hoping to come up with a compound which would serve as a catalyst for reaction and new energies.

The production operation at Progressive now runs with relative ease, and the lunchroom can still serve as switchboard for the company's communication needs. But there will come a time at Progressive when the employees cannot all group together around the lunch table in the morning for coffee and cigarettes. When that happens, Progressive Printing will have a real problem. It will no longer be Progressive Printing as it is now known. It will have become a large printing company with the inherent dampener of personnel anonymity.

Hopefully, the basic strength of Progressive Printing will always be the Luebcke family. As long as Walt, Betty and Jim are around, the company will retain its warm core. Every printing company, not just a small one, needs a Betty Luebcke, who never forgets employee birthdays, and who buys cigarette lighters for the entire crew when they keep running out of matches. A Walt and Jim Luebcke would be invaluable assets for any small printing company. The complementary fusion of their two personalities is critical for Progressive—the conscientious business conservatism of Walt working in harmony with the bulldozing energy of Jim.

This, then, has been the story-to-date of the Luebckes and their enterprise. It shares the classic elements of all the tens of thousands of its printing peers across America—their problems, their strengths, their forebodings, their underlying confidence in the soundness of their craft and of entrepreneurial independence.

Progressive Printing
244 West Fourth, South
Salt Lake City, Uath 84101

186

Anyplant Printing Company *

This is a true story. The names and dates have been altered to protect sources of information. We are publishing it to make our readers aware that without financial controls the best printer, businessman, creative or professional manager will fall flat on his face.—The Editors

Too Much, Too Fast, Too Soon.

Alexander Jacobs toyed with the pencil in his apron as he listened to the complaint over the telephone.

"You'll get the job tomorrow," he said soothingly. "I'm sorry you can't have it today, they didn't deliver the paper on time."

The phone clicked indignantly. Alexander remained standing at the window, watching the snarled traffic in lower Manhattan. Then he looked at his cluttered desk. He realized he wasn't keeping up with things. He was getting old.

It was 1956 already, his 30th year in business. Back in the shop the presses were humming and the linotypes were clicking. With 12 employees the Anyplant Printing Co. was doing an annual gross of $250,000 and making a comfortable profit. Maybe he should have felt satisfied. How many printers had done so well?

But he felt he had failed. He had failed because he had never learned to do things in a big way, the way young people learn to do. Like his son, Benjamin, who had a degree in business administration. Benjamin always spoke of millions. And when Benjamin came back from the army, he insisted that the millions could be had for the asking.

"Pop," he said affectionately, "as a supply officer I learned a few things in the army. Every piece of hardware, from a mortar to a missile, has to have an instruction manual. That means millions of manuals. Somebody has to print those manuals. Why don't you?"

The old man scratches his head. "I don't know. After 30 years . . ."

"You're in a rut, Pop. Why don't you just sit back, take it easy, and let me and my buddy put some new blood into the business?"

"Buddy?"

"Joe Green, Pop. We were roommates in college. And in the army we

*Ficitious

were supply officers. We've learned a bit about the manuals. And we've got the contacts."

The old man shrugged. Who was he to argue? What had he done in 30 years? Did he ever make a million?

And so he handed the management over to Benjamin and Joe. He liked both of the boys. They had pep. They had intelligence. And they had the guts to fight for the big orders, even in the Pentagon.

And when Joe became one of the family by marrying a daughter, the old man rented a tuxedo, drank champagne, and danced with the brides-maids. It was good to have a family business.

Things were really humming at the Anyplant Printing Company. The young blood was reaching for millions.

"Hey," the old man would sometimes say. "Not so fast . . ."

But the kids only laughed. They wore snappy clothes, drove sporty cars, and spent a lot of time on their boats. But they brought in the business.

When they had landed the first big contract to produce government manuals, the old man shook his head.

"It's too big for us to handle," he protested. "We haven't the equipment."

But the young men knew the science of subcontracting. With the help of another print shop, a bindery, and a paper house, they produced the big job on schedule. The next step, of course, was to buy more equipment, add a second shift, and move into a plant that was better designed for efficient printing production. With their own bindery, art section, and an enlarged composing room, they were now able to produce the big jobs themselves.

At this time there was a major change in the technical publications field. The government's prime contractors became increasingly responsible for furnishing printed matter with the hardware they supplied. To sell a bazooka to the government the manufacturer had to furnish a manual on how to handle the bazooka. The manufacturer, as a rule, knew how to produce a bazooka, but not how to produce a manual. So he dumped the entire problem into the lap of a printer.

The young men of the Anyplant Printing Company saw a new opportunity in this situation. They assembled a group of free-lance writers who would write the manuals. They called the new company the Anyplant Writing Service. Now they did the complete job, from the writing to the delivery.

The branching off into a writing service presented a problem. Up to now all the efforts of the young men had been to keep the presses rolling. Now they had to keep the writers busy. So they had to solicit work for the writers.

To handle these writers a three-man staff of executives was recruited. These men demanded plush offices, glamorous secretaries, and generous expense accounts. And they wanted to run things their own way. An increase in writing volume made it advisable to absorb a technical writing house with offices in Washington, D.C.

Old Man Jacobs shook his head. "But we're in the printing business, not the writing business."

His son smiled tolerantly. "We are growing upward, Pop. We are controlling the printed product from the writing through the delivery. We do it all now, art work, binding, everything. This is called vertical integration."

The old man shrugged. "Vertical integration? In my 30 years of business I never heard of such a thing."

"You never saw the kind of millions we'll be making. See, Pop, it works this way. The writing service is not for us alone. It's for all kinds of other clients. And when these writers finish their pamphlets, financial reports, books, and other things, who do you think is going to do the printing? We are. The Anyplant Writing Company will bring a lot of business to the Anyplant Printing Company. The two companies will work hand in hand. That's what we call horizontal integration."

"Horizontal integration?"

"The spreading out into other related fields. It all means more business. Eventually we'll become a giant in the communications industry. There's millions in it, Pop."

Up to now the Anyplant Printing Company had been operating with a small sales staff. The commercial printing department kept growing of its own momentum. And the technical publication department, which had been growing so rapidly, needed only a few contacts, principally with the government. The expansion of this department, however, to include all kinds of technical manuals made it necessary to open sales offices in other cities and to hire platoons of salesmen.

Old Man Alexander Jacobs had no reason for objecting. His young partners were really showing him how to run a business. They were making more money than he had ever dreamed of making.

When they took over the management in 1956, the 30-year-old business grossed $250,000 annually. A mere two years later, in 1958, gross sales approached one million dollars.

A million dollars?

The old man, scratching his head, went to look through the window as he always did when he had problems. He no longer saw the traffic snarl of lower Manhattan. Now that the plant had moved to a comfortable place in the Bronx, he saw green lilac bushes and a lawn. His desk was no longer cluttered with unanswered mail. A charming young secretary took care of such things. And he even had orange drapes at the windows. Mod orange, they called it. Imagine an old man like him with mod orange drapes.

Well, the young men knew what they were doing. As for himself, he didn't need fancy boats and racing cars and an expensive home on Long Island. Over the weekend he might do some fishing from a rowboat.

Onward and Upward   Bringing annual sales up to a million dollars seemed to be a tremendous accomplishment to old man Alexander Jacobs. But to his young partners it was just the beginning.

"The sky's the limit," said Joe Green, his son-in-law. "Nothing can stop us now."

Benjamin, the old man's son, laughed. "Right!" he agreed. "Let's aim for a hundred million."

The senior partner took off his glasses and rubbed his eyes. "A hun-dred mil-li-on?" he asked incredulously.

"Why not?" the boys asked in unison. "Pop, why not?"

The sales snowball was gathering momentum, getting larger every day. Because some of the sales offices, like the one in Pittsburgh, generated such a large amount of work, it became advisable to build a printing plant around it. This satellite offered a full range of composition, art, and printing. The writing was still done only in Washington and New York.

In the early 1960s the partners had a unique operation. On the one hand, they had a lot of cameramen, strippers, platemakers, etc., because technical publications usually had short runs. On the other hand, they had big presses for commercial work. If they got a rush order for a large volume of technical publications they could rely on their big presses. If they got a commercial order requiring a lot of camera work, stripping, and platemaking, they also had the facilities to handle it. Because of this balance, they had an advantage over both the tech house and the commercial printer.

Meanwhile, the young partners insisted on going public. The old man objected.

"I like a family business," he said. "And it's making a good buck. Why should we sell stock to strangers?"

"Because that's the modern way of doing business," Benjamin explained impatiently. "It's the way to get more money for expansion. And its the way to . . ."

The old man nodded. "I know. It's the way to settle the estate when I die." He had no more objections.

As a rule, print shops do not have too much public appeal on the stock market. Their investment in equipment is relatively too great for their annual gross. But the stock of Anyplant Inc., had romantic appeal because the company was branching off into many fields of communication.

In the middle of 1961 the stock was floated at 15. It went up to 27 by the end of the year, then leveled off to 16 early in 1962. It had about 1,500 stockholders, with the two young men, Benjamin Alexander and Joe Green, owning about 62 percent of the stock.

The company was doing exceedingly well, with a pre-tax profit of 20 percent. It became very strong financially as the management kept reinvesting in the firm.

Sometimes, however, they wished they had remained a family business. The stockholders were not satisfied with a slow, steady growth. They wanted to make a lot of money fast. They exerted a pressure which distorted the vision of management.

As Old Man Jacobs pointed out, "If we had remained a family business, we wouldn't be doing all these complicated things."

The stockholders really had nothing to complain about. Things were humming along beautifully. In the fiscal year ended February 28, 1962, sales hit a record of $7 million, a $2 million increase over the previous year. Net income after taxes rose from $400,500 to $600,000. The main printing plant in the Bronx had expanded considerably and the satellite in Pittsburgh had grown.

Six months later a Navy contract led to the opening of a plant in San Diego, Calif. That same year another plant was established in Cleveland. In addition, a color separation operation was organized and fully equipped in San Juan, Puerto Rico.

A subsidiary was set up to publish and market industrial publications. Furthermore, the corporation began producing about 1.5 million cassettes. But, almost as a portent of things to come, the company experienced its first loss.

By February, 1963, sales had dropped to $5.6 million, and a net loss of nearly $300,000 ($500,000 before taxes) resulted. The reasons given were these:

1. A former customer became one of the largest competitors.

2. An unexpected change in a large government contract resulted in a loss at the Washington, D.C., operation.

3. The San Diego plant's largest customer lost its government contract. Furthermore, its personnel was not as efficient as had been expected.

However, after this temporary setback, the corporation soon regained its sales and profit momentum. By the end of the next fiscal year, 1964, earnings had accelerated to 32 cents per share on sales of over $6 million.

The improvement was partially due to discontinuing the unprofitable technical writing group in New York, and to relocating the Washington operation to a larger plant in Virginia. Also during that year, the company landed a $1.2 million government composition and printing contract and began expanding its technical sales coverage by retaining representatives in Los Angeles, St. Louis, and Minneapolis. Technical publications were contributing 65 to 70 percent of the business.

Between 1964 and 1965, gross sales jumped another million to $7 million, but net income fell from $283,000 to $200,000. The decline in earnings was attributed to the market testing of an automatic tape repeater and to the relocation of the struggling San Diego plant to San Jose, Calif. There were two cheerful notes in the report that year. The color separation plant was profitable, and the employees had voted to defeat another attempt to unionize the company. At that time, in the mid-sixties, Anyplant, Inc., was employing 400 persons, including a full-time sales force of 32.

A year later sales were up to $8 million, with a net income of $412,000.

A prominent Eastern newspaper reported the company as having "six plants, 12 sales offices, and 485 employees." Its business was described as follows:

"... offers a total graphics portfolio of services, including art, photographic, cold composition, sheet and webfed offset, binding, motion pictures, and audio-visual devices. The company also provides technical writers, editors, temporary engineering and clerical help."

As the months passed, Anyplant, Inc., acquired three new companies—a book publishing house, a magazine in Arizona, and a public relations agency. It also developed a program for franchising quick printing shops throughout the country. They would be called Anyplant Rapid Copy Centers. There was a ground-breaking ceremony for a huge plant in New York and an announcement to found an Academy of Total Communications. The fiscal year ended on a happy note with sales of $10 million and a net income of $475,000.

The moving of the New York operations into the new 142,000 sq. ft. Bronx plant marked the third and final stage of the company's evolution as a total communications conglomerate. The first stage was entering the technical publications field, the second was going public, and the third was this huge plant capable of handling a tremendous volume.

As Benjamin explained it, "We had been subcontracting several hundred thousand dollars' worth of webwork annually. We felt we needed two web presses instead of only one. So we bought the other press in order to keep the business under our own roof. Our analytical projection led us to add a few extra sheetfed presses, an automated saddle-stitching line, and a perfect binding line."

To keep the big plant operating at maximum efficiency, the management reached out farther into horizontal diversification. A consumer magazine was launched, and then a magazine for teenagers. A division was created for the manufacture of point-of-purchase displays.

The franchising of quick printing shops seemed to be a good idea at the time.

"We had developed a technique," Benjamin said, "of teaching a beginner how to run a small shop. We'd teach him how to operate the direct image plate. He didn't have to be a craftsman. We told him that if he ran into a job too big for him to handle, he should farm it out to us. Thus every one of these printers, scattered throughout the country, would really be a salesman for us."

Old Alexander Jacobs, the father of Benjamin, no longer exerted his conservative influence. He let the boys have their way. One or two members of the board of directors objected to the headlong expansion, but they were overruled. Unlimited growth was the motto of the conglomerate.

By the time the annual report for fiscal 1968 came out the corporation had set up four divisions in its huge New York plant. They were:

1. The Marketing and Manufacturing Division with four web presses, six sheetfed presses and two automated bindery lines.

2. The Publications Division, which was publishing 100 specialized magazines.

3. The Consumer Products Division, which sold stereo players, popular records for a young audience, point-of-purchase displays, and motion pictures.

4. The Franchise Division, which promoted franchises for the Anyplant Rapid Copy Centers and for magazines.

Gross sales registered $11 million in fiscal 1968, a million higher than the previous year. But there was a net loss of $179,000. It was attributed to plant expansion and to "the development of new product lines and sources." After a three-for-one stock split, the per share net loss was reported as 14 cents.

The expansion continued. Two million dollars was poured into the plant itself, adding efficiency to the shop and elegance to the offices. The Consumer Products Division added three new audio units. The Publishing Division was granted copyrights to a 10-volume library on women's liberation. The Franchise Division planned programs for the copy centers and for a new sex magazine.

"We had assumed," said Benjamin, "that these new product lines would bring in profitable business. But we were wrong. We should have restricted ourselves to commercial and technical printing. That's where we were making money. These new ventures were merely siphoning off the profits. We would have been better off without them."

Disaster Strikes

The expansion of Anyplant Printing Co. into a total communications conglomerate created many problems. It was difficult to find the personnel capable of managing the various offshoots of the business. When the company had concentrated on printing, it had been doing something that its people understood. The father had been in the printing business for 30 years. Benjamin, the son, and Joe Green, the son-in-law, had been successful in expanding the printing business. Up to that point, all three men knew what they were doing.

But when they expanded into other fields they had to hire executives trained in those fields, and had to rely on their judgments. These men frequently wanted to do things their own way, even though their methods may have created a financial drain on the rest of the corporation.

Fiscal 1969 was another loss year for Anyplant, Inc. Although gross sales increased $3 million to $14 million, losses also increased by $50,000 to exceed $200,000. These six reasons were given for the loss:

1. Over-capacity—still not enough work to keep the machinery going.

2. A 28 percent increase in employment, bringing the total number of employees to 920.

3. Manufacturing costs still too high for the volume of sales.

4. Research and development costs of new electronic products.

5. Cost to develop the concept of subsidized publishing of magazines for national trade and professional associations.

6. Expense of administrative and sales teams to develop nationwide network of copy centers.

By the end of July of 1969, however, it seemed that the startup costs of the previous two years had been overcome. The quarterly report showed a profit of $152,000. That April, a 39 percent public stock offering in the company's subsidiary, Anyplant Rapid (copy centers), was made at $5 a share.

Things were looking rosier and rosier. The franchise rights to 250 copy centers were sold to several groups of investors for about $5 million.

It was estimated that these copy centers would bring in an annual profit of $1.5 million. But the profit was only $178,000 on gross sales of over $2 million.

In the summer of 1969, the main printing plant became unionized. This development, which had been staved off for so long, finally became inevitable.

Meanwhile, the company was busily engaged in meeting the principal objectives it had set for itself, namely "to interface these elements (the five divisions and 38 departments of the modular structure) so that they are mutually supporting in an infinitely varying pattern of service combinations. This ability to adapt to need, instantaneously, provides the clientele with customized communications services."

There was great enthusiasm about sales expectations for 1970. It was estimated that $17 million in sales would bring a net income of 75 cents a share. The sales projection was correct, but the earnings were only $90,000, or 7 cents a share.

The company was teetering. In the summer of 1970 it defaulted on two loan agreements totaling more than $2.5 million. Nonetheless, a few months later it acquired a 52-year-old advertising agency, which boosted the total sales volume to $19 million, with a net income of $150,000, or 9 cents a share.

But, in spite of all the efforts to get back on a profitable track, fiscal 1971 proved to be a bad year. The net loss amounted to $1.75 million and was attributed mostly to setbacks in Anyplant Rapid Copy Centers.

For fiscal 1972, losses exceeded $5 million, half of which was attributed to the copy centers. The board of directors decided to concentrate on the primary printing operations and get rid of everything else. The rapid copy centers were sold, the ad agency was sold, and the publishing department was also sold.

In October, 1972, the American Stock Exchange halted trading in the corporation's stock. The Securities and Exchange Commission suspended trading of the corporation's securities because of "the unavailability of adequate and accurate information" on its financial condition.

The SEC later revealed that financial reports filed by Anypalnt, Inc., showed assets with a book value of $6 million and liabilities of about $10 million, of which $4 million represented unsecured debt.

In October, 1973, the company filed for relief under Chapter XI of the Federal Bankruptcy Act. It was officially adjudicated bankrupt on March 25, 1974.

The provisions of Chapter XI, if accepted by creditors, permits a company to continue whatever profitable operations it may have while disposing of the unprofitable ones. Under this arrangement the creditors may benefit more than they would from an immediate liquidation.

Whys and Wherefores   We've studied the rise of Anyplant Printing Company from a modest, profitable print shop to a bankrupt collossus. Why did it fail? What are the lessons to be learned from its failure? Let the participants do the explaining.

"We tried to do too many things too quickly," said Benjamin, the son of the founder. "We started each one of these diversifications from scratch and we didn't have the management for doing so. If we wanted to diversify, we should have acquired existing companies."

A former manager of one of the divisions explained: "They had big guys and little guys, but no guys in between. The middle management was missing. Top management consisted of six people. These people tried to run five divisions and 38 departments. They couldn't possibly have the know-how. For instance, I was the head of one of the divisions, but I had nothing to say about policy-making. I was just a little guy. Without consulting me, they bought equipment for my specialty division and told me to make money with it. Well, it didn't work out."

The same conditions prevailed in the printing division, which was the largest unit in the conglomerate. According to one of the former managers, there was nobody between the man running the shop and the vice president in charge of manufacturing. Middle management was missing. It could have prevented a lot of losses.

A former supervisor commented, "Oh, yes, we had a lot of deadwood pulling down fabulous salaries, but they were friends of Benjamin or Joe. They were not hired for what they knew, but for whom they knew."

It was true that wherever possible the promotions were made from within the company. However, when seeking executives for the diversified fields, it was at times impossible for Benjamin or Joe to be good judges of capability. These were fields which the young men themselves did not understand. The conglomerate had grown too big too rapidly. It died of complexity.

As a former aide pointed out, "An awful lot of people made a lot of money out of that company, but Benjamin and Joe did not. Many of the executives were lazy. Instead of working, they just sat back and blamed the two boys."

One supplier, whose annual sales to the conglomerate averaged $275,000, suspected difficulties in the late 1960s. "I asked if they needed help and suggested a meeting with them and their other suppliers so that we'd all know where we were going. They said they needed no help. Trouble worsened after they added more people and more services they weren't familiar with. Our association tapered off."

An artist employed by the company for six years left because he didn't see much future. "The company used to be among the biggest and best tech printers. They had all the big accounts. It's a shame they didn't concentrate on what they really knew how to do. The young men wanted a printing empire, but they couldn't find the people who would help them handle it."

A salesman who had been with the company for five years complained about the money that was spent on the luxurious offices and the great number of personal secretaries. The salesman left when the company owed him several thousand dollars in back commissions. He later sued and won.

Because of the complexity of operations, it was difficult to hold people in some of the more important jobs. In the controller's office, for instance, there was a constant turnover. There were so many unrelated things going on at one time that a newcomer was completely swamped.

As one former member of the management team explained it, "They made a lot of bad moves: badly priced bids on printing; badly managed tech writing; badly conceived copy center franchises. They tried to do too much. They didn't hire the kind of executives who knew how to run the various departments."

Another former manager said, "They forgot about the salesmen. They were spending a lot of money on diversification, but they forgot about the guy who was going out getting printing jobs that made the money to support the diversification. Maybe they figured that by publishing their own magazines they'd have an automatic workload. But they forgot that magazines have to be published by a certain date each month. They had scheduling problems. When it came time to run the magazines, they had a commercial printing job on the press. They couldn't meet deliveries for their own magazines."

While the company was neglecting the kind of business that had made it rich, it was devoting too much attention to projects that were draining the cash. For instance, it would allocate $4,000 towards a magazine which cost $24,000 to produce. The balance would be absorbed by the rest of the company.

Another ex-division manager said, "The boys should have stuck to printing, like the old man wanted them to. They had a good thing going and it would have lasted forever. But they insisted on doing things they didn't understand."

Rebirth Controls

And what now?

Although bankrupt, Anyplant, Inc., is still very much alive in the intensive care unit of Chapter XI of the Federal Bankruptcy Act. It was admitted there after drastic surgery. The corporation may be on the critical list, but it is not yet in the morgue.

Benjamin Jacobs, son of the founder, recently outlined the therapy planned for the ailing, publicly-owned printer. The cure has already progressed through these three stages:

1. Amputation of subsidiaries that were a financial drain.
2. Shifting top management.
3. Closing and selling the high-overhead, 142,000 sq. ft. New York plant.

The fourth stage calls for an attempt to put each of the five satellite plants on a profitable basis.

"We were making our money in printing," Benjamin explained, "but we were losing it in the other ventures. So we decided to get rid of all projects that were unprofitable."

The rapid copy subsidiary was the first to go. In 1970 it had lost $900,000 on sales of $1,400,000, and in the following six months it lost another half million. It was traded for shares in a computer firm which had a guaranteed net worth.

The next to go was the specialized publishing service which was sold for its book value of $122,000. Other subsidiaries were merged or liquidated, leaving the basic printing business to cure itself. There were no more syndicated magazines, no more plastic-laminated recordings, no more books, no more tapes.

"We hope the company can rebuild itself on its commercial and technical building base," Benjamin said.

Step Two involved a shift in management and operating philosophy. The new emphasis was on administration rather than sales and marketing. The corporation decided to take care of what it had instead of reaching for things it could not handle. A plan to reach an agreement with the creditors did not get the necessary 85 percent vote. Therefore, the corporation filed for refuge under Chapter XI, which would give it time to try to get back on its feet.

Step Three closed the doors of the plushly carpeted, sunken lobby of its huge plant. One side door, however, remains open for a skeleton crew of 18. Clustered in a corner group of offices, they are the centralized accounting department for the field plants, administrative personnel, and a miniature sales and production staff operating in a brokerage capacity.

"We have been subcontracting to other printers a great deal of printing that we used to do here," explained Benjamin, who became president of the new management team. "We hoped to establish an association with another company to come in here. When we closed, our printing volume nudged $3.2 million, but it takes a minimum of $5.5 million to keep the plant profitable. Since we couldn't find another company doing $2.3 million to share the plant, we are selling it. Leaving it is extremely difficult. It's probably the best-equipped, best laid out printing plant I've ever seen."

Step Four of the recovery plan is to keep a tight rein on the five satellite plants, which have a combined annual volume of $4.5 million. Each of the plants is put on a weekly budget. Every Friday the manager of each of these plants has to give an account of his production, expenses, and profit. He is compensated according to the profit he shows.

"We didn't have time," said Benjamin, "for extensive studies or highly sophisticated management procedures. So we rolled up our sleeves to do the most we could with what we had. The system works. The managers understand a weekly budget system."

The future?

"We want to get back to where we were," said Benjamin. "Rebuild our reputation as printers. We've learned our lesson. In trying for a $100 million annual volume, we almost blew the whole thing. We'll grow again, but we'll remember the advice my father gave us. Stick to what you know, he used to say, and keep a good financial foundation. That holds true for any plant."

Anyplant Printing Company
500 Main Street
Anywhere, U.S.A. 00000